'CANE MUTINY

'CANE

HOW THE MIAMI HURRICANES OVERTURNED THE FOOTBALL ESTABLISHMENT

MUTINY

BRUCE FELDMAN

NEW AMERICAN LIBRARY

New American Library
Published by New American Library, a division of
Penguin Group (USA) Inc., 375 Hudson Street,
New York, New York 10014, U.S.A.
Penguin Group (Canada), 10 Alcorn Avenue, Toronto,
Ontario, Canada M4V 3B2 (a division of Pearson Penguin Canada Inc.)
Penguin Books Ltd. 80 Strand, London WC2R 0RL, England
Penguin Ireland, 25 St. Stephen's Green, Dublin 2,
Ireland (a division of Penguin Books Ltd)
Penguin Group (Australia), 250 Camberwell Road, Camberwell, Victoria 3124,
Australia (a division of Pearson Australia Group Pty Ltd)
Penguin Books India Pvt Ltd, 11 Community Centre, Panchsheel Park,
New Delhi - 110 017, India
Penguin Group (NZ), Cnr Airborne and Rosedale Roads, Albany,
Auckland 1310 New Zealand (a division of Pearson New Zealand Ltd)
Penguin Books (South Africa) (Pty) Ltd, 24 Sturdee Avenue,
Rosebank, Johannesburg 2196, South Africa

Penguin Books Ltd, Registered Offices:
80 Strand, London WC2R 0RL, England

First published by New American Library,
a division of Penguin Group (USA) Inc.

First Printing, September 2004
10 9 8 7 6 5 4 3 2 1

Ⓝ REGISTERED TRADEMARK—MARCA REGISTRADA

LIBRARY OF CONGRESS CATALOGING-IN-PUBLICATION DATA:
Feldman, Bruce.
    'Cane mutiny : how the Miami Hurricanes overturned the football establishment / Bruce Feldman.
        p.   cm
    ISBN 0-451-21297-5 (hardcover)
    1. Miami Hurricanes (Football team)—History.   2. University of Miami—Football—History.   I. Title.
    GV958.U528F45 2004
    796.332'63'09759381—dc22   2004006744

Set in New Baskerville
Designed by Helene Berinsky

Printed in the United States of America

CONTENTS

ACKNOWLEDGMENTS

This book was actually years in the making and wouldn't have been possible without all the help I got from the Hurricane family: Ray Bellamy, Melvin Bratton, Don Bailey Jr., Ed Reed, Mario Christobal, Art Kehoe, Tolbert Bain, Eric Winston, Lamar Thomas, Alonzo Highsmith, Andreu Swasey, Jim Kelly, Howard Schnellenberger, Pete Garcia, Jay Brophy, Darnell Jenkins, Randy Shannon, Greg Mark, Larry Coker, Vince Wilfork, Brett Perriman, Tolbert Bain, Russell Maryland, Arnie Romero, Ray Ganong, Ken Dorsey, Tiger Clark, Randy Bethel, Sonny Lubick, Ian Sinclair, Danny Stubbs, Ray Lewis, Clinton Portis, Bobby Harden, Paul Dee, Don Soldinger, Rob Chudzinski, Jon Vilma, Brett Romberg, Vernon Carey, Tony Fitzpatrick, Kellen Winslow II, Ted Hendricks, Rubin Carter, Bubba McDowell, Alfredo Roberts, Cortez Kennedy, Clem Barbarino, Ed Orgeron, Dr. John Green, Joe Brodsky, Gary Stevens, Greg Schiano, John

Square, Jarrett Payton, Willis McGahee, Jerome McDougle, Bryant McKinnie, Brandon Sebald, Kevin Patrick, Daryl Jones, Curtis Johnson; and also the Miami sports information staff: Doug Walker, Josh Maxon, Mark Prey, Sam Henderson, and Matt Winston. I am grateful to you for sharing your stories with me.

I am indebted to those who have also been a great help to this project, particularly my agents, Frank Scatoni and Greg Dinkin, and my editor, Ron Martirano, as well as Howie Schwab, Terry Egan, Rod Gilmore, Bill Curry, Mike Kuchar, Lee Berman, Chad Millman, Guff, Luke Cyphers, Luther Campbell, JB Morris, John Hassan, Ryan Hockensmith, Dan Le Batard, Eric Adelson, Seth Wickersham, Scott Burton, Stewart Mandel, Jorge Milian, Brian London, Chris Davis, Ed Dick, Richie Rosenblatt, Harry Rothwell, Mike Urranaga, Dave Revsine, Keith Goralski, Jeremy Bloom, Kay-Jay Harris, Mel Kiper, Brian Kenny, Eddie Shannon, Dax Grant, Katrina Ramsey, Jim Maxfield, Beano Cook, Bob Burda, Mark Snyder, Chris Demarest, Sam Johnson, Prof. Todd Boyd, Jeff Bowden, Bobby Bowden, Joe Wojciechowski, David Duffey, Ron Rhodes, T. C. Badalato, Brian Yauger, Jon Simon, and Rob Neyer.

Above all, I want to thank my family and Christie for supporting me through this project and in my life.

INTRODUCTION

What is behind that smoke?

That is the biggest question surrounding the most amazing twenty-five-year run in college football history. So much mystery, so much supposition lurks behind the puffy white clouds that the mighty Miami Hurricanes burst through every Saturday. The rarest of all things in sports has emerged from that smoke: a true dynasty much larger than any player or any coach or any rivalry. From that smoke roars a legacy, a brotherhood, and in a sense, it is a living, breathing thing.

Perhaps the best way to capture that spirit and passion isn't through a play or highlight, but rather through a moment—one that didn't take place on the field. It happened on October 13, 2001. Miami had traveled to Tallahassee to face the hated Seminoles. For many of the 'Canes, these were the same 'Noles who gutted them 47–0 when they were freshmen, the fuzzy-cheeked boys of Butch Davis's resurrection project. Only now the 'Canes were grown. UM captain Ed Reed reminded his teammates of that before the game. "Fo-tee-say-vin to NUTHIN'!" Reed kept hollering in the visitors' locker room.

The 'Canes were so wired they looked like they were ready to hang forty-seven right back on FSU, jumping out to a 21–0 first-half lead, but the Seminoles battled and narrowed the gap to 21–13 by halftime. Reed had already left the game by that point. He had separated his shoulder in the second quarter and gone to the locker room before the half was over. He sat in the training room glassy-eyed, while his teammates all filed past him. Who had control now? they wondered. They couldn't help but notice Reed, their charismatic leader, wincing as the trainers tried taking his shoulder pads off. Reed looked like he was done for the day. One by one, coaches and teammates came by to check on him.

Finally, the senior safetyman rose up and, through tearing eyes, screamed at his teammates, "Stop asking me if I'm hurt. I'm hurt, dawg. Of course I'm hurt. Don't ask me if I'm all right. Hell naaah! Joaquin [Gonzalez, the UM offensive tackle] said 'Dominate,' and we ain't dominatin'. I put my heart into this shit, dawg. Now let's go!" Reed led his teammates back out on the field, picked off two second-half passes and the 'Canes not only dominated—they conquered: 49–27. That moment was vintage Ed Reed, vintage Miami, and you couldn't find anyone who epitomizes the program any better.

Here, in his own words, is how Ed Reed feels about his experience as a member of the Miami Hurricanes.

———

People wonder how we keep producing all these first-round draft picks and all these Pro Bowlers. Well, that just goes to show you the talent that comes to this school and how we develop it. I guess it's an eye-opener to some folks, or at least it should be. Sure, other schools have talent, but honestly, I don't think other teams really compete like we compete on a daily basis. Even the older guys in the NFL, like me now, come back and work out with the younger guys. And you can't put a price on that. I know I got something from all the guys who came back because every older guy I ever came across, I paid attention to the things they did, and I took all the good I could.

Miami helped make me the man I am today. I went through a lot of things when I was at UM as far as football and training and life. That's why I still come back in the off-season and train there and why I always go back to talk to those kids to let them know there is more to life than just football. Miami taught me about how certain people and certain cultures are, and it really opened me up to the world. Miami is still teaching me.

I was always this person. When I was in high school, I was always following. I always looked up to the older guys on my team, and I always wanted to be like them, but I also wanted to be better than them, and I vowed not to make the mistakes that they made. So when I got to Miami, I looked for the guys who went to the NFL, and that's who you follow—only you try to be a little bit smarter than they are. Even now I do that, and right now, my guy is Ray Lewis. And I'm here to push him even more. I'm a perfectionist and I critique him and I critique myself—"Hey, man, you shouldn't do that"—because you can always be better. That's Miami.

That's what being a Hurricane is about because it's such a fraternity. It's got to be the best program in America because you have that brotherhood. Once you're part of the U, you're part of the U. It's just that simple. Kellen Winslow said it, only in some different words. But we're taught so much more in that program. I just see it.

I know the fraternity we have here. I know this brotherhood we have here, and when I was drafted in Baltimore, Ray displayed it best. We weren't in school together at all. We didn't know each other from nothing. We never even had a conversation till the first time I got to Baltimore. But when he watched me play, he could see "it" because he played at Miami and he knows what we go through to get to where we're at. He came up to me and we had a heart-to-heart, and he said, "Whatever you want out of this game, whatever you want out of this business, I'll give it to you," because he knew that I feel the same way about this game as he docs. I mean there's a reason why he's the best linebacker in the game, period. And he knew what I wanted when I got to the NFL: to be the best safety in the game, period. That's Miami.

What does it mean to be a 'Cane? It's my life, man. It's my life.

—Ed Reed

'CANE MUTINY

1

LAST RITES

"**D**ear Nigger," the letter began. "Do you know what Hell is? We will make your next 4 years at Miami hell." The envelope was postmarked February 2, 1967, and it was sent by a group calling itself Patriotism, Inc.

Ray Bellamy had been getting letters like this for two months. They all started out the same: "Dear Nigger . . ." They all went on to challenge his sanity, telling him to remember his place. If he didn't, they always reminded him, they'd *get* him. The letters always came to his school, Lincoln Memorial High in Palmetto, Florida. Bellamy was the president of the student body at all-black Lincoln, an honor student and a star wide receiver for the Trojans football team. He also had inside him the DNA for a college football dynasty and for the revolution that would spark it. Of course, he didn't know it back then.

Bellamy grew up a migrant worker in the sixties. That was what his family did, what they knew, so during winters the willowy kid would pick tomatoes, peppers, and cucumbers in Palmetto's fields. Then, during the summer, he and his family would move up to Maryland and do the same up there. It was a rough life for a man, much less an eleven-year-old. One day in the fields Bellamy witnessed one worker gun down another worker just because the guy couldn't count. Another day he watched as one man set another on fire while the guy was sleeping. Bellamy became numb to it all. He figured after high school, he'd enlist in the army, go fight in Vietnam. Afraid to die? Please. Anything, Bellamy thought, was better than this life.

But as he got older, his body continued to grow, fast and strong. Those callused hands, toughened by fifteen-hour days in the fields, proved to be perfect for snatching footballs out of the sky with one hand. By the time he turned seventeen, Bellamy was six-foot-five, 190 pounds, and could run the forty-yard dash in under 4.5. And he played on a powerhouse team that once beat a team from Clearwater 89–0—and that was with having seven touchdowns called back on penalties. They were so devastating, only five teams in the state would play them, so they had to trade home field with those five opponents just to have a full schedule. Throughout the deep South, there were many all-black schools like Lincoln, tucked away in every little hollow, loaded with disciplined, tenacious young bodies. Although it's doubtful any of those teams were better than the Trojans. In Bellamy's three seasons at Lincoln, the team was 25-0. One of his teammates, Henry Lawrence, a hulking tackle, would later become a first-round pick of the Oakland Raiders and make All-Pro twice.

Coach Eddie Shannon took kids, just like Bellamy, who had been raised hard, with unforgiving work ethics honed on one kind of field, and turned them loose on another kind of field:

a gridiron. Besides, after what Bellamy had gone through, how tough could football be? Bellamy's story wasn't that different from too many other top black football players in the South back then. The next step for a player of Bellamy's gifts would be college. That meant Florida A&M or Bethune-Cookman College or maybe mighty Grambling down in Louisiana.

What about Florida's Big Three, Miami, Florida State, and Florida? Not in that day. Colleges in the South were petrified about even recruiting a black player. (Wake Forest had three in the mid-sixties but still wouldn't acknowledge their existence four decades later.) Maybe this is why some experts say the best teams weren't Texas or Alabama in those days, but Eddie Robinson's Grambling teams that were always stocked with future first-rounders. However, the University of Miami, a school that once canceled a game against UCLA in 1940 because Jackie Robinson was playing, set out to change that.

The green light was given by Miami president Dr. Henry King Stanford, a country-as-corn-bread Southerner from Americus, Georgia, who wanted the school to be seen as a leader. College football, like the rest of society, was divided into two halves: the South, and the rest of the country. Other programs in the North and Midwest began recruiting black players from the segregated South in the early fifties. In 1953 J. C. Caroline, a black sophomore running back from Columbia, South Carolina, became a consensus all-American for Illinois, leading the country in rushing with 1,256 yards in a nine-game schedule. Illinois fans loved Caroline's dazzling style. So did rival Big Ten coaches. Within the next two years, a new wave of black football talent migrated to Big Ten country. Illinois plucked Charles Butler and future Hall of Famer Bobby Mitchell; Wisconsin recruited Sidney Williams, while Michigan landed Jim

Pace and Willie Smith. And these were just the kids from the state of Arkansas. Michigan State built a powerhouse, winning six national titles in the fifties and sixties with the barred black stars from the South as its foundation. "Segregation is what brought me to Michigan State," said Jimmy Raye, a mid-sixties Spartan quarterback from North Carolina. "I didn't go there thinking about pro football. I went thinking about an education and getting a good job." Raye's presence helped bring another African-American QB from North Carolina, Tyrone Willingham (now Notre Dame's head coach), to East Lansing too.

Sherman Lewis, who went on to a longtime career as an NFL coach, came to MSU from Louisville and finished third in the 1963 Heisman Trophy race. All-American rover George Webster was from South Carolina. Dominating defensive end Bubba Smith and receiver/track star Gene Washington came to Michigan State from Texas. Other key Spartans came from North Carolina, Alabama, and Georgia. Charlie Thornhill was a top linebacking prospect from Roanoke, Virginia. The coach who pushed him to East Lansing? Bear Bryant. The legendary Alabama coach, like Clemson's Frank Howard and a few other coaches in the South, steered some of their coaching buddies players they wanted but knew they couldn't take.

"It was the unwritten law," said Beano Cook, an ESPN college football analyst/historian. "It wasn't the coaches who didn't want to use African-Americans. One thing about coaches, if Ghengis Khan could turn the corner, he'd be recruited."

The South was an entirely different world, on and off the field. In 1955 Autherine Lucy was the first black student to attend the University of Alabama. But after angry crowds rioted on campus, Lucy was expelled three days later. The administration claimed it was for her own safety. It was eight years before another black student would enroll at the Tuscaloosa campus.

Life wasn't any more progressive anyplace else in the Southeastern Conference—a conference that had not hired a black head football coach until December of 2003, when Mississippi State announced Alabama grad Sylvester Croom as its new top man. (Croom got the job over, among others, Charlie Strong, Florida's defensive coordinator, who some say never had a real shot, since many Southern boosters wouldn't approve of him as a head coach because he had a white wife.) But that's the twenty-first century in the deep South. The sixties were the era of church bombings and lynchings; of Alabama governor George Wallace making his infamous stand in the schoolhouse door and proclaiming "Never"; and of the National Guard being called out to escort James Meredith to class at Ole Miss.

According to *The Journal of Blacks in Higher Education*, the league's color barrier was finally broached in 1967 when Greg Page walked on to the practice field at the University of Kentucky, the northernmost of the SEC schools. One day in practice the entire defensive squad of his own team piled on Page after a play. Page was paralyzed from the neck down and died thirty-eight days later. One year later, another Kentucky Wildcat, Wilbur Hackett, shook off death threats and took the field at Ole Miss, under the watch of armed guards—Mississippi highway patrolmen—to become the first African-American to play in an SEC game.

Alabama, the Southeastern Conference's flagship school, wouldn't suit up a black player until 1971. Legend has it Alabama coach Bear Bryant realized it was time after the Crimson Tide's 1970 game against Southern Cal, when a black fullback named Sam Cunningham led the Trojans to a 42–21 romp over the Tide at Legion Field. After Cunningham rushed for 135 yards and two touchdowns against Bama's vaunted defense, Crimson Tide assistant coach Jerry Claiborne attempted to describe the game's impact. "Sam Cunningham did more to integrate Alabama in sixty minutes than Martin Luther King had done in twenty years," Claiborne said. Alabama, which had won three national titles in the sixties, finished 6-5-1 in 1970, after having gone 6-5 in '69. The next season, the Tide suited up its first two black football players, Wilbur Jackson and John Mitchell, and went 11-1.

It's a nice story and a clever quote, but the truth is that Alabama had already started the process of integrating before facing USC. Jackson and Mitchell were actually freshmen on that 1970 team, but in those days, freshmen weren't eligible under NCAA rules. But there had to be an official first, and that happened in Coral Gables.

Miami, Dr. Stanford believed, was the ideal proving ground, because, yes, it was Southern, but it really wasn't the South. The 'Canes played many teams from the South, and had many players who were Southerners, but also had many who were from the Northeast and Midwest as well as South America, explains Hall of Fame defensive end Ted Hendricks, who came to UM from Guatemala. Stanford had informed his head coach, Charlie Tate, that the time was right, and soon the search was on for the right student to cross the color line. Back then, though, recruiting was different. There were no real recruiting coordinators or scouting services. Colleges didn't have the budgets to deploy their assistants all over the country, or even to the outer reaches of their parts of the country. Instead they relied on the part-time help of well-placed alums, who would moonlight as recruiters and get paid in game tickets. Guys like Ed Dick.

An insurance agent, Dick covered Jacksonville and the Tampa area for Miami. Over a fifteen-year period starting in 1961, Dick sent fifteen players to Miami. Dick was a Miami grad, he sat on the local school board, and he was a staunch civil rights advocate. He hired the first black insurance agent in the state of Florida. "I got called 'N-lover' more times than anyone in the history of Manatee County," Dick says. He started pushing UM to recruit black players in 1961, he says. That was the same year Miami's board of trustees voted to allow blacks into the school. But suiting up a black football player proved to be a struggle all by itself. "They kept saying no, they couldn't," Dick said. "There was always an excuse, though. They kept saying how they were afraid of schools canceling games against them because they wouldn't play a team with a black player." That argument didn't wash, though. Even Alabama was playing teams with black players. That started in 1959, when the Crimson Tide accepted a bid to play an integrated team from Penn State in the Liberty Bowl and attitudes began to soften. Not that the school loved it. Sure, death threats were made on the lives of Bryant and the Alabama university president, but the '59 Liberty Bowl was played without incident. Throughout the 1960s, Bryant continued to accept bowl bids to face integrated teams. Before each of these bowl games, Bryant would give his players, many of whom had never played against a black player in either high school or college, the same speech: "Treat 'em like any other player. Knock 'em on their ass and then help 'em up."

In the summer of 1966, Dick and fellow UM recruiter John Holcom, a Bradenton optician, got the green light. "Find us the right young man," Fran Curci, a UM assistant, told them.

Dick knew exactly where to start looking: the little school

right across the river, Lincoln High School. "We were looking for a special kind of person," says Dick. "Like a Jackie Robinson kind of person."

Eddie Shannon, Lincoln's head football coach, introduced Dick to Ray Bellamy, the school's student body president and star receiver. Shannon knew a thing or two about what pioneering athletes were made of. Before coming to Lincoln, he had been a track coach at Florida A&M and had worked with tennis legend Althea Gibson. He had also spent three years in the navy and understood the kind of discipline that would be needed to try to break through into segregated culture. "Ray had the hands, the speed, but he had the character too," Shannon said. "I didn't worry about him academically, and I knew he was humble enough that he could handle adversity."

Shannon believed that Bellamy had developed the thick skin he would need from his years spent toiling in the fields as a migrant worker. The coach said he was always impressed by the way Bellamy never seemed to let anything slow him down. "It's like we used to say, 'The more knocks you get, the easier it is to accept more knocks when you get 'em.'"

Shannon sat down with Bellamy to see if he was interested in being "the first one," the one who would break football's color barrier in the South. Bellamy was. But first, Shannon had to make sure that Bellamy understood what he was getting himself into. "Do you think you can take people throwing stuff at you?" he asked. Bellamy nodded. "Do you think you can take people spitting at you?" Again, Bellamy nodded. "Well, then," the old coach continued, "if you think you can take a little bit of hell, then you can go on and get that education."

Dick's first meeting with Bellamy came after watching a Lincoln practice. Dick's immediate reaction? Wow! "He was

bright, he was charismatic, he had a lot of leadership qualities," Dick said. "He was just very impressive. Right from then,
I knew, Ray Bellamy was the fit. He was exactly what we wanted."

Dick lobbied Miami's head recruiter, George McIntyre, to
drive up to Palmetto, a 4.5-hour ride north from Coral Gables,
to watch Bellamy. Not so much to see if he was good enough,
but really just to see how the kid carried himself. Sure enough,
McIntyre thought, Dick was spot-on. Bellamy, McIntyre reported back to Coral Gables, was their man.

On December 12, 1966, flanked by his older brother, Sylvester, Coach Shannon, and Dick, Ray Bellamy made history.
He signed to play football at the University of Miami.

Bellamy was prepared—well, as prepared as he could be—
for the animosity he would surely face. Once word got out
about his decision to play for Miami, the hate mail started to
show up at Lincoln. He'd get it every week, telling him how
they would kill him, kill his family. Bellamy vowed he wouldn't
let "those people" stop him. "I'm fearless," he said. "Even when
they threatened to kill me, I wasn't scared. My mom was more
concerned with her baby being hurt than I was."

Still, by the time Bellamy arrived on campus, the university
had already admitted twelve black students. Before the first
week had passed, Bellamy knew the name of each one. He'd
spend time gabbing with black cafeteria workers or go to
church with the team equipment manager, who also happened
to be black. Dr. Stanford had already invited Bellamy over to
his home for dinner, and the two hit it off. "He was an unbelievable leader," Bellamy said. "He looked beyond color. He
really made the difference. He had a commitment to blacks."

Of course, that didn't mean Bellamy's transition into Miami
was seamless. "When I first got there, no one knew how to act

around me," he said. "I paralyzed people. They just didn't know how to deal with me." Some, though, were quite certain how they wanted to treat Bellamy. One night he came home from practice and found a hate letter tacked to the door of his dorm. The next night he got another one. A week after that he had to dive out of the way after someone tried to run him down with a car. Bellamy just dodged it all and moved on. He never saw those people's faces, so why sweat them? he figured.

Bellamy recalls one of his teammates, a player from Liberty, Mississippi, talking down to him, acting like he expected the young wideout to be his slave. "I told him, 'I'm not that black man who cleaned your mama's house back in Mississippi,'" Bellamy said. And with that, he won the respect of many of his teammates who weren't quite sure how to deal with him. He was fully aware that no matter what he said or how well he played, there would still be a few players on the team who would resent him solely because of his skin color. "But," he said, "they never said anything to my face. There was a respect there."

Not that it stopped all of the exterior threats and venom that were coming his way. He says when the school felt things were serious enough, they did "some things" to protect him. Like before UM faced Auburn in 1968, the school notified the FBI about a death threat against Bellamy. Teammates would often joke with Bellamy to try to lighten the mood: "Hey, Ray, lemme taste that first before you eat it," they'd tease him in the cafeteria at pregame meals.

It didn't hurt his cause that his teammates knew right away that the kid was legit. "Ray truly was a great athlete," said Ted Hendricks, who played defensive end from 1966–68. "His teammates had to respect that." Bellamy could outrun all the defensive backs, he could make these never-seen-before one-handed snatch catches, and they couldn't tackle him. More important, he could help them win. Against the Florida State freshman team in '67 (back then freshmen were ineligible for the varsity), Bellamy soared above the mass of humanity piled up at the line of scrimmage to block a game-winning field goal and preserve a tie for the Hurricanes. The next year he led Miami in receptions with thirty-seven, the most ever by a Hurricane sophomore. Bellamy followed up that with a great junior year and looked primed for an NFL career.

But on January 3, 1970, while driving back to school from his home in Bradenton with his girlfriend, Bellamy fell asleep at the wheel a few miles from Miami. His blue Chevy Nova went off the road and smashed into some pine trees. Bellamy's girlfriend emerged virtually unscathed, but he broke his arm and his leg and suffered a head injury. He was hospitalized for four months and missed his senior season.

Bellamy, though, was convinced he would leave his mark on UM. He ran for student body president in 1971, and—imagine that—he won. Anyone who met him in Coral Gables bought into Bellamy's mantra of "It ain't a black thing or a white thing; it's a people thing." He was right. Before Bellamy left UM, Miami had fourteen black players on its team. Even Florida State and Florida had both signed black football players.

Funny thing is, after Miami football made history, it almost became history. The Hurricanes had some great players in the early years: Hall of Fame center Jim Otto, QB George Mira, Hendricks, running back Chuck Foreman, defensive back Burgess Owens. But in reality, Miami was hardly a blip on the national college football radar. The 'Canes were fodder. A nice balmy road trip for the Penn States and Notre Dames of the world, something for those powerhouses to pitch to recruits as well as a ticket to a fatter record. Alabama, Auburn, and LSU all took their turns too. Miami football, though, was a program lost in the margins; it never had an identity. It was a program without pride.

The low-water mark came in 1971 against Florida, in a game now known as "the Florida Flop." With Florida leading 45–8 late in the fourth quarter of the season's final game, Gator defenders lay down and let the Hurricanes score so quarterback John Reeves could have the ball back and get the fifteen yards he needed to break Jim Plunkett's record for NCAA career passing yards.

Miami coach Fran Curci refused to shake hands with Florida coach Doug Dickey after the game. Then some Gators headed to the Orange Bowl's east end zone and jumped into a pool that housed Miami Dolphins mascot, Flipper, during NFL games.

During one stretch in the seventies, Miami had five different head coaches in six seasons. Attendance dropped every year. Rumors swirled in 1975 that the administration was going to drop football just as it had done the basketball program in 1971. UM trustees were shocked to learn the university had lost $3.5 million the year before. Football had to go, most of the board concluded. It was hemorrhaging money. Even in south Florida, Miami football didn't matter. The 'Canes were lost in the shadow that came on the other side of the afterglow from the perfect '72 Dolphins, from Don "the Jaw" Shula, the no-name defense and the Butch-'n'-Sundance backfield of Jim Kiick and Larry Csonka. "Dadgum Dolphins in the paper ever' day," Charlie Tate, the 'Canes coach, groaned. The beloved Dolphins would draw seventy thousand to the Orange Bowl, and the 'Canes would get seven thousand.

"Back then there was a genuine fear that they would drop football just like they dropped basketball," said former Miami all-American middle guard Rubin Carter, who played from 1972–74. "With all the changes, we never could get comfortable. A new coach here, another new coach there. They were shuffling 'em in and out and it was difficult to understand what the philosophy of each coach was."

Miami football was on life support. The board was about to give last rites when it turned to its wolf. His name was Dr. John Lafayette Green, and unlike everyone else around UM, he knew the business of college sports.

Green had been an athletic board member at the University of Georgia, where college football wasn't seen as a sport, but a religion. Dr. Stanford, realizing his job was in jeopardy, along with his sorry football program, agreed to a reorganization ordered by the board of regents, including the creation of a new position, executive vice president of administration. That was Green's title. Green convinced the board to give football one more shot. But everything had to be done his way. The regents agreed.

Green was stunned to see just how miserable things actually were once he got a look under the hood. "It was pathetic," he said. "The program was as low in the cellar as you could get. You would've thought you were looking at the worst high school program in the country. The facilities were terrible. The showers were filthy. There was no weight room. It was in the pits. Morale was terrible. There was a lot of dissension with the players and with the coaches. The athletes made fun of the program. It was a joke. There was no spirit or enthusiasm." It didn't help that UM had just set a school record for its worst season attendance ever too.

Green's first move: telling the board to fire head coach Carl Selmer. "This guy will never be able to do anything with the program," Green explained to the board. Because word soon leaked to the press, Green had to hustle to tell Selmer before the papers did. So as the coach was attending a World Hockey Association game in Houston with the team while they were in town to play their season finale against the University of Houston, Selmer heard his name paged on the PA system. Selmer took the call and found out he was out of a job. Green says he hated that it went down like that, but he knew they didn't have any time to waste.

Next up: Find a coach. A big-name coach to front the program. Green traveled the country. "I must've tried to get twenty or thirty guys, all big-name coaches. Hayden Fry [from Iowa], [Notre Dame coaching legend] Ara Parseghian, Jackie Sherrill [then at Washington State]. I even talked to [former Kansas City Chiefs coach] Hank Stram, but nobody wanted to touch the job," Green said. "They kept calling it the coach's graveyard."

Green finally settled on Bill Dooley, the older brother of Vince Dooley, whom Green had worked with while Vince was coaching Georgia into the top twenty. Green and Bill Dooley had been college buddies in their days at Mississippi State. Dooley had agreed to take the job and was all set to sign a contract at a press conference, when he got to the airport at Chapel Hill and changed his mind. Green was bewildered. The press conference had to be canceled and everyone went home.

Once again, another huge embarrassment. Green started to wonder what he was going to do when the phone rang one day that winter. It was Otto Graham. "Think I got a name for you," the Hall of Fame QB told Green.

"Who?" Green asked.

"Lou Saban," Graham said.

"You're kidding," Green replied. But Graham was right. Saban, a guy who had won almost one hundred NFL games as coach of the Buffalo Bills, New England Patriots, and Denver Broncos, wanted the Miami job. Green got him for just $50,000. Green got creative to raise funds. With the help of a UM alum who was one of the owners of Caesar's Palace, he raised $125,000 with a $1,500-a-plate roast for Woody Hayes, the crusty old Ohio State coach. "We must've had twenty movie stars there that we got because of the casino guy's connections. Gerald Ford was one of the MCs. Ann-Margret was there," Green said. "It was really something."

Then there was the $250,000 UM netted from a Japanese marketing company after the 'Canes agreed to play Notre Dame, all expenses paid, in Tokyo in the '77 season. So what if UM got blasted 48–10? That quarter mil would cover the tab for the recruiting budget Saban would need to mine the country for talent looking to play in the south Florida sun.

Life at UM for Saban got off to a tragic start though. That spring, Saban told Green he would have to check himself into the hospital for a few days. Nothing serious, he said. Nah, just a triple-bypass operation. In September, two weeks before Miami's opener at Ohio State, Saban's wife of thirty years, Lorraine, who had just lost her sight battling diabetes, hanged herself in the basement of their home back in Buffalo.

Still, on the job, Saban worked his magic. He transformed Ottis Anderson from mediocre college tailback into bona fide NFL feature back, not to mention a future–Super Bowl MVP. Saban also implored one of his protégés from the Bills, O. J. Simpson, to schmooze Miami recruits. The sales pitch was simple: Get out of the snow, come to the sun, see the girls, and play in the Orange Bowl, a stadium where the NFL plays. That worked wonders too. Saban's first recruiting class was as good as any in the country. His prize prospect was Lester Williams, an aggressive run-stopper, considered the nation's top defensive lineman. Miami can thank defensive ends coach Arnie Romero for the coup. "They told me if I didn't get him we might not have a program the next year," Romero said.

Romero had started recruiting Williams when he was in the tenth grade. "Bobo [Williams's nickname] trusted me," said Romero. "He didn't trust too many people. He didn't talk to anybody. His grandmother trusted me. His girlfriend trusted me. Back then, recruiters didn't have any limits, so you could talk to a kid every day, and I did. I took him and his girlfriend to different places. He was always coming over to eat dinner. Whenever he'd go on his other recruiting visits, to UCLA, Ohio State, and Oklahoma, I was the one who was packing his stuff and taking him to the airport."

Saban's other key recruit was a bit more of a sleeper. He was a thick-legged, floppy-haired tough guy from East Brady, Pennsylvania.

Jim Kelly was torn between Miami and local favorite Penn State and its legendary coach, Joe Paterno. Kelly had gone to Paterno's football camps before his junior and senior years of high school. Trouble was, Joe Pa wanted Kelly to play defense and be the next cog in Linebacker U. Once Saban heard that, it was easy. "You want to play quarterback for us?" he asked Kelly. "You got it."

Kelly's recruiting visit to south Florida sealed the deal. "I flew in from Pittsburgh, they picked me up with some pretty Hurricane Honeys [the school's female recruiting hostesses], and they took me out to dinner and I had lobster for the first time in my life," Kelly said. "It was something like I'd never seen before. I was like, 'Where do I sign?'"

When Kelly returned home to Pennsylvania, all he heard was: "What are you, crazy? . . . You're throwing your football career out the window . . . You don't wanna go there . . . Why Miami? Saban will be gone after one year."

Kelly never wavered, although the skeptics were right about one thing: Saban didn't stick around long enough to coach the talent he had brought in.

In April 1978, three Miami players threw a twenty-two-year-old man into Lake Osceola on the Miami campus. The following Monday, Saban, just back from a recruiting trip, was asked by a newspaper reporter to explain. Saban had played football at Indiana, where being dunked had been a campus tradition. "The whole thing sounds like a nice fiasco to me," he responded through a chuckle. "Getting thrown in the lake? Sounds like fun to me."

Saban was never told that the man was an employee at a campus gathering place for Jewish students who said he was wearing a yarmulke and was walking to on-campus services when he was taunted and then attacked by the freshmen players. Miami's Jewish community said the incident had anti-Semitic overtones, and Saban's remarks triggered a flurry of protest calls. Saban apologized profusely, but the damage was done.

"Lou really got sandbagged on that," Green said. "He didn't know what happened. He had no idea of the ramifications. He was not anti-Semitic. He tried for three months to repair it and spent a lot of time working on it, but it just didn't go. He said, 'I'm never gonna be able to get past this.' He wanted to resign at midseason, and I said, 'Lou, don't do that. You have all these recruits coming in. You can't do that.'"

After Saban's second season, a season where the 'Canes finished 6-5, after going 3-8 in his rookie year, the old coach resigned, taking the head coaching job at West Point.

Saban's whirlwind stint with the 'Canes only gave the "Why Miami Should Dump Football" faction among the board more ammo. There was another vote. This time to deemphasize football down to Division 1-AA or to nuke it all together. Again there was a recess, and again Green lobbied for one more shot.

"I didn't want to lose the momentum," Green said, "so I scrambled."

Green realized after the way Saban left, sneaking out the door after dark, that he had to strike gold with his new hire. The next guy had to be perfect. He had to have a presence and a vision. And, as luck would have it, Green found such a man. Better still, that man found Green. He was a gruff, pipe-smoking former Bear Bryant disciple with a voice as thick and intimidating as a double shot of Kentucky bourbon. The guy showed up in Coral Gables the first week in January, just a week after Saban left, and made the darnedest proclamation. He stood there, looked at his new team, and announced, "Someday, we are gonna win a national *cham-pi-yon-ship* at Miami." The whole room got silent. Who the hell was this crazy colonel guy, the players thought, and what the hell was he smoking in that pipe of his?

2

PIPE DREAMS

The room was more like a cell than an office. It was eight-by-eight feet, smaller than the bathroom in FSU head coach Bobby Bowden's office. The plaster was peeling off the walls, the windows were propped open as wide as they could stretch, and the palmetto bugs (think cockroaches on steroids) were scurrying for cover. It was another sticky south Florida morning and the room had no air-conditioning. Ten men had piled inside and were seated shoulder-to-shoulder in front of a burly man with piercing dark eyes, a thick mustache, and a shiny Super Bowl ring. The guy looked like a cross between Colonel Sanders and General Patton. "*Gennn*-tel-men," he growled in a deep voice that sounded like an old chain saw revving up. "I did not come here to waste my time. I could've stayed in the National Football League for years and years. But I came here to win a national title and I have to do it in five years. Understand?"

This was how Howard Schnellenberger started his first staff meeting as the Hurricanes' new head coach. For a program desperate for an identity, it appeared to have found a man straight out of central casting. Schnellenberger didn't have to travel far to get to UM, since he had been working with the Miami Dolphins as one of Don Shula's top assistants. But in reality, the guy was light-years away from anything the Hurricanes had ever seen before.

Schnellenberger was as old-school as a pair of brass knuckles. He had learned football from some of the game's biggest legends. He played end for the professorial Blanton Collier at Kentucky, coached under taskmaster Bear Bryant at Alabama, then worked under the peppy George Allen, another Hall of Fame coach, with the Los Angeles Rams before landing with Shula, one of Collier's protégés.

Schnellenberger had a commanding presence. Folks could tell when he was about to enter the room. Of course, that probably had something to do with the cloud of pipe smoke that preceded him. But truth is, Schnellenberger's trademark black pipe only added to his mystique. It was a symbol of maturity, patience, and tolerance, he said. "Did you ever meet a pipe smoker you couldn't trust?" Schnellenberger asked. Even his name sounded dignified, as though you could hear it rattling out of John Facenda's mouth on one of those old NFL film clips. *SSSCH-nell-en-BURRR-GERRRR.*

He was the son of a German-born stonemason, and he grew up tough. Born in tiny Saint Meinrad, Indiana, he moved with his family to Louisville at age two, after his father, Leslie, borrowed money to buy a tractor-trailer so he could work as a wildcat hauler. Howard's mother, Rosena, working as a waitress, ran the family (consisting of Howard, his two younger brothers, and a sister) while Leslie drove the rig. But Rosena never gave the kids much wiggle room. Once, when Howard missed curfew, she phoned the cops. That was how Howard Schnellenberger learned his first lesson about discipline and responsibility. He said he didn't remember his mother kissing him till he was forty. This was a man who would always wear a sport jacket and tie on the sideline, but never an overcoat, not even if it was snowing or ten below. He'd also refuse to take his jacket off, even on the hottest Miami day. His reasoning, he would explain, was "because this is a profession, not a job. I think it gives me a better image."

"Howard just had this aura about him," Green said. "He was all about business."

"He wasn't a rah-rah guy; he was more like a statesman or something," said Clem Barbarino, an offensive guard who had been recruited by Saban.

To get Schnellenberger, Green had to give the coach a say in who the new Miami athletic director would be. It was an unusual move, something that just didn't happen, especially not for guys who hadn't even been college head coaches. But that was the kind of juice Schnellenberger had, and he knew how desperate Miami was. The university, especially the school president, wanted to name its popular baseball coach, Ron Fraser, as the new AD. But Schnellenberger wasn't sold on Fraser as the right man for the job, so Green agreed to keep the search open. Schnellenberger's candidate was Charlie Thornton, Alabama's assistant AD, who, like Schnellenberger, was a buddy of Bear Bryant's. Sure enough, the new football coach got his way and the forty-two-year-old Thornton was signed to a five-year deal. (Ten weeks later, Thornton resigned after his wife was diagnosed with cancer. Harry Mallios, a former UM fullback in the early fifties, who had been teaching in the school's health department, took over as AD.)

Why would Schnellenberger want to take over at the "coaching graveyard"? For all the reasons why most people said you *couldn't* win at UM. "Miami was a unique situation," explained Schnellenberger. "First, it was the only university in a subtropical climate. We played in the most recognizable stadium, at the Orange Bowl, and we were sitting on the hottest bed of prospects in the nation. And they had an independent, top-of-the-line schedule in place. What a great asset that became. I don't think we could have made the rapid growth we did if we had been in a conference."

The key there being that Miami, like Notre Dame and Penn State, wasn't locked into a set schedule. They didn't have to play Indiana like other Big Ten schools did, or Wake Forest like the rest of the ACC did. They could play a national schedule and, in essence, be a national program, especially in the eyes of the TV networks. "Being an independent meant we could have the best schedule in the country," said Schnellenberger. "And everybody wanted to come to play in Miami. We got intersectional exposure."

One of Schnellenberger's first moves was to bring with him Earl Morrall, a twenty-one-year NFL veteran and the Dolphins' QB during the perfect 1973 season, who had been working as the team's part-time quarterback coach since retiring in 1977. Back then few colleges had coaches solely to groom their quarterbacks, but since Schnellenberger wanted to install an intricately timed pro-style passing attack, he needed his QBs to work like pros.

Schnellenberger's offensive scheme was in sharp contrast to what most top teams were running those days. It was either

USC's Student Body Right ground attack, the Oklahoma wishbone, the Nebraska option, or some variation of the veer. But at UM, it would be an air show, just like in the NFL. Schnellenberger needed Morrall to develop difference-making passers, by refining their throwing mechanics and, maybe more important, teaching them where to throw the ball *and* when.

"If we'd put in the Dolphins' offense with the wrong quarterback, we wouldn't have won," Schnellenberger said. "It helped a whole lot. I always felt you needed somebody to work exclusively with the quarterbacks who didn't have a coordinator's responsibilities. Earl was a voluntary coach. He wasn't getting paid. He'd come to work an hour before practice. He wasn't involved with planning or recruiting. He just worked on the psychology of being a quarterback, the techniques of being a quarterback, what your reads are, when and how to audible. He'd watch their throwing motion, so if that got out of kilter, he could get them back in the groove."

"Coach Morrall meant everything to me," said Kelly. "He taught me so much, especially on the deeper throws, because when you're a kid, you just kinda throw it as far as you can. You never think about dropping it over the top. Coach Morrall taught me touch, how to put air under the football, and how to read defenses."

Schnellenberger knew that if he added speed to his system, opponents would be helpless. He had learned perhaps his most important lesson from Bryant: that you won with players, not assistant coaches, and that you "coached people, not football." To get that level of talent, Schnellenberger felt he had to keep all the shifty tailbacks, speedy wideouts, and aggressive linebackers from Dade and Broward counties at home. He coined the expression "the State of Miami." That meant that the U was walling off the fertile talent base that was south Florida—running from one hundred miles north in Palm Beach, through Broward County (the Fort Lauderdale area) and Dade County (the Miami area), stretching as far north as Tampa, Orlando, and Daytona Beach. All property "annexed" from the University of Florida, Schnellenberger loved to say. The Gators, back then, were *the* team in Florida, and they had plucked their share of stars, such as all-time leading tackler David Little and all-time leading receiver Carlos Alvarez, from south Florida. The powers of the Big Ten cherry-picked a few other choice playmakers too, like West Palm Beach's Anthony Carter (Michigan), as did small-college dynamo Florida A&M, nabbing future Hall of Fame linemen Tyrone McGriff and Larry Little.

Saban had started to close the doors on Dade, but Schnellenberger was determined to put a fence around it. Although just as Schnellenberger's staff was picking up momentum, "the shit hit the fan," Schnellenberger said. It was in January, the peak of recruiting season, when the football office got a memo from the school's comptroller saying their budget was frozen. "We couldn't spend any more money, not for erasers or pencils or phone calls to recruits," Schnellenberger said. "That scared all of us." So Schnellenberger and his staff began cobbling together all the dimes and quarters they could scrounge up and headed to the corner pay phone, where they dialed up recruits. One week later, Green shuffled some funds around and put some money in the football account and the freeze was lifted, allowing the staff to get back to tending to the State of Miami.

Schnellenberger's recruiting pitch was direct, as though he were challenging recruits. "This is what we're going to do,"

Schnellenberger would bark at them. "You want to be a part of it?" That not only appealed to the kind of player Schnellenberger wanted; it also fostered an us-against-the-world mentality. "He told you," said Don Bailey Jr., a Miami center in the early eighties, "'Someday we're going to win a national championship at Miami,' and you'd look into those eyes of his, and hell, yeah, you believed him." Schnellenberger was selling a vision. Good thing, because selling his run-down facilities or barren campus wouldn't have gone over quite as well.

"The facilities were utterly atrocious," said former Miami offensive guard Art Kehoe, who went on to become the 'Canes' offensive line coach and is the one link between all five national title teams. "It was all horrible. The locker room was just a bunch of rusty old lockers on concrete. The offices were horrible, and so were the film resources."

"There were no facilities," said Schnellenberger. "There wasn't even a place to hang a jockstrap." The weight room was the size of two cramped New York City hotel rooms. Strength coach Ray Ganong, a Hurricane fullback from the early seventies, took a sledgehammer to knock down one of the walls to make it one room. Inside were two weight benches with some of the padding missing, one power-lifting platform, a circa–Jack LaLanne squat rack, and some dumbbells. And there was no air-conditioning. "To call the place a joke would've been a compliment," said Ganong.

Schnellenberger closed a side shower stall to use as his de facto film lab, since back then everything in the NFL was done on 16mm film. Kehoe, a junior college transfer from California's Laney College, who, along with Smokey Roan, was among Schnellenberger's first Hurricane recruits, says the practice fields might've been the worst of all. On one side of the field stood an old tree that hung over a twenty-yard stretch of grass. Well, not exactly grass. "It always had this black mud and standing water," Kehoe said. "We used to have to do up-downs in that slop." Not that Kehoe knew any of this when he visited. "They just ran me through the locker room on my visit," he said. "And they really didn't want to show you the campus either. Kids came because we put 'em on a boat and showed them Key Biscayne, Coconut Grove, and Monty's, so we gave them a taste of the nightlife, because if facilities were graded from A to F, we were an F-minus."

The rest of campus wasn't that much better. Miami, which had been dubbed "Suntan U"—a school known more for its proximity to white-sand beaches than anything else—was essentially a marshland with a bunch of two-story buildings scattered just a nine-iron from U.S.-1. The place had all the charm of a doctor's office. Many students were the underachieving sons and daughters of rich Northeasterners. UM was a compromise school. It was part vacation, part education. Who cared what the classrooms looked like, when the beach was so close, right? Most of those kids didn't even know Miami had a football team, and they sure as hell weren't about to venture into "Little Havana" to visit the Orange Bowl to cheer the Hurricanes on.

Had he known just how low-budget the place was, would Kehoe still have come? "Of course. You just knew because of [Schnellenberger] and because of his background that this place was on the rise," Kehoe said. "I said to myself, maybe I can be part of something really nice down there. But I had no idea it would take off the way it did."

Schnellenberger and the Miami brass realized they would not only have to dupe recruits but prospective fans too. Especially since ABC was televising Schnellenberger's debut against

Louisville, and the school couldn't stomach the thought of cameras panning the stands of the 76,000-seat Orange Bowl and showing the rest of Southeastern America a vast array of empty bleachers. Instead, Miami officials would have those seats filled with Burger King customers, or at least folks who stopped at Burger King long enough to grab one of the 200,000 coupons for free admission to the game. Better still, for the allocation rights to 45,000 seats, Burger King kicked in $75,000 to Miami's athletic fund. "It was 'buy a Whopper and then take your tickets off the counter,'" said Tolbert Bain, then a Miami teen who would later play cornerback for the Hurricanes in the mid-eighties. "It was crazy. But, yeah, we'll go check that out." Miami beat Louisville 24–12 before a crowd of over 41,000—double what the 'Canes averaged the previous year.

Schnellenberger took on a ringleader persona, becoming a carnival barker for Miami football. In reality, he is a very private person, but since this was what the program needed, so be it. His first eighteen months on the job, Schnellenberger averaged two and a half speeches a day to the various gatherings he could find. "I'd talk to the Kiwanis Club, the Lions Club, the chamber of commerce," he said. "Anyplace where there were three or four people meeting, I was there." He did coaching clinics all over the state. He started a Long Name Club, with himself as president. He allowed the campus snack bar to tout "the Schnellen Burger." His weekly coach's show was beamed around the country by satellite. "Creating tradition" was how Schnellenberger saw it. He even took down the pictures from his days with the Baltimore Colts and Miami Dolphins that hung on the wall behind his desk and replaced them with an eighty-four-inch mounted sailfish. "*This* is Miami," he told reporters.

But that really wasn't what Miami football would be about under Schnellenberger. Like all good leaders—and generals—Schnellenberger's plan to build a powerhouse at Miami started with discipline. He harped on the "big three Cs: courage, commitment, and continuity." Kehoe estimates that Schnellenberger, through his demanding ways and practice habits, drove off twenty players that first spring. He ran off another ten in two-a-days at fall camp. "Howard never wanted to run anybody off," said Arnie Romero, the defensive ends coach from 1973–80. "He just stepped up the pace a lot."

"We were the Junction Boys," said linebacker Jay Brophy, evoking memories of Bear Bryant's famed first team of training camp survivors at Texas A&M. "We'd get up by six thirty, run 3.5 miles, go to breakfast, come back for a two-a-day practice, then have sprinting in the afternoon. There'd only be one water break per practice for two minutes, and then the water was taken off the field. Then you'd have meetings all night."

"I was always hiding ice bags underneath the yard markers because, other than that two-minute water break, he wouldn't let us have any drinks," said Kelly.

Schnellenberger had patterned his camp after the one that greeted him at the University of Kentucky in 1955. He had arrived in Lexington the summer before his freshman year as one of 132 first-year candidates for Bear Bryant's football squad. Only about forty survived that camp, and only a dozen completed four full years on the squad.

"That first camp at Miami was actually a lot harder than Junction, I tell you that," Schnellenberger said. "It was a lot harder and a lot longer than Coach Bryant was on his football team. I was with Coach Bryant at Kentucky when we went to Millersburg, and that was so much tougher than Junction. Millersburg made Junction look like a Boy Scout camp.

"Two things I promised the team when I came in: One, you'll be in better physical condition than anybody you play. I can control that. Two, you will be better prepared than anybody you play, and I control that too simply by a function of time. It was important that they buy into that, that they never go into a fourth quarter feeling tired."

Sure enough, after a few weeks Schnellenberger's survivors noticed the method to the man's madness, says Bailey. "You could tell we were getting better. 'Hey, this stuff is working.'

"He presses the physical and mental limits every way possible. But as hard as he pushes you, he has the ability to know when to pull off of you at the last second, which is an art."

"Right away he thinned out our troops and our depth, but he got the guys he wanted because of the discipline he instilled," Kehoe said. There were bed checks every night. At dawn, players had to be up for breakfast because there was a breakfast check too. Players had to be signed in for lunch and dinner also. "He wanted you at all the meals, not missing a class or anything," Kehoe said. "It was just a wholesale change in absolutely everything we did across the board. We felt like the Eye was always watching you, and if you brought a female into the dormitory, you were going to pay for what you did wrong."

Schnellenberger put building thirty-six, aka the football dorm, on lockdown. There was only a small window of time on Sundays when family was allowed to visit players' dorms. Friends or guests were forbidden. Only other players were allowed to come by. No women allowed, Schnellenberger warned. Or else. "I think he forced a lot of early marriages," Bailey joked. "Anything to get out of his dorms."

Two players sneaked girls in and got caught. Their punishment was "breakfast club." It was a nauseating blend of updowns, bear crawls, and full-length field rolls (in which you start on your side and roll the entire one hundred yards), and it started at six a.m.—not just for a couple of days or a week but for a whole month.

"Whatever coach was assigned to get you up at six in the morning, that guy was pissed off and he'd run you into the ground, and then they'd rotate coaches and that guy would be pissed to get up at six," Kehoe said. "You'd be dizzy. You'd be vomiting. You'd take a shower and say to yourself, 'I ain't ever gonna violate another rule again.' And that sent a message to everybody: You're gonna get up, go to breakfast, go to class, go to lunch, rehab your injuries, run, lift, study film, and then go to study hall, and if you wanted to be a part of it, you did it. And if you didn't you packed it in. It was a case of those who survived, thrived, and the word got out—this guy [Schnellenberger] is as serious as a heart attack—and along the way, you started to see we were getting better, we were tackling better, we were blocking better. We were becoming a team. We were scrapping our asses off, and because of that you start to care about one another, that bond develops, since you know what you sacrificed and what you went through together."

So Schnellenberger was stirring up a fan base and developing a hungry team spirit; all that was missing was a statement game. That would come November 3, 1979, up at Penn State, aka Happy Valley, the day Miami football officially turned the corner. Not that you could tell from the 'Canes' 3-4 record that a monumental event was about to take place. Miami was a forty-nine-point underdog. The Nittany Lions, 22-2 the previous two seasons, were again loaded with all-American types, defensive tackles Matt Millen and Bruce Clark, fullback Matt Suhey, and linebacker Lance Mehl, all athletic, lunch-pail guys in the Paterno mold. But Schnellenberger had a surprise for them—and for his own guys too. Just ten minutes before kick-off, Schnellenberger informed backup quarterback Jim Kelly that he would make his first career start. Kelly, the thick-necked redshirt freshman kid nicknamed "Big Country" who grew up just a two-hour drive from Happy Valley and was passed over so Paterno could sign QBs Terry Rakowsky and Frank Rocco, wasn't exactly expecting the news.

"He ran into the can, threw up, and he must've pissed his pants too, because he had a big wet spot there," said Romero. Kelly vomited a half dozen times during pregame warm-ups; he also threw up during the first huddle of the game.

Bailey, his new snapper, tight end Andy Baratta, and defensive end Greg Zappala were all true freshmen making their first starts. "I knew I was going up against their big star, Bruce Clark. I was pissing down my leg," Bailey said. Still, for all of the young 'Canes' jitters and expectorations, Miami blind-sided the Nittany Lions. Penn State's sellout crowd of 77,532 sat stunned as Miami opened the game with a scoring drive capped by an eight-yard Kelly touchdown pass to Jim Joiner. UM recovered a fumble on the ensuing kickoff, and added a twenty-yard Danny Miller field goal for a 10–0 lead before State had run an offensive play. Leading 13–10 at the half, Miami dominated the second half and put the game away with a twenty-five-yard pass from Kelly to Joiner in the third period and a six-yard strike from Kelly to Pat Walker. The rookie QB, the one Paterno had wanted as a linebacker, threw for 280 yards and three touchdowns as Miami pulled out a 26–10 victory.

"Kelly won the game single-handedly," said Schnellenberger. "He changed us from an ordinary team into a great team."

Schnellenberger waited to start Kelly not because he didn't think the young quarterback was ready, but because the rest of his offense wasn't ready to win. The upset over Penn State showed the country—and the 'Canes—that Schnellenberger knew exactly what he was doing. It also proved to Schnellenberger that Kelly was indeed his go-to guy. Schnellenberger had sensed in Kelly the same poise and command that he noticed in another western Pennsylvania quarterback he had worked with during his days at Alabama, Joe Namath. And Kelly had the guile that Schnellenberger loved so much when he recruited Kenny "the Snake" Stabler to Alabama.

Like Schnellenberger, Kelly was the son of a scrap-iron tough guy. Kelly's father, Joe Kelly, was raised in an orphanage and joined the navy when he was seventeen. The old man made Jim and his five brothers put on boxing gloves to settle things whenever the boys had a beef with one another. When Jim was ten, his father made him come home from school during lunch to practice football drills.

"All I can say is from that day, when he was in the huddle you knew you had a chance," said Bailey. "Every snap he took, I don't care what the score was, I don't care what the temperature was, when Jim Kelly was your quarterback, your ass was in the ball game. It's hard to explain, but you just knew he was the difference. He just had that mythical thing. That *it* thing."

Kelly knew how to inspire his teammates. He wasn't a kick-'em-in-the-ass, grab-their-face-mask kind of leader. "Jim was the other way, the better way," Bailey said. "If I made a mistake on the snap count, he would say it was his fault. If somebody didn't hear something, he'd take the blame. He knew the coaches would just say, 'C'mon, Jim, do better.' If someone else was guilty, then it was 'You stupid m-f'er,' and they'd be running forever. With Jim covering for you, you'd be like 'Damn, bro, how can I let that guy down?'"

Even though UM finished the '79 season 5-6, Schnellen-berger got what he wanted: a budding fan base, a hungry, close-knit team, and a poised young field general to pilot his offense. Best of all, everyone had expectations. It was just as he'd hoped.

3

HOWARD'S END

Schnellenberger's mantra for year two was "A bowl is the goal." Schnellenberger always was big on mantras. He understood how they gave people, particularly young people, something to grasp onto, something to believe in. "It gave him something to preach," said Don Bailey Jr., a Miami center in the early eighties. "That was like his sermon. He was always just so positive. 'You're getting there. You're getting there!'

"With Howard it was either 'Get on the bus' or 'Get the hell out of the way!' "

Armed with a talented young passer like Kelly and the feisty spirit Schnellenberger had inspired, the Miami Hurricanes were clearly no longer a punch line. They proved that by winning their first four games—including victories over Cotton Bowl champ Houston and Orange Bowl participant Florida State—en route to an 8-3 season. More than fifty thousand showed up for the win over FSU, a bigger crowd than the one the NFL's Dolphins drew in the same stadium the next day. The 'Canes finished the year in the Peach Bowl, making their first postseason appearance since 1967. Their opponent was Virginia Tech, coached by Bill Dooley, the guy who backed out at the last minute, clearing the way for Schnellenberger to take over at UM. The Hurricanes won, 20–10.

"The reason we won early [in Schnellenberger's tenure] was because he got us prepared mentally," said Bailey. "The physical part caught on later. He just outcoached people sometimes. He outcoached friggin' Joe Paterno with kids who probably shouldn't have been on the field."

Everything about UM football was punctuated, or better yet, preceded by Schnellenberger's audacious attitude. And heck, why should his players doubt him? Schnellenberger was always backing up all his claims, regardless of how crazy they may have sounded to the rest of the world. Just like the day before Notre Dame came to town in '81.

ABC, knowing Schnellenberger's penchant for promotion, asked him if he'd allow one of their cameras in the Miami locker room at halftime to record his comments. Schnellenberger balked. "It could be pretty lopsided by halftime." The TV producer acknowledged that given Notre Dame's lofty status and the fact that the Irish had perpetually blistered UM, having beaten them eleven times straight by an average of twenty points per game.

"No," replied Schnellenberger. "I mean we might be so far ahead I may not have to say anything." The producer opted to tape Schnellenberger's pregame speech instead, and sure enough, UM jumped out to a 30–6 halftime lead, en route to a 37–15 rout—just as Schnellenberger had said.

"Reaching higher" was Schnellenberger's mantra for 1981, and the Hurricanes did, going 9-2, including a shocking 17–14 win over then number one–ranked Penn State.

Year four's mantra was "Go for it." The *it*, of course, being the national title. That may've sounded even too optimistic for Schnellenberger, but not when you consider that in UM's two losses in '81, both games—at Texas and at Mississippi State—were decided by a touchdown, and in both games UM had touchdowns called back on questionable penalties. "We probably should've been playing for the title in his third year on the job," said Bailey.

Unfortunately for UM in 1982, Kelly, a senior Heisman Trophy candidate, separated his right shoulder in the third game of the season, against Virginia Tech. Miami lost four games, three of which were by a total of seven points. After the season, Kelly, along with six others, was selected in the NFL draft. That made twenty-three draft picks in the previous three years—as many as UM had produced in the prior six drafts. Perfect. Schnellenberger could sell that to new recruits. He knew what really mattered to high school stars—playing in a system that would get them ready for the NFL, and clearly UM was now on the League's radar. Just as important, he could tout instant playing time—if the player was ready. "We are the 'pipeline to the pros,'" Schnellenberger told prospects. The walls around the State of Miami just got a little bit higher. "Ninety-five percent of our recruiting was south of Orlando," Schnellenberger said. "We had been to all the schools to visit their principal, the guidance counselor, the head coach, and all the assistant coaches at least twice a year if they didn't even have a player. And if they did have a player we wanted, we'd be in there every chance we could get. The end result was we got the best players. We bloodied Bobby Bowden's nose. We shut [Florida coach] Charley Pell out, and we kept those carpetbaggers from the North from getting the best kids."

Although, with Kelly in pro football, a new field general had to be found. Again, Schnellenberger believed he had the ideal man for the job.

This time, though, the guy didn't have a linebacker's neck or spirit; he was scrawny with a concave chest and bony limbs. He had curly hair and big round eyes, the kind you might see on a Raggedy Ann doll. The dude looked more like a rabbinical student. But, oh, could Bernie Kosar play quarterback. Schnellenberger was so convinced he made Kosar his starting quarterback, ahead of another redshirt freshman with a more imposing build and stronger arm, Vinny Testaverde. Most schools had their doubts about Kosar: Pittsburgh and Ohio State, schools just an hour or two from his home in Boardman, Ohio, didn't give him a sniff.

Kosar joined an eclectic cast, many of whom were like 242-pound nose guard Tony Fitzpatrick, who came to Miami with only one other scholarship offer (from tiny Liberty Baptist). Fitzpatrick, who was told by a high school coach he'd never play a down of college football, was a gym rat who could bench-press twice his body weight. He was "discovered" by Bailey while both were playing in Florida's North–South All-Star Game after their senior years of high school. Fitzpatrick took home MVP honors at that game, then received a call from UM coaches after two days of practice at Liberty and got on the first flight he could find from Lynchburg, Virginia, to south Florida. These were guys who resented the college football establishment and felt like outsiders. There were also guys like middle linebacker Jay Brophy, who chose Miami over

Michigan because he trusted Schnellenberger. Brophy was from Akron, Ohio, and looked like an Oakland Raider, like he could've been Lyle Alzado's kid brother. He had a bushy black Afro and thick beard. The look was important because it told you that even though there was no stricter disciplinarian, Schnellenberger encouraged his players to be themselves, and he understood that might make them play even harder, freer, with more passion. "If you feel like high-fiving one of your teammates, do it," he implored them.

Brophy had played tight end his freshman year and was on the field that magical day when Kelly went back to Pennsylvania and knocked off Penn State. ("Screwed up real bad that day too," he says, of whiffing on a block near the goal line and forgetting a play that he was bringing in from the sideline.) Brophy also quit Miami after his freshman year. Maybe this isn't for me, he thought. Maybe he didn't have the commitment Schnellenberger was demanding. "Maybe I need to go into the real world," Brophy said. So he did; he took a job with his older brother working in West Helena, Arkansas, cleaning out the Mohawk Rubber Plant—"the scourge of the earth," in Brophy's words. One day he found himself standing on a bridge overlooking the Mississippi River thinking, What the hell have I done?

Brophy called his old position coach, Hubbard Alexander, and asked if he thought the old man would take him back. Schnellenberger accepted. One year later Brophy was the team's defensive captain and its conscience. "Yeah, we were cocky, but it really was out of confidence," he said. "We didn't want to lose anymore. Coach Schnellenberger instilled that in you. That's why we played with that chip on our shoulder. We knew we had it. We felt you had to come beat us."

Schnellenberger now had a rowdy brood of salty veterans who would soon get trumped by a brazen crop of newcomers that were drawn to Miami because they wanted to be part of the upstart program that had fostered a gunslinger's image. The program reflected the city's own persona. It was, in a word, hard.

The city had had its fists balled up since the summer of 1980. Tension began to stew in April, the beginning of a wave called the Mariel Boatlift that would bring more than 125,000 Cubans across the Straits of Florida, changing forever the immigration policy of south Florida—and its demographic. Of those refugees, about 10 percent were purported to be among Cuba's most hardened criminals and most dangerous mental patients. They fed a crime rate that had become Miami's dirty little secret, although suddenly it wasn't such a secret nor very little; murders soon averaged 1.5 a day. Miami became the nation's homicide capital. Many were casualties of the drug wars. The medical examiner rented a refrigerator truck to hold the overflow corpses.

One month after Mariel, in Liberty City, the heart of black Miami, one of the country's worst riots in history would break out and choke the city. The chaos stemmed from an incident the previous December, when a thirty-three-year-old black insurance agent named Arthur McDuffie made a rolling stop at a red light and popped a wheelie on his Kawasaki motorcycle. Police say McDuffie then gave the finger to a Dade County police officer parked nearby. The officer gave chase. By the time Arthur McDuffie was caught, eight minutes later, more than a dozen Dade County and City of Miami police units had converged on the scene. Accounts vary on what happened next. What is known is that at some point a rescue unit was called, for the victim of an "accident," and that four days later Arthur McDuffie died, without regaining consciousness, in Jackson Memorial Hospital. Following an investigation, nine officers were suspended, and four—all white—were charged by Janet Reno in the state attorney's office with manslaughter and tampering with evidence. A sergeant was charged with tampering and leading a cover-up.

The trial came before an all-white jury in Tampa, where the case had been moved after a Miami judge granted a change of venue with these words: "This case is a time bomb. I don't want to see it go off in my courtroom or in this community."

It took only three hours for the jury to deliver a verdict. Not guilty—on all charges. News of the four cops' acquittal hit the Associated Press wire that clear Saturday afternoon, May 17, by two forty-two p.m. The first police call reporting rioting in Liberty City came three hours and twenty minutes later, from the Miami Police Department. By nine forty-four p.m., when a call was placed to Tallahassee asking that the National Guard be sent in, there was rioting not only in Liberty City but in Overtown and around the entire Metro Justice complex, where doctors and nurses answering emergency calls to Jackson Memorial Hospital were being stoned and beaten and the Metro Justice building itself was being torched. The violence was confined to a relatively few blocks near the ramshackle James E. Scott Homes, the largest housing project in the state. Four days later, when the Liberty City riot was over, there were eighteen dead, eight of them whites who had driven down the wrong streets and been stoned or doused with gasoline and set afire, or, in the case of one, a twenty-two-year-old warehouse loader on his way home from a day at the beach with his girlfriend and younger brother, dragged from the car to be beaten, kicked, and struck—not only with bottles and bricks but also a twenty-three-pound chunk of concrete. Then he was pounded with a *Miami Herald* newspaper dispenser, shot, stabbed with a screwdriver, run over by a green Cadillac, and left, one ear cut off and lying on his chest, with his tongue cut out and a red rose in his mouth.

In all, four hundred people were treated at hospitals; seventy-one businesses in the community were destroyed and hundreds damaged; $100 million in property was lost.

Two years later, in 1982, in Overtown—just two miles from Liberty City—another riot was touched off after the fatal shooting of a black youth by a Hispanic police officer at an arcade. The officer, Luis Alvarez, was charged with culpable negligence and recklessness, and faced a maximum penalty of fifteen years in prison and a $10,000 fine. Ultimately, Alvarez was found not guilty. The verdict sparked another series of riots in both Overtown and Liberty City. (The city's reputation would take more hits at the end of the decade, when there were more riots after the Super Bowl came to Miami, giving the mess a national audience. Eighteen months after that, *60 Minutes* reporter Lesley Stahl actually would get mugged—twice—while working on a story about Miami crime.)

America, especially white America, shrieked. In the 1980s, the numbers of non-Hispanic white residents in Miami–Dade County decreased by nearly 170,000. This was no longer the Del Boca Vista–looking, pinocle-playing Miami most people pictured, and its football team wasn't the one that was getting bullied by the Notre Dames and Alabamas anymore either.

UM's rookie class of '83 came about when two of the top

three prospects in the state, Alonzo Highsmith and Melvin Bratton, both Miami natives, decided to play together when they met at a *Miami Herald* photo shoot for a story on great local talent. Bratton, a running back, had been leaning toward Miami ever since he and his best friend Tolbert Bain, an oversize cornerback, took a recruiting visit to Texas A&M. "I had wanted to get away from Miami so bad," Bratton said. "But then we're out in the middle of Texas, and I looked at Tolbert and said, 'Bro, we will not survive out here in the country. We're city boys. There's cows and shit out here. We're gonna end up in trouble and getting kicked out.'"

Highsmith, considered the top linebacker in the state and possibly the country, had become intrigued with UM ever since his junior year of high school, when he attended the Miami–Florida game in the Orange Bowl and felt a charge seeing the 'Canes bolt out of the tunnel amid a stream of white smoke. Highsmith, though, startled most of his friends when he chose Miami. "They all laughed at me," he said. "But I believed in what Coach Schnellenberger was saying. Whenever I talked to Notre Dame and Michigan, all they talked about was their tradition. Coach Schnellenberger just looked me right in the eye and said, 'If you go here with this group of kids, we can dominate college football.'"

Dominate? Yeah, Highsmith thought, I like the sound of that.

That group Schnellenberger had assembled included Bratton, Highsmith, and Bain, along with center Gregg Rakoczy, tight ends Charles Henry and Alfredo Roberts, wide receiver Brian Blades, defensive back Selwyn Brown, linebacker–defensive end Daniel Stubbs, linebacker Winston Moss, cornerback Darrell Fullington, and a tight end—soon to become a defensive tackle—named Jerome Brown. "We all just clicked right away," said Highsmith.

"Miami got a lot of players, especially from our class, because they let you be yourself," Bain said. Among the twenty-five recruits were two future first-round picks, four second-rounders, and one third-rounder—and another guy (Bratton) who was projected to be one of the top five picks had he not blown out his knee in his final college game. In all, twelve players from the class would play in the NFL. "That was the best recruiting class I believe that's ever been put together in the history of college football," Schnellenberger said. They were fast, fierce, and ornery.

"Our mentality of that class changed Miami football," Bratton said.

They realized they had a special chemistry their first week on campus, and the chip that was on Miami's shoulder became a mountain. "I'll never forget it," Bratton said. "*Cujo* [the Stephen King novel about a rabid dog] was out [as a movie] and we had all walked from campus to the Rivera Theater [about a mile]. Something happened in the movie when a guy lashed out in the theater. Jerome Brown stood up and told him, 'Shut the fuck up.' Someone made a comment in response, and we were ready to go to war. Everybody, all seventeen guys in the class, stood up." No punches needed to be thrown, but it became apparent that Cujo wasn't the only hungry beast on the loose. Miami football was salivating.

This class, though, didn't just bring spectacular talent; it brought a whole new culture to Miami, and in a larger sense to college football. Bratton and Highsmith, both charismatic characters, had developed icon status in their roughneck sections of Miami. Bratton came from the northwest area and brought his following from Liberty City. Highsmith brought his from the southside. "Now all of a sudden, even though we had shitty facilities, the Hurricanes became the 'in' thing,"

Highsmith said. "All the hustlers in town, they all embraced the Hurricanes. They were proud."

The 'Canes took their young bunch of rabid dogs up to Gainesville for the '83 opener, where 74,000 hostile Gator fans were waiting for Miami's redshirt freshman QB. Florida pounded Kosar and the 'Canes 28–3. But Kosar did tie George Mira's single-game record for completions with twenty-five. He also won over any teammates longing for Kelly when a woozy Kosar came to the sideline and huffed, "Those SOBs aren't going to put me out of this game! Where's the smelling salts?"

Still, many of the Hurricanes wondered if Schnellenberger started the wrong redshirt freshman quarterback. Some of them were more enamored with Testaverde and his rifle arm. "Most of the team wanted Vinny," said cornerback Rodney Bellinger. "Kosar had no athletic ability, but he had a brain. We didn't know that after the first game."

After the Gator rout, Schnellenberger considered "taking the players to the woodshed." Instead, though, when he entered the locker room he thanked the Hurricanes for their effort. "If I have made any good decisions, it was to reflect on what happened before I entered the locker room," Schnellenberger said. "Instead of displaying my ignorance and throwing chairs against the wall, I told them we lost because of errors and not because of a lack of effort."

Schnellenberger's head games worked. Just a few Saturdays later, on a steamy night in late September, with more than 52,000 in the stands, and a CBS national television audience watching, the Hurricanes—led by their rookie QB and an ornery defense—rattled the college football landscape again by shutting out thirteenth-ranked Notre Dame 20–0. Kosar picked apart Irish blitzes, completing twenty-two of thirty-three passes for

215 yards, while the D forced three turnovers and stopped the Irish inside UM's 10 yard line three times. Cornerback Reggie Sutton, one of Schnellenberger's finds from inner-city Miami, showed the Irish—if not the nation—the face of Hurricane football by blocking two field goals, batting down four passes, and making nine tackles. "We started talking to 'em," Sutton said after the game. "We started intimidating them, calling them names. We figured if we could make them talk back to us, they wouldn't have their minds on what they were doing."

The 'Canes reeled off eleven consecutive wins, earning Miami's first Orange Bowl bid in thirty-three years, and a shot at Nebraska. And if somehow they could upset the Cornhuskers and things broke just right, meaning the other unbeaten team, Texas, also had to lose, the 'Canes might even have a chance at claiming the national championship. But who thought Miami had a prayer against Nebraska?

Big Red had been steamrolling opponents. The Cornhuskers were averaging an unbelievable fifty-two points per game. Many were touting them as the best college team ever, and why not? Tom Osborne's program was on a twenty-two-game winning streak. They were the epitome of farm-fed Midwest-strong-boy football. Led by Heisman Trophy–winning tailback Mike Rozier, elusive QB Turner Gill, and speedy wingback Irving Fryar, the Cornhuskers' ground attack was hammering opponents for over four hundred yards per game. Their vaunted offensive line, anchored by beefy all-American Dean Steinkuhler, would outweigh their Hurricane opponents across the line of scrimmage by an average of thirty-six pounds per man. Miami didn't even have one all-American player on its roster. "No one gave us a chance in hell," Brophy said. "But I'll never forget it. We're staying at the Omni Hotel and we just had one of our first meetings and I remember Bernie and our center Ian Sinclair walking out saying, 'We are going to pass all over them. They haven't seen the pass.'"

So what if Vegas had made the upstart Hurricanes an eleven-point underdog? Schnellenberger strutted around in his Oriental smoking jacket and red felt slippers on the eve of the game like a guy clinging to the world's best-kept secret. Was he crazy? The media, now with no choice but to focus on Miami, was smitten with the quirky colonel, who one day would refer to his undersize linemen as "rejects and retreads," and the next day arrive for a press conference via helicopter.

Just how could Schnellenberger look so . . . well, smug? reporters wondered. "My guys are about to face the Russian army, and they don't care," Schnellenberger informed them.

Why should Miami have been scared? Turns out, the Hurricanes were the ones with the blueprint for how to topple Nebraska. "Weight only works against you if it's leaning on you," Schnellenberger preached. "If it's not, if it has to stop to figure out where to lean, it's not a factor." To do that, to bewilder the Cornhuskers, Miami's defensive schemes would rely on a variety of looks. Defenders would jump in and out of gaps. Safetymen would feint blitzes and then back out. Schnellenberger and his staff had also noticed on film that Nebraska center Mark Traynowicz snapped the ball on his own count, when he was ready, so the Hurricane linemen—just like the Cornhuskers front—keyed Traynowicz, giving Miami a much-needed split-second jump. "It'd look like he [Traynowicz] was cocking a shotgun when he was snapping the ball," said Fitzpatrick. Schnellenberger also would dare Gill to pass, by unleashing his corners Rodney Bellinger and Reggie Sutton to attack the Nebraska backfield like linebackers.

Beating Nebraska was one thing; overtaking two other teams ahead of the fourth-ranked 'Canes in the polls was another. The Orange Bowl was the last game of the evening, and wouldn't you believe it, UM got its big break: Second-ranked Texas, the country's other unbeaten, was knocked off by Georgia, 10–9, in the Cotton Bowl.

"After we saw that Texas lost, everybody was so fired up that we left the hotel early," said Brophy. "When we got to the Orange Bowl, people were shaking the buses."

Actually, the whole city of Miami had been shaking. All week leading up to the game, the city had been bracing for the Alvarez arcade shooting trial, and the riots that would follow the verdict. In contrast, the Hurricanes, with their blend of Hispanic, black, and white players, had become a source of unity in south Florida. Through Schnellenberger, the team had taken on a leadership role in a PR campaign touting "Miami Is for Me." All of the players wore the slogan on their helmets. Schnellenberger wore a big button on his jacket. And as soon as Miami charged out of the tunnel through the blast of white smoke, the deafening roar from the Orange Bowl crowd almost had Schnellenberger feeling sorry for Nebraska.

"South Florida rose up that night as one," said Schnellenberger. "Nebraska had virtually no chance to win. I would hate like hell to have been the coach of Nebraska that night."

In the locker room, Hall of Fame quarterback Joe Namath, whom Schnellenberger coached at Alabama, spoke to the team before the game. Namath, Schnellenberger's "honorary captain," didn't hesitate to point out the irony that the Orange Bowl was, of course, the site of his heroic Super Bowl III victory where he had the gall to predict that his New York Jets would upset the supposedly invincible Baltimore Colts. Namath,

though, had been right that time back in 1969, and he was predicting another shocker in the Orange Bowl.

When the game unfolded, it was just as Schnellenberger
and Namath had pictured. Well, almost. Nebraska switched
the jerseys of two defensive backs, a legal ploy as long as referees were informed, an hour before the game, in an attempt to
confuse Kosar. Didn't work. Kosar picked apart Nebraska's defense anyway, hitting on all three of his pass attempts in the
midst of a fifty-seven-yard touchdown march, capped off by a
two-yard TD pass to tight end Glenn Dennison. It was indeed
too easy. Before the first quarter was over, Kosar would connect
with Dennison again, this time on a twenty-two-yard touchdown toss, to give Miami a 17–0 lead.

Nebraska would rally, eventually making it 31–24. Then, after a UM field goal attempt sailed wide, the Cornhuskers got
the ball back with 1:47 remaining. In fifty-nine seconds Gill—
even without Rozier (out after twisting his ankle in the third
quarter)—took Nebraska seventy-four yards. The Huskers
would score on a fourth-and-eight from the Miami 24 when reserve tailback Jeff Smith took a Gill pitch, dashed around the
right end, and dove into the end zone. Just like that, it was
31–30. If Osborne kicked the extra point and ended the game
in a tie score, Nebraska would still win the national title. Instead, he opted for the two-point attempt and the lead.

Gill took the snap and rolled right. Miami's defense was
playing something called "55 Double Dog Trio," and rover
Kenny Calhoun, seeing Fryar release to the inside, broke to
the right flat to pick up Smith. Gill fired, but the ball was a bit
behind Smith and Calhoun batted it away. "I got three fingers
of my left hand on the ball," Calhoun said of swatting away
Nebraska's number one ranking. "I do that kind of thing all
the time," he said with a wink.

Think that was brash? Kosar said he *wanted* Nebraska to convert on the two-point attempt, so Miami would've trailed 32–31 with forty-eight seconds remaining. "There was plenty of time for us to at least get in position for a field goal," he said. "We would've done it too, the way we were moving the ball. Forty-eight seconds was more than enough time. It would've been fun." No matter, Schnellenberger had done just as he said he would; he brought a national championship to UM.

Everyone called it "the Miracle in Miami." Everyone except, of course, the colonel himself. Schnellenberger scoffed when he heard that. "A miracle?" he said incredulously. "I'd prefer to say this was a team of destiny. I wasn't surprised. All along I'd felt it coming."

Maybe so, but few around Coral Gables could've expected what happened five months later. Hurricane Howard was leaving UM. "We were all shocked," said Highsmith. Schnellenberger had accepted a $3 million deal to run a team in the USFL, a springtime competitor of the NFL. The announcement put an end to the whispers around Coral Gables over a power struggle between Schnellenberger and the new athletic director, Sam Jankovich, and UM president Tad Foote. Among the issues that Schnellenberger had been stewing over was the reluctance from university officials to build an on-campus football stadium and a projected cutback in funds for the athletic department for 1984 after the football team had earned an extra $1.8 million for the school as a result of being invited to play in the Orange Bowl.

"No one at the university wanted much to do with the football program when we got there, so we did a lot of things that were innovative and different," Schnellenberger said. When Jankovich took over in July 1983, replacing Harry Mallios, who retired, he set up new chains of command, new lines of communication, and new areas of responsibility. "A lot of red tape," Schnellenberger deemed it.

"Coaches coach. Administrators administrate. Boosters support," Jankovich said. "We're here to service the coach, to make life as easy for him as possible. But the coach is not supposed to be out merchandising and selling his people. That's not his job."

Schnellenberger exited Miami the same way he entered, on a power play. He had done just as he said—won the national title within five years—and just like that, he was gone. An era was over. His legacy, though, is open-ended. "If [Schnellenberger] had stayed at Miami, he'd be the greatest coach in the history of football, bar none," predicted Kehoe. "We'd have ten titles and he'd be more legendary than Bear Bryant." (Schnellenberger resurfaced at Louisville in 1985, where he built that program into a top-twenty team before he spent one season at Oklahoma in 1995, going 5-5-1. In 2003, he led Florida Atlantic, a school that didn't even have a football team three years earlier, to the semifinals of the 1-AA play-offs.)

Ten days after Schnellenberger turned in his resignation, Jankovich announced the hiring of Miami's new coach, Jimmy Johnson, a chubby, beady-eyed Texan who had quietly built a strong reputation at Oklahoma State as a defensive guru. When he arrived, Johnson griped about two hurdles facing him: a ridiculously tough schedule facing eight bowl teams (including four in a twenty-day stretch to start the season) and the fact that the change happened one month after spring ball ended. Johnson didn't know it, but an even bigger hurdle was awaiting him in Coral Gables—his new staff.

4

THE RENEGADE

Scarhead wasn't trying to be a prick. It's just that sometimes the fast-talking boy with the devilish grin, blond buzz cut, and perpetual I'm-up-to-something-squint couldn't help himself. Like during those days back in history class at Port Arthur's Jefferson High. Scarhead—the nickname buddies pinned on young Jimmy Johnson because the guy was always diving headfirst into something—would whip around in his seat and make some obnoxious crack about "Beatweeds," the homely beatnik girl sitting behind him. Scarhead just couldn't resist. Maybe it was because he got bored so easily. Janis Joplin, aka Beatweeds, never did forgive him for that.

Everybody else, though, around the old refinery town in east Texas loved Scarhead. He was C.W. and Alleen Johnson's middle child, he supposedly had an IQ of 162, and yeah, he was always up to something. Yet Jimmy never seemed to get caught. That was part of his charm. Jimmy loved the idea that he could outfox someone. Always did. Once when his big brother, Wayne, was nine and Jimmy was six, their old man caught them smoking in a movie theater. C.W., a supervisor at the local dairy, took the boys home, gave each one a fat stogie, and made them both light 'em up. "Jimmy knew how to smoke just as much as I did," Wayne would say. "But when Jimmy lit his cigar, he started blowing the smoke out the end, rather than drawing on it. Daddy said, 'Aw, Jimmy, you don't even know how to smoke. Wayne put you up to it.' Daddy made me smoke both of 'em, and I got sick. And Jimmy was lying in bed laughing. He knew what he'd done."

Jimmy was slick like that. At twelve, he and his best friend, Max, had charmed their way into the hearts of the men who ran the local bordello. The women working there didn't let the boys partake in any action, but they all thought the little tykes were cute, so they let Jimmy and Max hang around. Soon the boys were charging other kids twenty-five cents for a "tour" of the place, which basically meant having one of the women, wearing nothing more than her nightgown, sit on some amazed twelve-year-old's lap. After a month or so, the coins were rolling in—till C.W. found out and chased the boys home.

Still, for all of Jimmy's antics and his penchant for playing people, he had a genuine human side. There was something very real about him: an openness to people, all people, something you didn't expect to see much of in segregated Port Arthur. Maybe it was because his old man put him to work the summer after fourth grade at the local dairy. Little Jimmy worked side by side with the black and Mexican women working there. Some afternoons he worked as a route helper and

rode a delivery truck with a Cajun named Blackie. The inter-
actions were so normal he never seemed to notice the change
from the town's segregated ways. When he got older and attended all-white Jefferson High, Johnson would snap at anyone who made a racist remark.

"I remember one time this real tough kid in town said
something negative toward blacks, using the N-word, and
Jimmy stopped it right there," said Johnson's childhood buddy
Jim "Max" Maxfield. "But Jimmy did it in a way where there
wasn't a challenge; it was like, 'We don't need to talk about
people like that.' Jimmy always was able to look at a person as
an individual." Maxfield reasons that that was why he never saw
Scarhead initmidated by anyone. Not by bullies, not even by
the pro wrestlers who came to town. "If John Wayne had
walked into our classroom, all of us would have been blown
away. But not Jimmy. He would've walked up, shook Wayne's
hand, and said, 'I'm Jimmy Johnson.' "

Johnson's grit and guile enabled him to become an all-state
lineman for coach Buckshot Underwood, an old pal of Bear
Bryant's, at Jefferson High. It also got him the distinction of
captaining Arkansas's national title team of '64, where he
earned the nickname "Jimmy Jump-up." No doubt that same
spunk surely played a big part in his transforming an Oklahoma State Cowboys team that had just fifty scholarship players (due to NCAA probation) and patching together a squad
that won seven games his first season as coach. Although after
his fifth year at Okie State, a year in which he led the Cowboys
to an 8-4 season and signed blue-chip Texas tailback Thurman
Thomas, Johnson was ready for a new challenge.

Sam Jankovich had been headhunting at a coaches' convention for Schnellenberger's replacement when he pulled

Johnson aside to get some advice on other coaches. Johnson's take? "I wouldn't mind living on the beach, Sam."

Part of the deal when Johnson took over in Coral Gables, though, was that he had to retain Schnellenberger's staff, some of which, particularly defensive coordinator Tom Olivadotti, felt like they should've gotten the top job. Before Johnson met the media in Miami, Jankovich told him he wanted Johnson to meet his new coaching staff. They met at the Miami Airport Marriott. At the time Johnson had no clue that Olivadotti or offensive coordinator Gary Stevens or Schnellenberger's administrative assistant, Bill Trout, had applied and been considered for the job. Johnson says in his autobiography that he was also unaware that each of the ten assistant coaches waiting for him had been told to make an evaluation of Johnson—and if they wanted to stay on, fine. If they didn't, they would still receive their salary for the year. Jankovich introduced Johnson and then ducked out of the room. Johnson admits he was clearly unnerved. "I was stammering and struggling for words," he said in his biography. "Remember, I didn't know they had an option. I thought we were all supposed to make the best of this. I said, 'Well, to get things started, why don't we go around the table, you introduce yourself, tell me who you are and what you coach, and a little bit about yourself.'

"The whole time I was talking, Olivadotti was sitting there with a set of keys in his hand, continually dropping the keys on the table, picking them up, and dropping them. Picking them up . . . and dropping them . . . clink . . . clink . . . clink . . ."

Johnson walked around the table, asked some questions, and was greeted with one- and two-word answers. And through it all: clink . . . clink . . . clink. "Finally," Johnson wrote, "Olivadotti spoke up and said, 'I've seen your teams play, and I really don't think our philosophies could coexist. I can't coach defense the way your teams play defense.'"

Olivadotti, the man Schnellenberger recommended to get the position, resigned two days later. Johnson, taking over in June, wanted to install his 4-3 defensive package, but knew it was too far into the off-season, so he stuck with the old 5-2 system that would be run by Olivadotti protégé Bill Trout. It turned out that neither the defense nor many of Schnellenberger's coaches meshed with J.J. Players weren't quite sure how to handle the change either. Maybe they just felt a huge sense of relief, as though they had just been discharged from Howard's army. Or maybe it was as Schnellenberger had warned them in spring ball: They had developed a case of "championship-itis."

"I think we tested Jimmy," said Ian Sinclair, who was a fifth-year senior and UM's starting center in Johnson's first season. "It was almost like he had to earn it from us more than we did from him. We shouldn't have done that, but we did."

Some players, like Highsmith, the budding star fullback, discussed transferring as they watched Johnson find his way. Others, like dominating sophomore defensive tackle Jerome Brown, reveled in the freedom that the new coach afforded them. The freshmen crop, led by dynamic safety Bennie Blades, linebackers Rod Carter and Randy Shannon, defensive tackle Bill Hawkins, safety Bubba McDowell, and a pair of brash wide-outs, Brett Perriman and Michael Irvin, not only added an astounding boost of speed but more attitude and rage too. Johnson got wind of that during fall camp after one of the UM assistants reported back that there had been a fight in the cafeteria between Irvin, a spindly 190-pound receiver, and Mike

Moore, a 245-pound fifth-year senior offensive guard. "It was a mismatch," Johnson was told. He figured that meant Moore mauled the eighteen-year-old. Instead, it was Irvin who had dropped Moore after the upperclassman tried cutting in front of him in line.

Johnson, like most football coaches, relished the competitiveness, but what UM seemed to have was beyond that, more like combativeness. And now there was room for it to breathe, to grow, and feed off itself. Players suddenly weren't just *allowed* to be themselves; they felt compelled to be themselves. And so what grew out of Schnellenberger's absence was a mangy garden that had some brilliant red roses but also some very sharp thorns.

"I saw the same group of young men's attitudes change with the type of leadership they had," said Ray Ganong, the former UM strength coach. One day during a workout session, Ganong got into it with the 285-pound Brown. "We were nose-to-nose, and neither one of us is backing down, and I'm thinking, 'Oh, my God, I hope he doesn't swing because I will lose this battle.'" The two men were separated before punches were thrown, but Ganong realized maybe it was time to rejoin Schnellenberger, who was taking over at Louisville. "Things had really changed. That thought [of challenging a coach] never would've entered Jerome's mind if Howard was still there."

The players, though, had been caught in the middle of a power struggle among a fractured coaching staff, and in the last four games the Hurricanes' defense yielded an average of thirty-five points per game. UM slogged its way to an 8-5 season, losing its last three games in heartbreaking fashion. In one game Miami led Maryland 31–0 at the half, only to lose 42–40 after the Terps pulled off the biggest comeback in

NCAA history. Thirteen days later, on Thanksgiving weekend, UM lost in a shoot-out to Boston College, 47–45 on Doug Flutie's famous Hail Mary pass. In the locker room after the game, Trout resigned over "philosophical differences."

Trout had been blunt about the fact that he wanted out. "The last four games, we'd come in and hear our defensive coordinator saying, 'I'm quitting after this season.' And we were thinking, 'Wow, these guys could care less if we win or lose,'" linebacker Bruce Fleming said.

Then, in the Fiesta Bowl, Miami lost to UCLA 39–37 on a last-minute Bruins field goal. Players sensed the nervous tension that had hovered over the team all season. "A lot of finger-pointing," Johnson called it. He would make sure after the season that the 'Canes would have his imprint on them the next time they took the field.

Trout's departure was followed by that of assistants Chris Vagotis and Marc Trestman. Johnson later would kid with reporters about his relationship with his staff. He picked up a letter opener, placed it between his arm and side so that it appeared he had been stabbed in the back, and said, "This is the picture of me they should have used in the media guide."

Off the field, the 'Canes' reckless renegade image was starting to take hold too. In February of '85, seven Hurricanes were arrested during one two-week stretch on charges ranging from disorderly conduct to trespassing.

During the off-season, Johnson cleaned house and brought in coaches he trusted. He decided to have one bus for the offensive players and one for the defensive. That way players didn't fall into riding on a "black" bus that played one kind of music (rap), while another bus of 'Canes usually full of the white UM players listened to another kind of music (rock).

Johnson also cut loose his young players and challenged them. Maybe more important, though, he listened to them. Johnson wasn't new to football, but the Miami culture—and the Miami athletes—did take him some time to figure out. "Jimmy had to learn," said Bratton.

Johnson created weekly nine p.m. Thursday-night meetings, when he would go around the room to each player and make him tell Johnson what he planned on doing in ten years. Some guys would do imitations. Some guys would crack jokes. Johnson's only caveat was that the player wasn't allowed to just say, "Football." Then Johnson would press them about what they were doing to work toward that goal. "We'd just sit around and shoot the shit," Bratton said. "Say whatever we felt, and Jimmy'd motivate you. He'd get in your head."

The idea, cornerback Tolbert Bain said, was that Johnson would start getting your mind right forty-eight hours before kickoff. "He'd make you think, 'You don't wanna be that weak link,' and hell, no, you didn't."

Johnson challenged the players at the place where he could dig the deepest: their manhood. The former psychology major had indeed gotten them believing in him, a guy whom some in the Miami press had (baselessly) pegged as a rube from the day he replaced Schnellenberger. But in reality, his players were teaching him more than he ever could've taught them.

Johnson got an advanced lesson in Hurricane football October 19, 1985, when UM went to Oklahoma to face the second-ranked Sooners. Miami, 4-1, having again lost its opener to Florida, was unranked. But that didn't seem to bother the 'Canes. Neither did the sellout crowd of 75,000 awaiting them in Memorial Stadium, or the fact that Johnson had never beaten OU, going 0-5 against the Sooners from his days coaching at Okie State. In fact, if anything, it did the opposite. The 'Canes, jumping around in their dressing room, were getting off on this. All of it. "Coach Johnson was really uptight," said Highsmith. "We were laughing about it. The coaches were like, 'They never lose at home. Those guys never lose here,' and we were like, 'Man, we're gonna go out there and punch them in the face. We're gonna run through their practice lines. Tell them about it and then kick their ass.' "

The players were right. Testaverde, a backup to Kosar for two seasons, connected with flanker Michael Irvin for a fifty-six-yard touchdown in the first quarter, then ran four yards for the score that put UM ahead to stay in the second quarter and broke the game open with a thirty-five-yard scoring pass to the split end Brian Blades in the third quarter. Testaverde, playing against the nation's top-rated defense, completed seventeen of twenty-eight passes for 270 yards without an interception. Meanwhile, Brown dominated the game on defense, blocking a field-goal attempt, which set up Miami's go-ahead touchdown. Then, with nine minutes left in the first half and the Sooners driving, Brown snatched OU sophomore quarterback Troy Aikman and flung him to the ground for a loss. Aikman left the game with a broken ankle.

"We didn't just want to beat them," said Highsmith. "We wanted to beat the hell out of 'em."

If the 'Canes' dismantling of the Sooners showed Johnson what his players were capable of, UM's meeting with Notre Dame in the '85 season finale would show the whole country. The game would be the last in the dismal five-year term for Irish coach Gerry Faust. The affable Faust was handed the reins in South Bend after going 70-1 and winning five state high school titles in his last six seasons at Cincinnati's Moeller

High. But without any college coaching experience, Faust drove the Irish program into the ground. Not that Miami felt very inclined to show Faust or his team any sympathy.

Even though UM had beaten Notre Dame two in a row, ND still led the series 13-4-1. More than that, though, the Domers epitomized everything the 'Canes hated about college football, and clearly the 'Canes saw the Miami–Notre Dame rivalry as a yin-and-yang thing. The Domers were pretentious blue bloods who, even when they were down—and under Faust, they were pretty down—still carried themselves as if they were college football royalty. Notre Dame people like to claim they invented the game. The 'Canes were the outsiders, the cold-blooded ones who felt like they perfected it.

"Everybody always views Notre Dame as 'the ideal team,'" said UM tight end Alfredo Roberts. "Everybody paints this pretty picture of these white choir boys that never do anything wrong, and then people paint us as the Raiders of college football.

"We had great games beatin' on 'em."

The Irish didn't have a prayer that day in the Orange Bowl. The 'Canes weren't only out to prove a point to Notre Dame, but to the pollsters too, who had been voting one-loss Oklahoma ahead of one-loss Miami, despite the 'Canes' romp at OU.

Miami scored on its first four possessions of the game. UM safety Bennie Blades added in more humiliation for the Irish by intercepting a second-quarter pass and returning it sixty-one yards for a touchdown. But before he reached the end zone he slowed down near the Irish 2 long enough to high-five a teammate. The 'Canes rolled up a 37–7 lead by the end of the third quarter, but they were far from satisfied. Johnson allowed his quarterbacks to keep throwing till there were only six minutes left in the game. And if that didn't tick off the Irish faithful, then the 'Canes' blocking a fourth-quarter punt and running a reverse with seventy seconds remaining sure did. Brent Musburger, Pat Haden, and former Notre Dame coach Ara Parseghian, calling the game for CBS, bashed Johnson for not calling off the dogs. Haden called Johnson "bush."

By the time it was over, it was 58–7 Miami. The 'Canes piled up 534 yards of total offense, including 399 yards passing, the most ever allowed by Notre Dame. The media railed against Miami for running up the score, something Johnson denied. Almost. "We had our second and part of our third unit in the game in the last twelve minutes or so," he said. "We're going to run our offense regardless of the situation.

"Nobody apologized to me when Oklahoma did it to me," Johnson added, referring to Barry Switzer's 63–14 rout over Johnson's Oklahoma State in 1980.

As for Faust, Johnson said, "I feel for the man. I sympathize with him," which sounded downright sappy compared to what some of the 'Canes were saying postgame. "I'm glad we did it," said defensive lineman Kevin Fagan. "I don't feel sorry about it, and I don't feel sorry for [Faust] either."

"Oklahoma has been pouring it on everybody," Irvin explained. "We thought about Oklahoma, and knew we had to impress everybody watching this game. I think we did."

Perhaps Allen Pinkett, Notre Dame's star tailback who managed seventy-seven yards in the game, summed up the day best: "It goes back to the old adage—maybe nice guys do finish last."

Johnson was a visionary of sorts. Coaching icons like Bryant, Vince Lombardi, and George Halas had ruled with iron fists. Those men, like the military heroes they idolized, weren't so much cut from the same cloth but rather shaped by the same blade. They were short-tempered men with deep creases in their faces. Lombardi's credo—"Winning isn't everything; it's the only thing"—became the coaching gospel. He, like many of his contemporaries, believed in the fire-and-brimstone delivery, or as one of his players, Hall of Famer Henry Jordan, once explained, "Coach Lombardi treated us all alike . . . like dogs."

Johnson, too, could be a hard-ass. (Later in his coaching career with the Dallas Cowboys, he cut second-string running back Curvin Richards after two fourth-quarter fumbles in a regular season-ending win over the Bears. The Cowboys won a Super Bowl a month later. The next year Johnson released second-string linebacker John Roper because he fell asleep during a team meeting. Dallas won a Super Bowl that year too.) However, his way was different. He was a "button-pusher," probably the best one who ever coached. His philosophy, background, and grasp of the cultural shift of the eighties athlete who grew up listening to rap music and loving movies like *Scarface* were rare in his profession.

Johnson was a master manipulator. He had the 'Canes at their sharpest when they felt like they had the most to prove, or the most people to prove wrong, which explains, in part, why Johnson's 'Canes were 4-0 in his career against opponents who were ranked number one at the time. Payback was a virtue. His players loved that. (After Arkansas athletic director Frank Broyles passed on Johnson in 1983 and hired another former Razorback, Ken Hatfield, to be head coach, Johnson added Arkansas to the 'Canes' schedule. Then, in 1987, UM smashed the Razorbacks 51–7, Arkansas's worst loss ever in Little Rock. After the game, the players gave Johnson the game ball.) You never wanted to disappoint Jimmy Johnson.

It may have been a shotgun wedding, but after a rocky honeymoon it turned out Johnson, he of the Teflon hairdo, fit in better around Miami than a tube of sunscreen or Crockett and Tubbs. Johnson may have been perceived as a "player's coach," especially compared to Schnellenberger and Miami's other football coach, Don Shula, but in reality he could be so cold-hearted he could've made Lombardi blush. After one uninspired day of practice, Johnson ripped into his team. "You guys think you have four-year scholarships," Bubba McDowell recalls Johnson yelling. "But they're not. Those are one-year scholarships, and if you don't get your shit together, I won't renew them."

Johnson didn't care about what you did last week or what you might do next week. All he cared about what could you do for him right now. His players understood that, and Johnson loved the rep that came with it. "That way," he explained, "we'll weed out lazy players before I ever get to them."

Johnson's unforgiving rep meshed well with UM's budding 'Cane-eat-'Cane work ethic that radiated from the Greentree practice fields. "Jimmy got *us*," said Brett Perriman, referring to what some deemed Miami's inner-city thug players. "He understood what it takes to win."

And no one delighted in the "us against the world" charge more than Johnson. If you weren't part of his inner circle, you were an "outsider." He didn't care if you liked him or hated him. Although if it came down to it, he'd probably prefer that you hated him. It served his cause better. So when his players ran roughshod over Oklahoma or kicked the Irish while they were on the ground in the fetal position, Johnson wasn't bashful about pumping his fist. And if the media and the rest of the country wanted to put a black hat on his team, bring it on. Johnson made sure his guys embraced the image. They became the Oakland Raiders of college football. "We had some players who came from very deprived backgrounds," Johnson said in his autobiography. "That in no way hindered their quality as men and as citizens. It did, in some cases, leave them with insecurities they had to work out and overcome. If you've grown up in the hard environments of Pahokee or Homestead, and suddenly find yourself walking the well-to-do environs of the University of Miami campus in Coral Gables, there is some adjustment to be made. And so to mask nervousness, anxiety, and insecurity, some of our players behaved quite the opposite on the football field: cool, supremely confident, joyful. They exulted in their success, and they were demonstrative about it.

"Confidence is necessary to play football. Different players have different ways of building confidence. Both my formal training in psychology and my decades of firsthand experience with human beings told me that if I stymied and handcuffed the players who needed to be demonstrative, I would stymie and handcuff their confidence. Because of a lot of our players' backgrounds, we had to be somewhat flamboyant. And so we the Miami Hurricanes got our national reputation as 'hot dogs.' The tragic irony is that if America had understood the true reasons our players were demonstrative on the field, we might have been more popular, or at least less criticized."

Johnson always figured that much of the resentment about his 'Canes was born out of bigotry, plain and simple. After all, most of his star players were black. Not only that, they were brash, always acting "out of line." Some people, Johnson maintained, couldn't stand that. It was like they had taken over. "We had a lot of black players out front," Johnson told *Sports Illustrated.* "I think a lot of resentment came that way. The black players knew that, and the black players knew how I felt. I don't know that there was racism involved in the resentment, but there was some ignorance involved—people who had few dealings with other ethnic groups. I mean real relationships, not getting somebody to clean your house."

Johnson identified with the black players. "I could relate to the passion of Michael Irvin and Jerome Brown," he explained after retiring from coaching. "We weren't going to be successful with white kids from suburbia."

Irvin attributed Johnson's ability to relate to black players, many of whom had grown up rough and poor, as the key to his coaching success. "He'll sit there and listen—I mean, really listen," Irvin said. "You know he's in your corner, no matter how the media caves in on you. It takes the load off. Then when you go on the field and the man says, 'I want you to run down there, catch that ball, and run into that wall,' who are you to say no? You say, 'Okay, Coach, you were there for me, and now I'm going to give it up for you.' And you run into the wall.

"He is a shrewd man. A very shrewd man. He can get you to do things you don't really want to do. You know you don't want to do them, and you know he knows you don't want to do them. But—and I still haven't figured out why—you'll do them. And you'll not only do them—but you even end up enjoying doing them. He knows what buttons to push."

"Nobody can play mind games like Coach Johnson plays mind games," said defensive lineman Jimmie Jones. "He wants you to keep your edge, so he'll play mind games with you to help you maintain your focus. If he sees the team is a little uptight, he'll come out and joke around and keep things loose. If things get too loose, he'll do something to fire the team up."

Johnson relied upon a standard textbook theory, the "Pygmalion effect," to get his players to hit harder, run faster and work longer. Pygmalion, in Greek legend, is the symbol of a lifegiver, and later became the name of a George Bernard Shaw play about phonetics professor Henry Higgins's attempt to tutor the very Cockney Eliza Doolittle and transform the common flower girl into a sophisticated duchess. The story would evolve into the Broadway show *My Fair Lady*. Johnson, though, had no inclination to make his 'Canes prim or proper.

The basic application of the Pygmalion effect is that a strong self-perception will lead to vast self-improvement. "It goes back to the basic psychology of treating a person as you want him to become, and he will grow to fulfill your expectations," Johnson would tell all his assistants. "Treat a person as he is, and he will remain as he is. Treat a person as he could be and should be, and he will become as he could be and should be. It has to do with high expectations and self-fulfilling prophecy. I treat people as though they've already become what I want them to be."

The trick in all this, Johnson would point out, was to find out what turned each person on and made them respond.

Johnson's translation of the Pygmalion effect to his players often was made in more blunt terms, said Highsmith. "He'd say, 'I can treat you the way you are. If you act like a dog and you work like a dog, then I'll treat you like a dog.'"

"My decision to major in psychology," Johnson once said, "was also the decision that would eventually make the difference between a good Xs-to-Os college coach and a national championship coach; between a good, solid NFL coach and a Super Bowl coach."

Folks who knew him best liked to say that Johnson probably had a used-car lot somewhere, which in today's game, dealing with the modern athlete, is an essential quality for a coach. Yet there wasn't the phony plastic exterior to his pitches. If there was, the players, especially these players, would've seen right through it upon first glance. Still, Johnson took pride in his ability to manipulate people—even if that wasn't the way he described it: "I always try to get the most out of the people around me—my assistant coaches, players, trainers, administrative assistants, secretaries, everyone," he said. "I try to put them in situations where they're motivated. I try to guide them in a way that they make the decisions I want them to make. But not in a way that says, 'This is the way I want you to do it.'

"No doubt I drive people, but I also drive myself. I'm obssessed with one thing in life: winning, especially big games. That means more than anything with me." The image of master manipulator, though, meant almost as much. Later in his coaching career, he loved to gush to the media, using references about Hannibal Lecter, the cannibalistic shrink from the movie *Silence of the Lambs*. "He [Hannibal] was able to make the guy in the next cell kill himself by talking to him and making him swallow his tongue," Johnson raved. "Now, that's an influential speaker."

Unfortunately, Johnson's motivational tactics would soon have the 'Canes spiraling out of control, making them a list of enemies, starting with the school's own president.

5

EMBRACEABLE U

Hannibal Lecter probably would've appreciated Jimmy Johnson's 'Canes. Especially the stunt they pulled the morning of September 27, 1986, when top-ranked Oklahoma visited Miami looking for payback. It was a spur-of-the-moment thing; even Johnson didn't know what they were up to.

Barry Switzer's Sooners had been the preeminent bad boys of college football. Their star was Brian Bosworth, "the Boz," a fast-moving, fast-talking, 240-pound Texan who, en route to leading OU to the 1985 national title, won the Butkus Award honoring the nation's best linebacker. Bosworth had a hideous, postpunk flattop that, depending on the week, could be red and blue or green or black or whatever color felt cool at the time. It was shaved on the sides and weaved to a three-inch long rattail down the back. After *Sports Illustrated* made him their cover boy for its 1986 college preview issue, the Boz developed into a cultural phenomenon, especially for feisty white teens, and the hairstyle, which became known as "the Bozcut" was the rage in every hollow of the football-mad Southwest. In the *SI* cover story, Bosworth boasted about loving to gouge the eyes and twist the heads of fallen running backs at the bottom of piles. "I like to spit a loogie in a guy's face after I tackle him," Bosworth proclaimed. He bragged about his youthful indiscretions—including hiding loose screws in the doors of new cars while working one summer at the General Motors plant in Oklahoma City, thus driving their new owners crazy. He went on to trash two of OU's rivals, Texas, whose burned-orange color, he said, "reminds me of puke," and then likened playing the University of Miami Hurricanes to "playing the University of San Quentin."

Miami couldn't wait to get a crack at Bosworth. The 'Canes were number two in the country, and the game was going to be on national TV. Kickoff was high noon. "We couldn't sleep," said running back Melvin Bratton of game day. "It's five thirty in the morning and I'm just lying there looking around. Me and High [roommate Alonzo Highsmith] are like kids at Christmas. We are so ready to get in their ass. Oklahoma's been getting all the hype. It's all Bosworth this and Bosworth that. We are ready to tear his ass up. I was going crazy. I said, 'High, fuck the Boz and fuck that fade haircut of his. Let's call that sumbitch and wake his ass up.'"

Bratton had read in the paper that the Sooners were staying at the Fontainebleau Hilton. He dialed up information and got the number for the Hilton's switchboard. He called the Hilton and asked for Bosworth's room. The woman at the front desk told Bratton the phones were turned off. "I said, 'Tell him it's Melvin fuckin' Bratton,' and Alonzo's in the back ready to tear the lamps out of the walls. She says, 'Melvin, I know you from high school and I don't like him anyway. He's a jerk. I'll put you through.' "

Bosworth's roommate answered, "*Hay-lo?*"

"Put Brian Bosworth on the phone," Bratton screamed.

"Aw, hold on, dude."

Another creaky voice said, "Hello?"

"Is this Boz?" Bratton yelled into the receiver.

"Yeah . . ."

"Well, this is Melvin fuckin' Bratton and Alonzo Highsmith, and this is your fucking wake-up call, mutherfucka. And at high noon, we'll see your sorry ass in the Orange Bowl and we're gonna kick your fuckin' ass."

In the background, Highsmith is screaming, "Yeah, son of a bitch, kick your ass!"

"Okay, dude, okay," Bosworth finally answered after a few seconds of silence. "That's fine, but why y'all gotta wake me up so early?"

Bratton wanted to laugh, but instead screamed, "Fuck you," and slammed down the phone.

Then Bratton and Highsmith ran down the hall and banged on Jerome Brown's door to wake him up. It was time for the defense to wake up Sooner QB Jamelle Holieway. First Brown summoned the entire UM defense to his room, and then he dialed up the Fontainebleau and asked for Holieway's room. "Jerome was like, 'Ja-*may*-yal,' in this falsetto voice, 'Come out to *paaa-lay-yay*,' " recalled cornerback Tolbert Bain.

Holieway stuttered, "Who . . . who . . . the hell is . . . is . . . this?"

"Jerome was cussing and starting to sweat," said Bain. "He was so excited. The next week after he faced us, Holieway couldn't play. He had taken such a pounding, he couldn't even lift his right arm."

J.J. loved the wake-up call idea when he got wind of it. He also probably didn't mind when Brown led the other UM captains to midfield for the pregame coin toss, looked the Sooners captains in the eye, and told them, "Don't be afraid," before refusing to shake hands. Brown loved saying outlandish stuff like that at the coin toss. Anything to see the freaked-out look on the other guys' faces. Some games he'd just start screaming at the refs, "We don't need a coin flip; have them take the ball. In fact, place the ball on the fifty and we will get started; we don't want the ball first!"

"We probably won ninety percent of our games before kickoff just because we scared the hell out of the other team," Bratton said. "We had a theory: We'll go into your backyard, turn over your garbage can onto your lawn, and we'll just walk out. That was our motto. We didn't give a shit. People could say we were cocky and arrogant, but whatever they say it was, it was working."

Maybe the Sooners were part of that 90 percent, or maybe the 'Canes were just that much better than OU. Whatever the case, UM roughed up Holieway and the Sooners' vaunted wishbone attack. The 'Canes held OU to 186 rushing yards—almost three hundred below Oklahoma's average. Brown splattered Oklahoma's inside game, containing Sooner fullbacks to fifteen yards, while Testaverde emerged as the Heisman frontrunner, lighting up OU's defense for four touchdown passes and running off one stretch of fourteen consecutive completions as the 'Canes cruised to a 28–16 victory. "Testaverde is the best quarterback we've ever played against in my twenty-one years here," said Barry Switzer, Oklahoma's head coach for fourteen years and an assistant for seven before that.

Bosworth, who had looked up in the stands before the game and noticed that he was being hanged in effigy, left the stadium without making comment. Brown's assessment of the Boz? "He couldn't start" for the Hurricanes.

"It's the University of Miami football players against the world," proclaimed Brown.

The domination of Oklahoma was Miami's answer to the growing image that UM had trumped the Sooners as *the* outlaw program. In the weeks leading up to the game, several stories had come out portraying a program out of control. Just three days before the showdown with the Sooners, news of a telephone credit card scandal hit the papers. UM officials had acknowledged that thirty-four players illegally had charged more than $8,000 in phone calls to an MCI credit card number that was posted on the wall of a dormitory.

However, the phone card scam was far from the most serious charge Miami players faced that summer. Willie Smith, who before moving on to the NFL had been UM's starting tight end in '84, was arrested and charged with possession of cocaine and a handgun. Miami had to declare starting linebacker Winston Moss ineligible for the season opener because he violated an NCAA rule by using a car leased by a part-time instructor, David Glassberg, who also has acted as a professional sports agent. (The NCAA later examined the school's review of the incident, and cleared Moss, Highsmith, Brown, and running back Cleveland Gary after it was found that relatives of the players leased the cars through Mel Levine, who represented two members of the Miami Dolphins.)

Paul Dee, who became Miami's athletic director in 1993,

was UM's attorney at the time and said "the cars case" was the start of Miami's bad-boy reputation. A *Miami News* investigation was started after Brown rolled his corvette on the Florida Turnpike near Fort Pierce on his way home to visit his parents for the weekend. Brown was okay, but the car was totaled. Richie Rosenblatt, the UM beat writer for the *News,* was suspicious of where the car came from and returned to the parking lot near the Miami football offices with a photographer. They ran a check on every license plate and discovered some of the cars had leases that led back to an agent. Miami brought in outside counsel, a lawyer from New Hampshire, Mike Slive (later the commissioner of the Southeastern Conference), to work the case. "He came in and really helped us," said Dee. "We wrapped it up in two weeks and none of the people were found guilty of anything. Turns out there was paperwork, there were loans, and the parents were making payments, and these were similar agreements being offered throughout the banking community locally."

Rosenblatt laughs that UM emerged virtually unscathed from the investigation, losing only Moss for one game. "Sam [Jankovich] hired Slive and he ran interference for them," Rosenblatt said. "There's no doubt in my mind they should've done two or three years' probation for this. Sam knows he was caught, and it was basically, 'Thank you for warning me.' "

But there were other incidents: Starting linebacker George Mira Jr. was arrested August 19 and charged with possession of an illegal drug (steroids). The charges were dropped when a nonathlete told the Dade County State's Attorney's Office the steroids were his. Brown left a handgun in a shopping cart on campus. Dan Stubbs, a starting defensive end, ran out of gas and was caught siphoning some from a nearby car. Jimmy

Johnson, the head coach, said he would have done the same thing if he had run out of gas.

"When it rains, it pours," Jankovich told the *Washington Post.* "It would be great if Vinny [Testaverde] were getting all the attention now, but . . . it's unfortunate to have this series of problems. But, thank God, they have been minor incidents."

If they were, *Sports Illustrated* didn't think so when the magazine wrote a scathing article about the UM program. "Miami may be the only squad in America that has its team picture taken from the front and from the side," *SI*'s Rick Reilly quipped.

The cover story at first shocked the team, but then it became a rallying point, more gas on their fire. They believed they were being misunderstood, persecuted even.

"We didn't have bad guys," Highsmith said. "Yeah, we might've had some guys who did some stupid shit now and then, but people were making us out to be a bunch of gangsters and outlaws. We didn't have any drug problems. We didn't have guys getting paid under the table by some rich boosters. Everybody swore that we did. Please. We didn't even have fucking boosters. We're not Oklahoma with these millionaire oilmen. Guys just come to Miami out of pride because they wanted to play like the Hurricanes and because they wanted to win championships and so they could play in the NFL."

"A lot of young guys have freshmen-type problems," tight end Alfredo Roberts said. "It comes out now that Penn State, Oklahoma, and Notre Dame have had similar stuff. It can happen anywhere, in Miami, Florida, or in Bumfuck, Indiana.

"And when you have success like Miami does, the media is there to report on anything you do. If you spit on the curb, you could probably read about it the next day in the paper."

"It made us want to go out on that field and destroy," Bratton said.

The 'Canes whupped up on everyone they faced in 1986, with only number thirteen Florida managing to stay within two touchdowns of UM. The 'Canes' average margin of victory: twenty-six points. They had also become America's favorite wrasslin' villain, going an astounding 19-1 in nationally televised games. Their television record was even more eye-popping when you consider that back then the networks usually showed only high-profile matchups, not one-sided potential blowouts.

UM's offense featured not only Testaverde—the Heisman Trophy–winning quarterback—but also a trio of wideouts (Irvin, Perriman, and Brian Blades) who would all get snapped up by the NFL in the first two rounds of its next draft, as well as Highsmith, the third-overall pick in the same draft, and Bratton, a projected first-rounder in the '88 draft. On defense, Brown, a consensus all-American, anchored the middle. Stubbs, one of the defensive ends, set a school record with seventeen sacks, while hard-hitting Bennie Blades (Brian's younger brother) led the nation in interceptions with ten.

All that stood between Miami and going down as one of the all-time great college teams ever was a Fiesta Bowl date with Penn State. The media loved the juxtaposition of the black-hat 'Canes against the "good-guy" Nittany Lions and their leader, Joe Paterno, aka Saint Joe, a virtual icon of clean living for white-bread America. Joe Pa's boys were nothing flashy. They wore black shoes and had plain white-and-blue uniforms without any names on the back. They didn't say much, or at least much worth repeating. They appeared to be the anti-'Canes.

The media ate up the good-versus-evil theme, especially after a pregame Fiesta Bowl function that came off as though it were staged by Vince McMahon. Three thousand people turned out to see both teams at a steak-fry. All the Penn State players were there in coats and ties. All the Miami players showed up in black sweat suits. The event was pretty ordinary by Fiesta Bowl standards—till Penn State punter John Bruno Jr. took the stage as part of some good-natured skits that were the norm for the event. Bruno told a couple of jokes, then dragged out a huge garbage can covered in white masking tape with the words *Jimmy Johnson's Hair Spray*. He followed up with a bit about his team's racial unity and why Penn State was such a wonderful place to play: "We're one big family because we even let the black guys eat with us at the training table once a week," Bruno cracked.

There were a few nervous laughs and then it was Miami's turn to perform. Brown rose up, thanked the Fiesta Bowl for dinner, and then unzipped the black sweat suit he was wearing to reveal green army fatigues. "Did the Japanese sit down and eat with Pearl Harbor before they bombed them?" Brown barked. "No. We're outta here." He waved his arm, and just like that the rest of the 'Canes unzipped their sweats to show their fatigues and stormed off.

"They were expecting us to act in that way," Brown explained later, referring to the public's perception of Miami as the villains as opposed to Penn State's clean-cut image. "The way we look at it, the only person who can talk about Coach Johnson is us. If we want to crack on Coach Johnson, fine.

"A couple of guys got ticked off, and to make everything short and sweet and before the thing got out of hand, we just went up there and did what we had to do and left."

News of the 'Canes' fatigues-clad exit made headlines everywhere, although the setting wasn't quite as black-and-white as it came off. "The Fiesta Bowl gave both teams sweat suits," Highsmith explained. "Guess what colors ours were? Black. The bowl people wanted us all to wear them to the steak-fry. They said the Penn State players would be wearing theirs. So we show up for the steak-fry and there are three thousand people there, and guess what the Penn State guys have on? Suits and ties."

Johnson chuckled when reporters asked him about his team's latest stunt. "Every morning I can't wait to pick up the paper and see what they've said next," he said.

Brown and company, though, were just warming up. "You know what I think of [Penn State quarterback] John Shaffer and [running back] D. J. Dozier? I think they're nothing," Brown said at a pregame press conference. "Shaffer thought he had a bad bowl game last year. That was nothing. After this game, he'll wish he'd graduated. The dude's about to star in a nightmare. . . . We don't care what people think about us, as long as we win, our fans are happy, and we bring our school more money. We could care less what people think about the University of Miami. We take an attitude, 'We're on a mission, Miami, and we'll do anything to win.'"

Brown said the idea for the fatigues was to pump more intensity into the 'Canes, but stopped short of saying they were a prop just to try to intimidate Penn State. Of course, if that was a by-product of the warrior look, then so be it. This was a tough guy's game, Brown explained. "If football is made for clean-cut guys, priests would be playing the game. It was made for men, trying to kill somebody."

Johnson, no doubt, loved what his guys had become—and how they sounded. So, too, did the TV execs. The oddsmakers made the second-ranked Nittany Lions seven-point underdogs. A television audience of seventy million people tuned in, the largest in the history of collegiate sports.

The game more than lived up to its hype. Miami came out flat. Testaverde, the all-American quarterback who had one stretch during the season throwing 116 passes without an interception, struggled to find his rhythm against the Penn State defense that mixed in blitzes while playing a three-deep zone. His touted receiving crew dropped seven passes, four in the first half. Penn State's offense was helpless against Miami's defense, but UM's six turnovers gave the Nittany Lions all the breaks they needed.

Still, even with Testaverde playing the worst game of his life, UM had one final chance. Miami, trailing 14–10, faced second-and-goal on the Penn State 5 with forty-eight seconds remaining. The entire state of Arizona was expecting Highsmith to get the ball. After all, the 230-pound back had chewed up the Lions' defense on sweeps all night long, rushing for 119 yards on eighteen carries. Plus, the 'Canes did have two time-outs remaining. Johnson wanted to run. So did Gary Stevens, UM's offensive coordinator. But Testaverde wanted to pass. "We all pretty much agreed that we wanted to run on second-and-five," said Johnson. "We were all very frustrated, but we gave in. He wanted to throw it, and he felt good about it, so we went with it."

Testaverde faded back, spotted Irvin open crossing the middle of the end zone, only defensive tackle Tim Johnson got to Testaverde first for the sack. Third-and-goal on the 13. Testaverde, hurried again, overshot running back Warren Williams, setting up a fourth-and-13 with eighteen seconds remaining.

Testaverde settled in behind the center. Johnson was screaming for a time-out, but with a stadium-record 73,000 fans howling, Testaverde couldn't hear him. Penn State dropped eight men into coverage and each focused on the quarterback's eyes, just as they'd been taught. "We knew in key situations he would stare at the receiver he was going to throw to," safety Ray Isom said after the game. "On first-and-ten, he may be the best quarterback in the country, but on third-and-eight or fourth-and-eight, he maybe needs to work on it."

Isom was right. Testaverde locked on Perriman breaking down the left side and then flung the ball toward the wideout. Only there were four Nittany Lions flocking to that area. Linebacker Pete Giftopoulous got to the ball first and snared it. The greatest college team ever had been beaten. Miami had gained 445 total yards and twenty-two first downs while holding Penn State to Fiesta Bowl record lows of 162 total yards and eight first downs, and still lost.

Johnson broke down in front of his team in the locker room afterward. "I still can't believe we lost to them," said Highsmith. "The worst part is, there's no doubt in my mind that they were the worst team we played that year.

"It was just a bad, bad night."

UM president Tad Foote chastised Johnson for the walkout and said he was putting J.J.'s contract on hold because of the embarrassment to the university. Johnson profanely threatened to resign. Just a few weeks before the Fiesta Bowl, at the Hurricanes' football banquet, Foote had announced that he wanted to give Johnson a contract extension. But that plan was tabled after Foote became enraged at the antics of Johnson's players. From Arizona, Johnson flew to the Japan Bowl and returned home to a press conference, where Foote not only broke the news to him that he might go against his word, but also demanded an apology to the Fiesta Bowl for his team's behavior and a promise to take steps to prevent any more headline-grabbing incidents like the steak-fry episode. He also said a dress code would be implemented. "It's something that I've given a lot of thought to primarily because we had an 11-1 football team, we went through an undefeated regular season, and yet it was one of the most trying and frustrating years of my coaching background," he said. Foote gave the players a forty-two-page code-of-conduct book, telling them they were "expected to conform to all federal, state, and city laws." In his mind, Johnson vowed to deal with Edward Thaddeus Foote II later.

Two days later, the 'Canes had their say. "I apologize for nothing," said Highsmith. "The only thing I apologize for is losing the game. That's it."

"If we would have won, fatigues would have been the new fad in Miami, just like *Miami Vice* and the Don Johnson clothes and haircut a year ago," Bratton added. "Now we lost and everybody puts us as the goats."

Highsmith also took issue with the bad-boy rep of the 'Canes program. "How many times have I gone to junior highs and elementary schools and talked to the kids about behavior and drugs?" said Highsmith. "I've done countless speeches since my freshman year. Now they're telling us we're a bad example. That's ridiculous."

Brown conceded that the fatigues were just part of the head games that helped make the 'Canes a special football program. He made his point by bringing up Foote's alma mater. "Ask Tad Foote what Yale's record is," said Brown. "They wear suits and tuxedos to every game and they end up 0-10. That sure brings the school a lot of money."

"If Tad Foote is so concerned about our dress, why doesn't he come out of his air-conditioned office and pay for our suits?" asked Highsmith.

Suddenly, the Nittany Lions, the Irish, and the Sooners weren't the 'Canes' most hated rival. Tad Foote, the Ivy League–educated school president, came to embody everything they believed they were up against. "We felt we were getting a raw deal," said defensive tackle Russell Maryland. "Looking back, I think they [the administration] could've handled things a little better. We always felt that they were trying to get rid of the program anyway. Miami wanted to be the 'Harvard of the South,' and they were trying to take away something that we enjoyed so much and [that] ultimately brought a lot of recognition to the school.

"It was very frustrating. Back then, it was an 'us against the world' attitude. I think it made us a little stronger, though. And I don't think we received any backing from the administration. They were just placing all the blame on the football program, instead of searching out the problem. There was always a guilty-until-proven-innocent thing there."

"Foote was always the first one to jump on a plane when it came time for us to play in a national championship game or go to the White House, but he's never there during the season," said wideout Brett Perriman. "All he did was criticize, but as soon as we achieve the status of number one, the best in the world, now here comes the man who downgraded us and was embarrassed by us.

"He and his entourage . . . Here it is, we're making millions of dollars every year, and Foote doesn't say anything. With us winning, it brings X amount of dollars in TV rights. But since the time I got there, there has always been a problem with Tad Foote. He told us we've got to be this certain way on the field. We were like, 'No, no, no. You're the president, you've got to behave that way, we're playing football, this is a rough game, it's not a sissy game.' If he wants a sissy game, he can go play badminton.

"He came to practice one time and I remember the whole team was screaming: 'Tad Foote, kiss our ass. Tad Foote, kiss our ass.' This was the president of our school; we weren't supposed to say that. It was wrong, but it was unjust for him to do us a certain way, and he didn't try to get to know us. To come to practice and reconcile with us was one thing, but to come out and just tell us to do this and that . . . We weren't gonna take that. We went against all the rules, if it meant dogging us as a team. Tad was just one of the persons that got caught up in that."

It appeared the inmates were indeed running the asylum. Although from the inside a different picture formed. Scarhead was pulling all the strings, and he had a different set of priorities than did the UM president. Using his school's stuffy president as a foil only helped his cause.

After losing a game, freshman defensive back Charles Pharms told reporters that the Foote-imposed emotionally handcuffed Hurricanes would get back to celebrating and taunting. To appease Foote, Johnson announced that anyone who taunted would be benched. Then Johnson made Pharms his captain for the upcoming game. Johnson's way was all about winning football games. He could've cared less about Foote's initiatives. Still, for all their recklessness and rambunctious attitudes, Johnson's players had discipline. Only Johnson's definition of *discipline* wasn't what Joe Paterno or Ara Parseghian preached to their players.

"Discipline isn't saying, 'Don't throw your hands up in the air when you score a touchdown,'" Michael Irvin told the *Miami Herald*. "Discipline is when it's a hundred and ten degrees in the Orange Bowl, no breeze, fourth quarter, a minute left to play, fourth-and-three for the other team, you are dead tired, they come to the line, and that opposing quarterback gives you a hard count: Hut. Hut! And you don't jump offsides because you're disciplined mentally and physically. That's Jimmy's discipline."

"As personalites, I would say Howard and Jimmy are as opposite as it can get," said Kehoe, Miami's line coach. "They are both very intimidating, but Jimmy was a guy who loved to talk to his players and have his coaches involved. He was so gregarious and outgoing, but he was also a staunch disciplinarian. You didn't screw with Jimmy. You were never late for a meeting. If you were two minutes late for a bus, Jimmy would just take off and you'd get the bus fumes. In many ways Howard and Jimmy were actually the same."

There was one thing, above all else, that boiled Johnson's skin—losing. He wouldn't tolerate it, and to make sure that his players grasped that fact, he made it clear that they would be punished severely for it. (Again, another psychological model at work. Something akin to Pavlov's dog.)

"Jimmy had us where we were scared shitless to lose a game," said Bratton. Johnson's punishments following a loss were gruesome. Normally, conditioning meant a twelve-minute run in which the players would sprint forty yards and then jog back the other forty. "If we lost, though, we'd have to sprint both sides of the forty," said Bratton. "We'd be in the huddle of a close game saying 'Goddammit, think about Monday!'"

Maybe that's why there were so few losses and why Johnson's teams never lost to an unranked opponent. Despite having three players (Testaverde, Highsmith, and Brown) selected in the first nine picks of the NFL draft, the 'Canes opened up the '87 season against three ranked opponents—Florida, Arkansas, and Florida State—and won by a combined score of

108–36. Still, many skeptics wondered if UM or its new QB, Steve Walsh, was national-championship caliber. Walsh was touted as another 'Canes discovery, an intangibles guy whose only other offers came from Iowa State and Schnellenberger at Louisville. Miami's litmus test would come Thanksgiving weekend, when a familiar foe would come to the Orange Bowl—Notre Dame. The Irish had been remade in new coach Lou Holtz's image. They had fostered a physical ground attack and found a game-breaker in receiver/returnman Tim Brown, who, thanks in part to the glow of the Golden Dome, had emerged as a Heisman Trophy favorite.

Apparently, Brown had popped off and said Miami's secondary wasn't as good as USC's. Or at least that was what 'Canes secondary coach Dave Campo told his players Brown had said. Holtz gave the 'Canes some ammo too. Earlier in the week, he said the Hurricane players "aren't afraid of the FBI, the police, or the opposition." By the time that made its way onto Miami's scouting report, it became: "Miami is a team of plantation boys, white trash, and criminals."

The new and improved Fighting Irish came to Miami ranked tenth and had revenge on their minds for the 58–7 thrashing Miami had put on them two years earlier.

It turned out that UM dominated the '87 battle with the Irish even more than they did in '85. Miami coasted 24–0 and the 'Canes defense permitted Notre Dame, a team averaging thirty-three points per game, to cross midfield only twice. The score would've been much more one-sided had UM not been intercepted at the ND 33 or fumbled the ball away at the Irish 1, 13, and 34 yard lines. "If we hadn't had so many turnovers, they'd have accused me of running it up again," said Johnson.

The 'Canes also upheld their vow to not let another player

win a Heisman on them. They contained Tim Brown to ninety-five all-purpose yards, almost half his season average. His totals: three kick returns for forty-two yards, three punt returns for fourteen yards (and a fair catch), three receptions for thirty-seven yards, and one carry for two yards. He also dropped four passes. Bennie Blades, Miami's all-American free safety, bragged that the 'Canes "intimidated" Brown. "We told him in a nutshell that he wasn't worthy of being an all-American," Blades said.

Tim Brown's response? "If they can taunt you and talk about your mama . . . well, that's the way they play," he said. "They play with no class, definitely no class. They were the worst, a million times worse than anyone else. But that's the way they feel the game should be played."

The second-ranked 'Canes again were stampeding to another national title matchup, this one in the Orange Bowl against top-ranked Oklahoma. But there were other issues brewing around the university. Foote's determination to raise the school's academic profile was coming at the expense of maintaining big-time football, according to Johnson. In '84, Foote had led an initiative for UM to phase out all of its undergraduate majors, including the "jock majors," i.e., recreation and physical education. The move, no doubt, could make it harder for athletes to retain their academic eligibility. Foote also discussed making a radical change in UM's six-week Freshman Institute, a required summer program for borderline students, who had only to attend classes. Foote considered introducing a "pass/fail" system, meaning if a student (or student-athlete) were to fail, he couldn't attend UM. Jankovich and Johnson railed against it, arguing they couldn't recruit and then tell a kid he *might* be allowed to get into school. The pass/fail proposal was subsequently scrapped, but Foote stressed that UM would not let anything (including its power-house football program) impede his plan to make Miami an elite academic institution. As for what that meant to the status of his moneymaking football team? "I don't think we should be too hung up on being number one," Foote told *Sports Illustrated.*

In October '87, the *Miami Herald* obtained a confidential memo from assistant academic support coordinator Steve Carichoff to Jankovich that read, in part, "If . . . the standards are going to continue to rise along the lines of a 'Harvard of the South,' then it appears to me that the athletic department and the University of Miami administration and faculty will be on a very real collision course. From an athletic department standpoint, it could mean that our department could become another Rice or Northwestern—what a thought!"

The memo touched off more chaos within Miami's executive committee. (The school was smack in the middle of a five-year fund-raising drive that would end in 1989 and generate $517 million—one of the most lucrative such campaigns ever, and one no doubt related to the 'Canes' success on the grid-iron.) Foote had become vilified around south Florida as an elitest snob, but he did make a dramatic difference in raising UM's academic profile. In a ten-year span, Miami's mean SAT score for freshmen jumped from 940 to 1104. Under Foote, the school also spent more than four times the money to at-tract academically exceptional freshmen than it had before he arrived in 1981—although what that had done was create a bigger gulf in the classroom between the average Miami stu-dent and the football players. The upshot was that some Hur-ricane football players, feeling the academic heat, resorted to cheating, claimed a *Sports Illustrated* article that hit the newsstands ten days before UM faced Oklahoma.

"Cheating seemed to be endemic on the campus when I was there," Alan Beals told *SI*. Beals was an academic counselor for the football team from 1985 until he resigned in the spring of '86 out of disgust, he says, with the direction of the program. "It wasn't just in the football team, either. In a history class, the whole class, including six football players, had the exam in advance."

More bad press. So what? Bratton said. "We didn't care what people thought. We'd just take it out on our opponent." They did, beating OU 20–14 to capture the school's second national title. Against the country's top-rated defense, Walsh hit on eighteen of thirty passes for 209 yards and two touchdowns and looked like the second coming of Kosar, particularly after he coolly converted on a crucial fourth-and-4 from the Oklahoma 29 late in the third quarter. At the time, UM was nursing a 10–7 lead and the rain was pouring down. A field goal, especially after seeing UM's Greg Cox hammer an Orange Bowl–record fifty-six-yarder on the previous possession, seemed to make sense. But Johnson smelled blood. The gamble paid off. Despite a heavy rush in his face, Walsh connected with Bratton for a six-yard pass. Three plays later, Walsh tossed the game-clinching touchdown pass to Michael Irvin.

"He's less emotional than Bernie," Johnson said of the sophomore QB from Minnesota. "I don't want Steve to be emotional. I can be hyper, but not my quarterbacks." Walsh's own teammates actually roughed him up more than the Sooners did. After the game, Walsh tended to a black eye that resulted from hugging Hurricane offensive lineman Mike Sullivan following the TD pass to Irvin. But as impressive as Walsh was, there was an even better example of just how loaded the Miami program had become.

Before the game UM offensive tackle John O'Neill and star middle linebacker George Mira Jr. flunked a pregame drug test. Mira's understudy Bernard "Tiger" Clark, a stocky sophomore with lightning bolts shaved into his head, didn't register on the OU scouting report, but it took all of about a minute of game action for the middle linebacker to assert himself. "I knew they thought I was the weak link," said Clark, who piled up fourteen tackles, a fumble recovery, and a sack to win MVP honors. "The very first play I hit [Lydell] Carr and said, 'Hey, it's going to be a long night. You think I'm the weak link? Bring it on. Bring it on.' " Against UM, the Sooners didn't have anything to bring. They managed just one sustained scoring drive, and that lasted just forty-nine yards. OU's only fireworks came on a trick play—the fumblerooski—in which the 280-pound senior guard Mark Hutson picked up a ball that had been intentionally left on the ground by the center and rambled for a twenty-nine-yard touchdown run with two minutes remaining. Funny thing: Hutson's twenty-nine yards rushing matched the total of OU's speedy wishbone QB Charles Thompson, the same option whiz who burned Nebraska for 126 rushing yards earlier in the season. Thompson got his twenty-nine yards, though, on twenty-seven carries. The lasting image of the game is of a drenched Johnson flopping around on his players' shoulder pads, exulting, kicking his arms and legs in the air. "This wasn't just a national championship," he said in his autobiography. "We had taken on a world of bullshit, and Florida, and Florida State and Arkansas and Notre Dame, and Oklahoma, and Edward Thaddeus Foote II. And we kicked their collective ass."

The next April, twelve 'Canes—a school record—were drafted, with Bennie Blades and Michael Irvin both going in the first round. They would've had a third first-rounder, but Bratton—considered a top-five pick going into the Orange Bowl—tore his ACL (anterior cruciate ligament) in the fourth quarter and ended up as a sixth-round pick. The season opener was against top-ranked Florida State. Bobby Bowden's Seminoles had been trying to follow Miami's lead. They had emerged in the eighties as a force, kind of a 'Canes knockoff. Before the season, the 'Noles, who finished the '87 season number two behind UM, even produced a rap video, "The Seminole Rap," to promote the football program. Bowden said before the game that he didn't know about the video until it was completed, and that he then told the players they might be forced to "eat it."

Sure enough, Bowden was right. Johnson got hold of the video and played it for his team two days before kickoff. Even with ten new starters (five on offense and five on defense), the 'Canes ambushed FSU, 31–0. Seminole Heisman hopeful Sammie Smith was held to six yards on ten carries. The 'Canes picked off five passes. "I've had nightmares about this game since last May," Bowden said afterward. "Every time I woke up and thanked God I was asleep. My nightmares weren't as bad as this game. I can't believe we were this bad."

"What really annoyed me about the rap," Miami cornerback Donald Ellis vented, "was if we'd done all this crap, the entire country would be on us like we'd shot the president. It would be 'Oh, Jimmy Johnson has no control over his team.' But Bobby Bowden's team does it, and it's 'Oh, how nice. Let's sell it.'

"That [video] was the last straw. It's just that for the last three months all we've been hearing about is Florida State.

The verbal abuse went too far. And now here comes this rap about how good they are. . . . Well, one of the reasons we beat them is because their whole team was 'I, me, my.' No 'us' and 'team.' We leave the 'me, my, and I' at home on the dresser."

The 'Noles' marketing ploy was nothing compared to what was waiting for Miami in South Bend. The Irish were 5-0, their best start in nine years, and ranked number four in the nation. Industrious ND fans capitalized on the lingering hostility from the Miami beat-downs, creating a T-shirt business that was booming by October 15, when the 'Canes came to town. For $10, you could get an *Even God Hates Miami* T, or *Jimmy Johnson: Pork-faced Satan,* complete with a sketch of Johnson as the devil. Another one said, *Top ten reasons to hate Miami.* (It ranked reason number ten as, *They think* Leave It to Beaver *is a method for getting homework done,* while number one was simply *Jimmy Johnson.*) But the big seller would play up both schools' images: *Unfinished Business—Catholics vs. Convicts.* Funny thing was, Walsh pointed out, all of the 'Canes' offensive linemen as well as himself and tight end Rob Chudzinski were Catholics, and Notre Dame's QB, Tony Rice, was a Baptist.

Before the game, a brawl broke out during warm-ups between the two teams, near the tunnel back to the locker room, that had to be quelled by police. Johnson pointed the finger at the Irish: "They attacked us." Holtz said the 'Canes instigated it: "They taunted our players and hit our players." The outcome of the game would be just as muddled. The 'Canes had to rally from a 21–7 deficit, similar to their comeback one month earlier at Michigan, where Walsh led them out of a 30–14 hole with less than six minutes left in the game to a 31–30 victory.

The game's most-talked-about play would come midway

through the fourth quarter with Miami driving. The 'Canes, trailing 31–24, had a fourth-and-7 at the Notre Dame 11, when Walsh connected with fullback Cleveland Gary on a swing pass. Gary scrambled between tacklers and dove for the goal line, stretching the ball over. But as his wrist slammed down on the turf, the ball squirted free. Notre Dame recovered. The officials didn't make a call on the play, other than first down, Irish.

"I caught the ball and I broke the goal-line plane. And I thought it was a touchdown, regardless of if the ball pops out," Gary said after the game. "The referee told me that my knee had hit the ground. He said, 'I'm sorry, son, the ball is dead.' If the ball is dead and it's not a touchdown, we still should have maintained possession of the football."

Miami would get the ball back, and score with forty-five seconds remaining when wideout Andre Brown caught an eleven-yard touchdown pass. With Miami trailing 31–30, Johnson opted for the two-point conversion. This time, it was Miami whose two-point pass attempt would get batted away. Irish fans stormed the field.

Johnson railed about the fumble call. Holtz, meanwhile, seemed more concerned with the animosity between the two schools: "I think the two schools really and truly need to talk about playing in the future. I am talking about next year. I think we need a cooling-down period."

Three months later, the rivalry would indeed lose some of its heat. Jimmy Johnson, aka Pork-Faced Satan, was leaving Miami to replace coaching legend Tom Landry as the new head coach of the Dallas Cowboys. Johnson was lured to Dallas by his longtime buddy and former Arkansas teammate and roommate, Jerry Jones, who had bought "America's team." Johnson took with him most of his coaching staff and a 52-9 mark, including a 44-4 record in his last four seasons. "The one thing I'm proudest of—obviously the winning record and record against the top-notch teams [I'm proud of]—but the thing I'm most proud of is when I first got there Miami had a reputation of not being strong academically," Johnson said. "The graduation rate was thirty-two or thirty-three percent when I first got there. My last year we had built it up, purposely did not recruit Prop 48 players even though the school would accept them. We really worked at the academics very hard and ended up my last year graduating seventy-seven percent of our players. Miami's been strong ever since. That's one thing I'm very proud of, the academic progress we made while I was there."

The 'Canes lobbied for offensive coordinator Gary Stevens to take over. Stevens, a glib, cigarette-puffing holdover from the Schnellenberger staff, was a local favorite. He had his own swagger. Kosar, Testaverde and Florida coach Steve Spurrier all voiced their support for Stevens. Walsh threatened to jump to the NFL if Stevens didn't get the job. Students even hung pro-Stevens posters around campus. The Miami police and fire departments issued statements endorsing Stevens for the job. But Jankovich bypassed Stevens for a family friend, Washington State coach Dennis Erickson, citing head coaching experience as the primary reason for his decision. Jankovich said choosing Stevens would've been "rolling the dice."

The forty-one-year-old Erickson, 50-31-1 as a head coach, brought six members of his old staff with him. Erickson's suburban-insurance-salesman look left most 'Canes scratching their heads. "He wasn't accepted right away," defensive tackle Russell Maryland recalled. "Our first team meeting, these guys from Washington State show up with these big tweed jackets. They looked like they had just got off a plane from the tundra.

"After having had Jimmy Johnson for three years, when Coach Erickson and his staff showed up, it was like, 'Who are these guys who are going to try and take over what we've established?' That just goes back to us tightening up and coming together and being wary of outsiders after all the trouble we'd been through." It also showed that Dennis Erickson had clearly entered a whole new world.

6

IT'S A 'CANE THING

Lamar Thomas grew up the way most people did in Gainesville, Florida—as a die-hard Gator fan. Thomas, a fast-talking, dimple-cheeked sort, was an all-state shooting guard and wideout. He had his heart set on playing both sports for the University of Florida. But a buddy of his, Gator basketball star Vernon "Mad Max" Maxwell, tipped Thomas off that the NCAA was on to UF, and that the Gators program was about to get rocked by an investigation. Thomas wasn't sure what his next move would be, especially after the Gators fired Mike Heimerdinger, the coach who had been recruiting him and had been in his house just a week earlier. He considered visiting Georgia Tech, Syracuse, North Carolina, and Miami.

The six-foot-three, 170-pound Thomas, though, had his doubts about visiting UM. Actually, he said he crossed the 'Canes off his list and canceled a visit so he could check out

North Carolina (the Tar Heels were playing NC State in hoops). Then, a few hours after he told UM coaches his plans, his phone rang. The voice on the other end had a deep rumbling sound, the kind that made all the words seem to blur together. The caller was Michael Irvin, the 'Canes' standout junior receiver. "Man, izzzallllzetuppp," Irvin hollered into the phone. "You gonna go out and hang with me—and I'm gonna show you what Miami iszzzalllllabouuuttt." Thomas was intrigued. He nixed the trip to Carolina and came to Coral Gables, and was indeed floored by the way Irvin owned south Florida. "Wherever we went, people knew him and yelled out, 'Playmaker!' " marveled Thomas.

Irvin drove Thomas around, got smiles from all the pretty girls and nods from all the suits, and then turned to him and said, "So, do you wanna be the next Michael Irvin?" Thomas, who fancied himself as a bit of an extrovert too, liked the sound of that. But he still told Irvin he was on the fence about UM. "Let me tell you something," Irvin continued. "I'm on NBC, CBS, ESPN, and PBS. Every station. Every Saturday. You come here, you're going to be on them, too." Irvin was now speaking Thomas's language.

The UM game Thomas saw was against his hometown Gators. It was a rout. The 'Canes rolled 31–4 and Irvin made the game's sickest highlight, turning a simple, quick out into a sixty-five-yard jaunt after he juked Gator DB Dwayne Glover and left him grasping at air. From that moment on, Thomas believed he had to be a 'Cane. Irvin promised him he'd teach Thomas everything he knew. Irvin, however, wouldn't be at UM by the time Thomas arrived on campus. He had opted to leave early for the NFL draft. Still, Irvin stood by his pledge. He called Thomas. "I told you I would teach you and I will."

And he kept calling and calling and calling. "He'd talk to me a hundred times during the year, but it was primarily just to talk about himself," Thomas said. "I would just listen. I was in awe of him. On the field, he was just a studmuffin. He'd start off and say, 'Good game, young buck. Keep trying to catch me.' Then he would go on for about an hour and talk about himself. 'You see how I did Darrell Green Sunday? They say he runs a *fo'-two*. I run maybe a *fo'-five*, but when I put this big, fine body on him, he can't get *ahh-roooound* me! He runnin' Mike Speed.'

"I enjoyed it because I knew he'd call every week and I knew I had to do something spectacular to keep up with the wide-receiver tradition." Irvin gave Thomas tips on how to better disguise his routes so he could set up defensive backs, how to maneuver in traffic, and how to read defensive backs' body language. He also reminded Thomas "how to be a 'Cane." Irvin would leave messages on Thomas's answering machine, encouraging, "I'm watching. Do *something!*" Thomas always did.

Irvin was an ideal spokesman for the program—even if UM president Tad Foote may not have seen it that way. Irvin grew up in a family of seventeen children in Fort Lauderdale. His father, a preacher, died a year before Irvin caught his first pass at St. Thomas Aquinas High. Irvin dedicated his football career to his father's memory. He was big for a receiver, at six-foot-three, but hardly fast. In fact, he may have been the slowest of the UM receivers, but he was relentless. No one outworked him. He attacked passes like a power forward going for a rebound, rustling for position, using his shoulders and butt to carve out space. He earned all-American honors and graduated with a business management degree in four years. After he announced his decision to enter the NFL draft, Irvin boasted, "Hey, I'm like Kentucky Fried Chicken. I do one thing, and I do it right," about his ability to catch. Nobody loved being a 'Cane more.

Irvin's mentorship of Thomas isn't uncommon at UM. Around the program, they have an expression to explain, or at least answer, how things happen at UM—whether it's about a miraculous comeback, a bit of eye-popping bravado, or how a team can lose one star and replace him with an unknown who turns out to be even better: "It's a 'Cane thing . . . you wouldn't understand."

A "'Cane thing" is about the closest you can get to summing up what has made the program a football phenomenon. It's about mentoring and it's about mind games. Belief and bravado. But the biggest reason why most people don't understand is because it's about swagger *and* selflessness too. Jessie Armstead, a standout linebacker for Miami in the early nineties, made the mantra mainstream when he got some *'Cane Thing* T-shirts made up for his teammates. The spirit, though, started well before the shirts did. It's the thing, even more than sheer talent, that has separated Miami from everyone else, explains UM defensive coordinator Randy Shannon, a former star linebacker for the 'Canes in the mid-eighties. "If it's me and you playing the same position and I'm the older guy and you've got talent, I'm gonna teach you what I know to try and beat me out," Shannon said. "I want you to take my position, because if you take it, we'll be a better team, and if not, when I leave you'll be smart enough to get it done. That's what 'A 'Cane Thing' means. No matter what happens, I want the best players on the field. It ain't an ego thing or about 'I'm this,' or 'I'm that.'"

Almost as important, the "'Cane Thing" doesn't end when

the star player leaves campus and starts wearing an NFL uniform.

Jerome Brown had been in the NFL for two seasons playing for the Philadelphia Eagles when his buddies down in Miami started telling him about a guy they were touting as "the next Jerome." Cortez Kennedy, like Brown, grew up in a small country town. Kennedy was from Wilson, Arkansas (population 900). He was big, boisterous, and had a menacing scowl. He could also do amazing things for a man his size, like burst through the A-gap before the guard could get out of his stance, or chase down ball carries from behind. Kennedy also had some class clown in him, same as Brown. He was another gentle giant and he was charismatic. Kennedy earned honorable mention all-American honors at Northwest Mississippi Junior College in '87 and broke the hearts of Razorbacks fans all over the state when he decided to sign with Miami and Jimmy Johnson instead of his home-state team. But when he arrived in Miami in August of 1988, he weighed 319 pounds, thirty-nine more than his playing weight. Johnson put him on the scout team and ordered him to lose nineteen pounds. Kennedy struggled in the south Florida heat, and his new 'Cane teammates dubbed him "Two-Play Tez."

"He'd kill you for two plays, then take the next twenty off," said Shannon, who was a senior during Kennedy's first season at UM. "He had the talent and he was a good person mentally. He just couldn't sustain it. He'd get past one drill, then be halfway through the second and flop down. He'd say, 'I can't make it.' We'd have to hold him up and say, 'Don't you quit on us!' "

It wouldn't have been hard for Kennedy to have gotten lost

in the transition when Johnson bolted for the NFL and Dennis Erickson came in from the Pacific Northwest. Erickson flirted with the idea of redshirting Kennedy, but Shannon, who got drafted by Johnson's Dallas Cowboys that spring, made sure that wasn't going to happen. He moved into Kennedy's apartment and put him through boot camp. Up at the crack of dawn to run three miles. At noon, he had him lifting weights. At five thirty, he ran him some more. Shannon insisted that Kennedy adhere to a low-fat diet. All he would let him eat were subs and salads. Shannon wouldn't allow Kennedy to eat after seven p.m. either, and he slept on the sofa to make sure Kennedy didn't raid the refrigerator at night. "I put a padlock on the fridge and I took away his [car] keys so he couldn't leave," Shannon said. "The only way he could go out was if I went with him."

In late June, when Shannon left Miami for Cowboys training camp, Russell Maryland, a rock-solid junior defensive tackle nicknamed "the Conscience," took over as Kennedy's drill sergeant. Maryland got his nickname because he nagged teammates about their grades and their practice habits. Maryland himself had been quite a reclamation project. He was a self-described "fat kid from Chicago" who eventually remade himself into a two-time all-American. He weighed 330 pounds as a senior at Whitney Young High School, and he was more highly regarded as a student than as an athlete. Only one college recruited him for football, 1-AA Indiana State. Maryland did, however, have the grades to get into the Ivy League and was considering trying that route in the spring of 1986 when, by a twist of fate, Hubbard Alexander came to town. Alexander, Miami's receivers coach, was one of Johnson's ace recruiters. He came to the Windy City to try to sign another defensive tacklc, Mcl Agee, only at the last second Agee backed out and chose to sign with Illinois. Alexander rechecked his list of D-line candidates in the Chicagoland area and noticed the only one who hadn't signed a letter of intent was Maryland. Once at UM, Maryland's dogged work ethic in the classroom showed up on the field. He dropped thirty pounds his first year at Miami. His mentor was Jerome Brown. Maryland was an honor student too, majoring in—what else?—psychology. He prodded Kennedy: "If I can lose the weight, so can you."

But the real driving force behind Kennedy became Brown. Big Jerome had never laid eyes on Kennedy till the spring of '89, when the Eagles' defensive tackle barged into the UM weight room and yelled, "Where's the kid who's supposed to be like me?"

Brown eyeballed him for a moment, broke out his big white smile, and then wrapped his arms around Kennedy's broad back. "You come with me," he told Kennedy.

Brown showed Kennedy how to read an offensive lineman based on his body lean. He also taught him how to use his hands better and how to navigate a double team. When the '89 season rolled around, Kennedy weighed 285. He led all Hurricane linemen with ninety-two tackles (twenty-two for losses), had 7.5 sacks, and was named all-American while helping Miami win the national championship.

Brown and Kennedy grew so close that Jerome's mother used to refer to Tez as Jerome's twin brother. When Brown bought a white BMW 750iL, so did Kennedy. When Brown bought a Corvette ZR-1, so did Kennedy. Whenever Kennedy sacked a quarterback, he busted out the Tez dance, a double-pump pelvic thrust he learned from Brown. Every Monday night during the season they'd dial each other up and compare stats.

On June 25, 1992, the day before Kennedy was supposed to fly to Miami to meet Brown to go on a cruise together, Brown, driving with his twelve-year-old nephew, Augusta, lost control of his Corvette and smashed into a power pole—both driver and passenger were killed. For the remainder of his football career, Kennedy wore number 99 to honor his fallen brother.

The closest parallel you can find to a legacy steeped in such tradition is the fraternities on most college campuses. The Greek system offers brotherhood that is forged through hazing rituals and links through its IDs, such as tattoos and brands. These body markings are born out of the excruciating burning processes that create them. (In the case of the brands that you often see from black fraternities, the frats' logos are seared across the biceps at 1,500 degrees Fahrenheit.) Among the 'Canes, especially from Johnson's teams in the eighties, joining frats wasn't acceptable. "We are our own fraternity," said Bratton. Some UM players have further adopted this concept by getting tattoos of the UM logo, a logo they all believe defines them and is a tribute to how they play the game.

One day Bratton and his best friend, cornerback Tolbert Bain, were walking across campus and spotted freshman wide receiver Doyle Aaron in line for one of the fraternities. Even though Bratton was the big talker of the two, it was Bain who went off. "You don't do that here," Bain told Aaron. "That's a no-no. It would be hard on us walking by seeing some little wimp talking trash to you. You play for the Hurricanes, the greatest show on turf. We are our own fraternity. Why you wanna be in a fraternity anyhow? You go through enough for the two and a half hours at practice. Then you're gonna put up with some bullshit. 'Go find me a rock!' 'Go get me this or get find me that.' What kind of bullshit is that?"

"Being a 'Cane is more than a fraternity, because in a fraternity you have to pay dues," former UM defensive tackle Warren Sapp said. "Being a 'Cane, you have to give part of yourself. Each one of us has a special bond with each other."

"We are so close, we're brothers. A real family," said former UM linebacker Ray Lewis. "It's about the blood, sweat, and tears, and your brother has been right there with you through all of it. That's why you have that trust.

"My mentality was always like that, and when I got to UM I was like, 'Wow, you mean to tell me there's a place like this where guys trust and believe in each other, on and off the field? Man, there is nothing like it and how that makes you feel or what it can do for you."

Players joke that the only thing a 'Cane fears is an injury. Because they believe that if they go down and just miss one game, they might never get their job back. Irvin tells a story about tailback Warren Williams, who had hurt his leg during two-a-days in 1985. Irvin's message to his fallen teammate? "Heal fast. If you miss two practices, you might not get your job back," he said. Irvin was right. Miami was so loaded at running back with Bratton and Highsmith and Darryl Oliver, Williams didn't get to be a feature back again until he joined the Pittsburgh Steelers. "It's true," said Bratton. "If you got hurt at Miami, your ass might not ever touch the field again, so you were scared to get hurt and leave the field. Jimmy [Johnson] had this rule: You don't practice by Wednesday, you won't start on Saturday, and you did not want that to happen." The strength of Miami depth regularly surfaced—Bernard Clark filling in for middle linebacker George Mira Jr. and winning Orange Bowl MVP honors, or the 1992 Orange Bowl, when starting fullback Stephen McGuire missed the game with an injury and his understudy, freshman Larry Jones, came from nowhere to run for 144 yards and won MVP honors in the national title–winning game over Nebraska. But it was also the cocksure attitude of those guys waiting behind the curtain. Like the time in 1987 when Purdue quarterback Jeff George, an all-everything recruit, seeing a vacancy after Vinny Testaverde left, wanted to transfer to Miami. UM offensive coordinator Gary Stevens told George, "If you come here, you *might* play." The message? George's rep and fabled arm strength were worth nothing. (George opted to transfer to Illinois instead.) "I didn't think he'd ever play here anyway," UM QB Steve Walsh said of George. "For him to change his mind [about coming to Miami] showed he didn't have much confidence in himself."

Those dues that Sapp spoke of can come at a heavy price, especially when dealing with insecure teenage boys and young men struggling to find their way on a college team. Egos can get crushed. So can dreams. Wide receiver Tony Page came to UM from Lawton, Oklahoma, where he was the state's long-jump and sprint champion. He wasn't bashful about telling his new teammates about his track exploits. So one day before practice, another receiver, Brian Blades, called Page, aka "Mr. Oklahoma Sprint Champ," out and challenged him to a race. The whole team gathered around and Blades torched Page. "If you came here as a 'top-ranked' guy, you got challenged," said Highsmith. "And the truth is, Miami ruined a lot of the 'big-time' kids. You just can't be sensitive at Miami. They'll beat it out of you." One player, Mick Barsala, a linebacker from California, bolted after he didn't like the haircut his new teammates gave him. Head shaving—or comically botched head shaving—was part of the 'Canes' freshman orientation, something that had started under Schnellenberger. (Before transferring to Cal, Barsala protested about the process to the administration. UM's athletic director at the time, Dave Maggard, responded by outlawing the practice. The 'Canes' response to that? The freshmen themselves decided to uphold the tradition by shaving their own heads to show their commitment.)

The bond can do wonders in terms of success breeding success. It explains why the 'Canes always seem to have the essential ingredient that's always labeled as chemistry. "The main reason Miami stays at the top is that the players are always competing against the past, and the past is standing right there on the sideline, watching them with pride and high expectations," said Maurice Crum, a Miami linebacker in the late eighties.

At most Miami games, the 'Canes' sideline looks like a players' reunion. Most old 'Canes, if their NFL teams have the week off, return for UM's game to show their support. Bain said their presence can sometimes mean the difference between winning and losing. He points to the 1988 Orange Bowl against top-ranked Oklahoma. Part of the Sooners' game plan was to split all-American tight end Keith Jackson out wide to neutralize Bain's efforts in helping contain OU's running game. The Sooners' first series, OU kept running to Bain's side and gaining yards. "I just couldn't get off him," Bain said. "At Miami, in the huddle, you had to be accountable for yourself. I get back in the huddle and all the boys are looking at me. I said, 'My bad.' They don't say nothing. They would just look [*making an irate stare*]. We get off the field and I'm like, 'Fuck!'

"[Former UM linebacker] Winston Moss used to be my roommate, and he had moved on to the League [the NFL]. He leaned over to me and goes, 'You're playing too far off him.' I was five yards off. Winston goes, 'Walk up on his head and when the ball is snapped, engage him and find the football. Just play football.' They came back out and ran the triple option my way and this time—*bam!*—I slammed the running back. That was the end of that. They never ran that again and we won. That kind of thing happens a lot at Miami."

The old 'Cane–'Cane relationship can create a gray area for coaches. It certainly did for Erickson's staff. The potential for chaos, what with players getting coaching from men who aren't actually their coaches, was a concern.

"I think it could've been a problem," said Sonny Lubick, Erickson's defensive coordinator at Miami. "But we learned to work with it, and it was all very constructive. A lot of the time the players would listen to their ex-teammates before they'd listen to us."

The time, though, that Miami got its biggest edge over everyone else was smack-dab in the middle of south Florida's summer swelter. Back in the 1980s and even deep into the nineties, most colleges were empty at summertime. Players were more like regular students. They left campus for a few months, recharged their batteries, got flimsy summer jobs, and played the role of small-town hero coming home. Not at Miami, though. There was no such thing as an "off-season." Since Miami was running a high-powered passing attack, they could fine-tune their routes in seven-on-seven drills (featuring all the "skill" players—minus only the linemen). At option- or wishbone-based programs, it's hard to replicate such a scheme without contact or linemen working in unison. Better still, Miami players could battle. Same as in games, only because of NCAA regulations, coaches aren't permitted to supervise. But Miami developed something that might've been an even better teaching tool: Old 'Canes returning home from their NFL teams to train side by side with the youngbloods. Tips are shared. Bonds are strengthened. Spirits are challenged. Robert Bailey, a Miami cornerback who spent a decade in the NFL, said, "[Former all-American wide receiver] Eddie Brown came back and ran every single drill with us, and I remember challenging myself to stay up with him and I could not. He won every time. His work ethic left a lasting impression on me."

"The off-season regimen was, and still is, I believe, unlike any other," Clark adds. "The workouts were 'voluntary-mandatory,' that was our saying. They were brutal. You're already competing in July against the best before you even line up against your opponent. If you beat those guys all summer you felt you could beat anybody."

Winning every head-to-head battle wasn't essential. "All you gotta do is beat him one time. That does it," said Bratton. "Because you ain't gonna beat him too many times. Winston Moss was one year ahead of me and he had gone off to the NFL and made All-Rookie [for the Tampa Bay Buccaneers], and I beat him one time, and everybody was like, 'Whooo!' I looked at him and said 'You're the best in the NFL?' I spiked the ball in his face and said, 'Man, I know I can play on Sundays.'"

Not that the younger guys didn't hear their share of trash from the older 'Canes. Linebacker Darrin Smith came to Miami in 1989. A few days after the Miami native moved into suite 36A, his phone rang. When he picked up the receiver, Smith heard an unfamiliar voice on the other end of the line. "Who dis?" the voice barked.

"What do you mean?" Smith answered. "Who's this?"

"I asked you first," the voice growled. "Who is this?"

Finally, Smith relented. "This is Darrin Smith. Now who is this?"

"This is Michael Irvin, and you're in *my* room," the voice said.

The voice actually was Irvin, who like many of the old 'Canes took to calling their old numbers to find out who had taken over their old digs—and to make sure the legacy was in good hands. The old 'Canes become godfathers to the young guys, as Smith said Irvin became to him or as Brown became to Kennedy. "Having former players call you is like having a big brother," Armstead said. "It's like a big family. At Miami, nobody is jealous of anybody." Irvin and Smith hit it off that day after the rocky phone introduction. A few weeks later, Irvin returned to UM and crashed in Smith's suite.

With Irvin stoking the fire, Lamar Thomas not only became the epitome of the fist-pumping, butt-wiggling, let-me-get-this-helmet-off-so-America-can-see-how-pretty-I-am 'Cane; he also smashed the 'Canes' career receiving record, a record that was held by Irvin. The Dallas star congratulated him by sending him a lithograph of himself. It came with a note that read, "If you ever forget what a great receiver looks like, just look at my picture."

Thomas said UM brought something out in him that he didn't know was in there. "Once I found out I was going to Miami, a lot of things changed for me," Thomas said. "My confidence changed. It just happened. Wherever I walked, I carried that swagger that I picked up on my visit. Whenever I thought about being a Hurricane, it was, 'I'm the best, and if you wanna be aroun' me, you gotta be zummmbah-dee!'"

Thomas, like Irvin, was the fuse for his team's combustible psyche. Only under Dennis Erickson, a more laissez-faire type top dog than Johnson and Schnellenberger, the fuse didn't seem to have as far to burn to reach the dynamite pack.

Erickson had come to Miami from Pullman, Washington, and if he didn't realize the difference in climate, he needed only to watch his new team perform in the 1989 opener at Wisconsin. The 'Canes romped 51–3. They also celebrated after plays, not just touchdowns, by dancing and head-butting each other. After UM receiver Randal "Thrill" Hill caught a four-yard touchdown pass in the second quarter to make the score 34–3, he bowed to the Badger crowd. The *Chicago Tribune* described Miami as having players "you wouldn't want your local motorcycle gang to be associated with." Two weeks later, the 'Canes took their show on the road and blasted Missouri 38–7 in a game that saw UM safety Bobby Harden, on his way to the end zone, shaking the football in front of the faces of the entire Tigers sideline after he intercepted a pass. Late in the game, another Miami DB, Kenny Berry, KO'd Missouri's star tight end, Tim Bruton, who lay motionless on the field with trainers tending to him. Meanwhile, Berry did his version of the Ickey Shuffle. After the game, Erickson said, "I never liked taunting, I never will, and I'm going to do whatever I can to eliminate what could even appear to be taunting." For the most part the 'Canes toned it down the rest of the '89 season. In the Sugar Bowl, they beat an overmatched Alabama team 33–25 to win the program's third national title.

The 'Canes entered 1990 ranked preseason number one. They visited number sixteen Brigham Young in Utah and came out flat. There was no dancing. No styling. No hip-shaking. And there was no energy. Cougar QB Ty Detmer picked them apart. Miami fell 28–21. Irvin, like Bratton and many of his old 'Canes brethren, were irate. They believed the problem was that the 'Canes were being shackled by Erickson's buttoned-up edict. They needed to be dancing and showboating and, yes, taunting and intimidating. Irvin dialed up Thomas to let him know the deal. "This ain't right," Irvin told Thomas. "Somebody makes a big play and you guys don't do anything?" Other 'Canes received phone calls from the old 'Canes, imploring them to be "like the old Miami."

The next week, on the road at Cal in a nationally televised game, the 'Canes danced all over the Golden Bears in a 52–24 blowout. Hill exulted, thrusting his palms to the sky after each of his first six receptions, while linebackers Micheal Barrow and Jessie Armstead, after a sack, broke into a pelvic-pumping choreographed number that would've made Madonna squirm. The message was sent: The 'Canes needed to be the 'Canes. Foote told Erickson he was embarrassed by the team's actions. On the flight home, Jankovich tore into Armstead about his X-rated sack dance. Erickson declared that, from this point forward, he would bench those for the remainder of a game if "they celebrate in an embarrassing way."

Erickson's decree cut to the core to what many thought was Hurricane football—the swagger that had boiled over into a flamboyant house party in shoulder pads. That was, after all, a big reason why most of these players chose to become Hurricanes. "I visited Notre Dame, Michigan, Pittsburgh, and Florida, and it seems like they were playing football with ties on," Barrow said. "At Miami, the guys were dancing and stuff. It's a place where you can shine as an individual. There is no comparison."

Critics, many the same ones who cheered when Miami was upset by Penn State in the '87 Fiesta Bowl, said the 'Canes were making a mockery of the sport. AD Paul Dee, again, described the program as "misunderstood," which is perhaps the best way to look at it. Clearly, the "offenders" didn't subscribe to some of the same ideals as those chastising them. There was a divide along cultural and economic lines. "People complain about me celebrating after a four-yard catch," Hill told the *Mi-*

ami Herald. "I look at it like this: If you were poor and you didn't have a car and God blessed you with a Yugo, wouldn't you be happy with that Yugo? Why not be happy with everything you get on the field?"

"The rules didn't apply to them," *Miami Herald* columnist Dan Le Batard said. "They were not of the NCAA. It did not apply to them. The NCAA sportsmanship was not their sportsmanship. It was a complete disconnect. They were this group of kids who brought the street near the library. They weren't from Coral Gables and they weren't going to fit in there. And they brought whatever it was they were to Coral Gables."

"We played by the rules—the Miami rules," said Thomas. "Everybody only saw Saturdays, but no one knows how hard we go at it during the week. We hated each other, fought each other on the practice field, but then on Saturday, we come together and it's playland."

The bottled-up 'Canes struggled with their composure. Notre Dame beat them 29–20 in a game billed as the "Final Conflict," since Irish brass felt the series was no longer a healthy thing. Against Kansas, the 'Canes traded punches with Jayhawk players a half hour before kickoff after both teams got tangled up near the entrance to Miami's locker room as Miami broke its pregame huddle. Kansas coach Glen Mason called the incident "part of the intimidation factor I don't like in college football." Erickson took the blame. Miami won 34–0. Then, in the regular-season finale, the 'Canes eeked out a win at San Diego State and were baited into a bench-clearing brawl that lasted five minutes. As UM, ranked fourth in the polls, prepared for a Cotton Bowl meeting against number three Texas, the media had fun with the image of Erickson's "kinder, gentler" 'Canes—especially since it was the Longhorns doing all the trash-talking.

Texas, thinking it had an outside shot at the title, was hyping itself on a "Shock the Nation Tour." UT offensive tackle Stan Thomas did most of the yapping, talking about how he was going to take away the Outland Trophy that Miami defensive tackle Russell Maryland had won. He predicted a 28–10 Texas victory. Later Thomas likened attending a barbecue with the 'Canes to being in prison. "Typical gangsters," Thomas called them. "I can't wait to play those guys. I hope the first play lasts five minutes because I'm going to hit everybody." The 'Canes' response? Nothing. They just smiled politely for the media and tried on the white hat. Behind closed doors, however, gasoline had been heaved on the fire. Highsmith, Irvin, and a host of other old 'Canes were in Dallas and let the team know they didn't approve of these kinder, gentler Hurricanes. A few days before the game, the team had a players-only meeting. They decided no more Mr. Nice Guy. Players even began rehearsing their dance moves. Before kickoff, Erickson told the 'Canes to have fun, and then he walked out of the locker room. The 'Canes then reconvened and pledged to *really* have fun. "We fell in the poll one week when we didn't play," said UM cornerback Robert Bailey. "We all said, 'We're going to show the entire nation, show all the doubters that we're back. Let's give them the bad image they all want to see. The people watching on TV want to see the bad Hurricanes.'"

And that's exactly what they saw. Miami mugged the Longhorns, annihilating them 46–3. The 'Canes were flagged sixteen times for 202 yards, which included nine unsportsmanlike or personal-foul penalities. The only thing they didn't get whistled for was a double dribble violation.

Bailey, who had boasted to teammates before the game that he was gonna knock someone out on the opening kickoff, did.

He punctuated the lights-out hit on Longhorn returnman Chris Samuels by doing the Nestea plunge. The Hurricanes iced the game early in the third quarter on a forty-eight-yard touchdown pass to Thrill Hill, who roared past UT's Willie Mack Garza on a fly pattern and sprinted straight up the Cotton Bowl tunnel after scoring. Then Hill returned from the tunnel, shooting at the Longhorns with a pair of imaginary pistols. "It was an expression," Hill said, "to show I could take it all the way if I wanted. If the gate had been open, I probably would have gone on out."

Miami sacked Texas's sophomore QB Peter Gardere eight times. Maryland, working often against Stan Thomas, sacked him three times in the first half alone. After the game, the normally soft-spoken Maryland said he hoped the Longhorns had learned a lesson. "To shut up," he said. "If you're going to talk a lot of stuff like we do, you've got to be able to back it up. If you're going to be somebody, be them. Don't be half-steppin'.

"But they weren't ready for that. They were saying, 'These boys are crazy.' They're right; we are."

"Texas didn't respect us, and that doesn't happen with the Hurricanes," UM center Darren Handy told the *Miami Herald*. "So we had to go out and get that respect back. . . . We came out and said, 'Whatever it takes.' We didn't want to get two hundred yards in penalties, but we said, 'We're going to showcase. We're going to dance, talk trash in their face.' We just didn't care. We were going to do whatever it took to intimidate them, get them out of their game, and get that respect back.

"It might be embarrassing to the university and the coaches, but it's not to the players. We enjoy it. It's like a show. People from Texas came to see Miami's swarming defense, high-scoring offense, and what new dances we had come up with. We gave them their money's worth."

Sonny Lubick, the 'Canes defensive coordinator, said the coaching staff tried to tone the team down, but was flummoxed by the whole situation. "We tried to clean it up," he said. "The kids weren't bad. That was just their way, and that's the way they play. I don't know how to explain it. Maybe it's a Florida thing. I just don't know.

"I know a lot of people had their opinions about Miami, saying, 'Man, these guys are out of control.' But we saw them from a different viewpoint. These were some good kids. Russell Maryland is one of the best people I've ever known. We watched these kids working and practicing in ninety-degree heat with ninety percent humidity. They were disciplined, but I can imagine how it looked from the outside."

Not pretty. Like someone spray-painted over a Norman Rockwell. The media was outraged. So were many in the rest of the college football establishment. Former San Francisco 49ers coach Bill Walsh called the 'Canes' Cotton Bowl performance "the most disgusting thing I have ever seen in college sports."

Will McDonough, the *Boston Globe*'s football columnist, compared the 'Canes to a bunch of thugs running loose on gang rape. "The day of reckoning was inevitable," McDonough wrote forty-eight hours after the game. "This has been in the making for close to two decades. Sooner or later, the street would take over, and it did in the Cotton Bowl in Dallas Tuesday, when the University of Miami players delivered college football's version of wilding. . . . At Boston College this morning, they should be asking: Do we really want to be in the same conference with these people and expose our players to this garbage year after year? Is this college football? Is this what we want to bring into our stadium?

"Thankfully, the vast majority of college football is not like Oklahoma or Miami."

"This is a grubby bunch, this Miami menagerie, about as far from the college ideal as a tire iron is from an ear swab," wrote Bernie Lincicome in the *Chicago Tribune*. "And this is the best college football team in the nation. . . . I am not without some gratitude for Miami collecting dangerous young thugs and giving them a place to be angry. Better in Coral Gables than on public transportation."

The criticism only galvanized the team even more. To them, all those who sit in their sport coats, watching from above in their glassed-in, air-conditioned sky boxes, were just a bunch of whiny hypocrites. Who was bringing in all those millions to the school? The 'Canes. Who was making the TV ratings pop? The 'Canes. But were they seeing any of the windfall? Not a dime, said Mike Sullivan, who was UM's starting offensive guard and an MBA student at the time. "I don't see anyone refunding that $3.2 million we brought in this year," he told the *Herald*.

During the off-season the NCAA sent a videotape to member schools defining unacceptable conduct on the field. Of the thirty-seven examples cited in the tape, the first dozen featured Miami players. Anyone infringing would be slapped with a fifteen-yard penalty. The rule's definition: "The use of language, gestures or acts that provoke ill will, or incite spectators, or incite an opponent, or are demeaning to the game, shall be penalized." In layman's terms, it became known as "the Miami rule."

Bernie Kosar ices down on the sidelines
while Jim Kelly is just plain cool.

Warren Sapp and Rohan Marley (above);
UM athletic director Paul Dee with
Hurricane mascot, the Ibis (left).

Coach Howard Schnellenberger knew #12 Jim Kelly was more than just a linebacker.

Coach Larry Coker and his rival counterpart, FSU's Bobby Bowden.

Coach Butch Davis and Santana Moss.

(Photos Al Messerschmidt/Wire Image)

Vinny Testaverde on the sidelines with Coach Jimmy Johnson.

Coach Dennis Erickson and Earl Little pumped up before kickoff.

TOUCHDOWN! Lamar Thomas (above);
Najeh Davenport sends a message to the crowd (below).

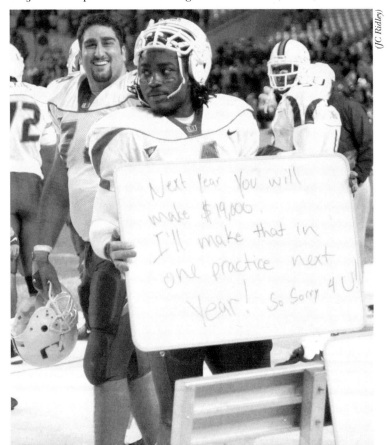

Gino Torretta flanked by (from left) Kevin Williams, Lamar Thomas, Darrin Smith, Micheal Barrow, Ryan McNeil, Rusty Medearis, and Darryl Spencer. All went on to play in the NFL, except Medearis, a UM all-American whose career was ended by injury.

Do a little dance! Ray Lewis (52) and Kenard Lang (96) get down (above); Jeremy Shockey puts up the big numbers (left).

Rabbit ears (courtesy of Victor Morris) do little for Winston Morris's reception as he and George Mira Jr. settle down for a long flight.

(JC Ridley)

(Alonzo Highsmith)

(Al Messerschmidt/Wire Image)

Edgerrin James stiff-arms his way to extra yardage (above); Ed Reed, after the turnover (left).

(Al Messerschmidt/Wire Image)

Can you smell what Dwayne Johnson's cooking? The Rock at UM (above); Kellen Winslow II moves the chains and any defender who can hang on (left).

(JC Ridley)

Clinton Portis dives for the end zone.

(JC Ridley)

Andre Johnson holding up
the Sears Trophy, with Daryl
Jones (1) and Ken Dorsey
(left); Ed Reed hanging out
with the Ibis.

Seat backs and tray tables
up, and rabbit ears stored
properly—Victor Morris on
board.

7

THE MIAMI VICE

Antonio Bryant had never heard of Tony Dorsett, Hugh Green, Mike Ditka, or other icons of Panther football royalty when he left his mama's Miami home to come twelve hundred miles north to the University of Pittsburgh in 1999. Bryant, a lanky six-foot-two, 190-pound wide receiver with willowy arms so long they seemed to droop down into his shoes, was actually known around Miami more for his academic prowess than for his football skills. Irene Bryant's place in Liberty City has a living room full of honors her little Antonio won—for being a scholar. "That boy's got more trophies at home for academics than he does for athletics," said Florida A&M DB Levy Brown, a childhood buddy. Bryant was so advanced that he was placed into a magnet program for gifted students in the second grade. Every school day for the next ten years, he'd get up at sunrise to take a bus and a train to ritzy, predominantly white Coral Gables. On game nights for Coral Gables High, he sometimes wouldn't get home until one a.m.

Bryant begged his mother to let him stay local for his senior year and go with his buddies from the neighborhood to powerhouse Northwestern High. Irene wasn't sure. She gave birth to Antonio when she was fifteen and says she broke ties with his father shortly after their son was born. She relented after talking to Northwestern's academic counselors, and her son enrolled in the school in time to join their 16-0 state championship season. Bryant maintained his grades, but, as he says, people don't start trippin' over someone getting a 4.0—unless, of course, that's your fortieth time. On the field, he put up good, but not gaudy, numbers—at least not compared to some receiver prospects. And while Bryant ran well, he wasn't exactly a burner. He was regarded by most schools as the Bulls' sixth-best college prospect. The Panthers' coaching staff, though, knew Northwestern's rep for developing talent and figured Bryant, a sleeper recruit, might be a good fit. "We only had to beat Louisville to get him," said Pittsburgh coach Walt Harris with an almost embarrassed chuckle. "And we even held off on him until the Monday before signing day."

Before taking over a dormant Panthers program, Harris was a top assistant at Michigan State, Tennessee, and Ohio State, and spent three seasons in the NFL with the New York Jets. The Panthers had won just fifteen games in the previous five seasons till Harris came to town and started making an attitude adjustment. Harris is quick to tell you that he's personally tutored eight players who've gone on to become first-round draft picks.

Harris liked Bryant's quickness and soft hands, but what he really loved about the kid was his confidence. Bryant was ultracompetitive. He was downright combative. He was the quintessential Miami kid. He played and—more important—practiced with a swagger. Bryant had what might well be called "the Miami vice." He played angry. Bryant expected the best out of himself and his teammates, and if one of them dropped a pass or ran the wrong route or made a bad read or missed a tackle, they were going to hear about it from him. "Antonio has such high expectations for everybody," Harris said. "Whatever he's into, it's a hundred and ten percent. Nothing is halfway.

"He's different from anyone I've ever coached before. His passion for the game is too strong, and he struggles with that. With some special people, their greatest strength can also be their greatest weakness. And that's Antonio."

Actually, that's not just Antonio, but many kids who grew up hard and played Little League or Optimist football (as it is known in south Florida) mimicked the 'Canes' swagger. The style became contagious. It seemed to be the one "trickle-down" element of the eighties that did reach the people of the inner cities. It spread from the likes of Bratton, Highsmith, Jerome Brown, and Irvin all the way up to the Florida panhandle, where Florida State coach Bobby Bowden allowed a similar star system, cutting loose Deion Sanders so he could be "PrimeTime." Other 'Noles followed suit, and then it became an epidemic of sorts—especially in Florida.

Just as at Miami, embracing the personas and allowing them to drive each other and flourish was the secret behind the Seminoles' rise too. "You make sure guys are disciplined," said FSU defensive line coach Odell Haggins, a former all-American nose guard with the 'Noles. "But you allow them to be themselves and have fun. We're not here to block talent."

"I believe we all have pent-up anger inside us," Bowden

said. "I tell 'em football is an excuse to lash out. Now, I want them to obey the rules during the week, but when Saturday comes, man, turn it loose. And sometimes I get a big kick out of the dances they do."

Sports' first soft-shoe took place on a rainy February night in 1964 in Miami Beach, but it wasn't done by a Hurricane. Muhammad Ali, known at the time as Cassius Clay, won the heavyweight championship of the world, knocking out Sonny Liston. Upon his triumph Ali declared, "I don't have to be what you want me to be. I am free to be what I want." And with that proclamation suddenly the values and ideals heaped upon athletes by coaches, the media, and fans no longer were attached to them with chains. Maybe more important, Ali's statement served as the next leap in the efforts of African-Americans to shake free from the bonds of institutional oppression.

Ali's motto was "I'm just a nigger gettin' bigger," and his stance was more about revolution than evolution. Ali got bigger not just because he was such a skilled boxer, but because he was a showman who could bring people into the tent, and because he had a surgical ability to get under his opponent's skin. His three biggest influences, he once said, were Little Richard, pro wrestler Gorgeous George, and Liberace.

Ali's arrival in America's consciousness in the days leading up to his big fight with Liston left the country with its mouth hanging wide open. Bursting through a door for the prefight weigh-in at the Miami Beach Convention Center, the twenty-two-year-old Clay, a seven-to-one underdog, strode in banging his African walking stick off the floor. With each step he and his sidekick and head cheerleader, Bundini Brown, yelled their battle cry: "Float like a butterfly, sting like a bee, rumble, young man, rumble! Auuuu*gg*uuuuuu!"

When Liston arrived, Clay howled: "I'm ready to rumble now! You're scared, chump! You ain't no giant! I'm going to eat you alive! You're a bear, you're ugly, I'm going to whip you so bad!"

"Clay is acting like a man scared to death," the commission doctor observed while taking Clay's blood pressure. "He is emotionally unbalanced, liable to crack up before he enters the ring."

Some of Clay's cornermen weren't exactly sure what their fighter was up to either. Clay's answer: "Because Liston thinks I am a nut. He is scared of no man, but he is scared of a nut because he doesn't know what I am going to do."

The head games worked. Ali, as he screamed to anyone who'd listen, "shook up the world," and he was only just getting started. So was the metamorphosis of the modern athlete, particularly the modern black athlete. Ali's style was a blast of hot air into America's face. Society, at that time, was comfortable with its sports heroes putting on the smiley-faced, milk-drinking, crew-cut-wearing, all-American image. Most of the football stars were cookie-cutter guys with the charisma of wood-paneled station wagons, and they all seemed to come from Army, Navy, or Notre Dame. The most prominent black athletes before Ali, baseball's Jackie Robinson and boxer Joe Louis, were encouraged not to show signs of defiance. Louis made sure he was never photographed next to a white woman.

Ali's persona grew out of the political and cultural waves sweeping through the early sixties—rock music, antigovernment rebellion, and black power. His energy was drawn from being a rebel, and being hated by the bigots and the establishment. He also came along at a time when television was exploding and changing the way society viewed itself. Suddenly the world was smaller and faster and harder. Everything was visceral.

Ali's braggadocio—and often outlandish ways—soon pulsed through the rest of the sports world. One year later Homer Jones, an unheralded wide receiver for the New York Giants, scored his first career touchdown, an eighty-nine-yard pass play against the Philadelphia Eagles. Jones wanted to fling the ball to the cheering crowd, but he remembered that the NFL fined players for throwing the ball into the stands, so instead he fired the ball down as hard as he could. Football's first spike. Jones begat Elmo Wright, who celebrated his touchdowns with a high-kicking dance.

The threads of Ali's psychological ploys and his flamboyance, though, were never so tightly intertwined again. All the lines were blurred. Still, the spirit had already spilled out of the bottle. The dancing and the styling that often get derided as showboating today have a larger meaning, some say. That it is about freedom and control. Ali's style was axiomatic for the black athlete—especially coming from a heritage where as slaves they were allowed no identity. And even after slavery was abolished blacks were still relegated to second-class status right up to the Ali era. This, the way "they" perform, is a by-product of that, said USC professor Todd Boyd, author of *Out of Bounds: Sports, Media and the Politics of Identity*.

"Ali was saying, 'I'm not just gonna beat you. I'm gonna humiliate you,' and that comes back to sports being much more than just sports for the black athlete," Boyd said, "because it's not just about winning, it's about winning with style. People always get this twisted, but it's real important for black athletes to be stylish so they can define themselves. It's like telling your opponent that, for instance, you are superior, and for a people who come from an environment where they don't have much to cling to or don't have things that they can call their own, this is something you completely control. That's huge."

For a generation that identity often has been tied into basketball, aka "the city game," which has been made a staple of the hip-hop world, in large part due to its playground hoops artistry and showmanship, but in reality, football operates on another level. As Luther Campbell, the notorious Miami-based rapper of 2 Live Crew fame, put it, football, because of its physical nature, digs even deeper into man's psyche. "Football showed we could rise above the slave mentality, the segregation, and be who we want to be," he said. "This game is our therapy. We can come out to the field and leave all our problems behind. It's therapeutic. While we're out here, we don't care about how they fuck us over and everything. We go out there and we can just focus on football and have that camaraderie. Football is all we got, man. They can't take this shit from us. We do own this game. I mean, y'all can take whatever the fuck you want to take from us—our land, our housing, our jobs, everything, man. But we got our pride and we got our dignity. We might not have ever had any leader to lead us to the promised land, but at least we got our football, and y'all aren't gonna take that from us too.

"Down here in Miami, football is like a rite of passage. It's even more so like that now because we have a reputation to uphold as the best football players. It's mandatory that we hold that down."

The 'Canes' example fed off that fire. Their impact also

created a feeder system that was loosely formed on the club football model of international *fútbol* (soccer). "The success of the University of Miami inspired a lot more inner-city kids to play Optimist football, which has really improved the overall quality of football in Dade County," said Miami's Killian High football coach Billy Rolle, who won a state title at Northwestern High in 1995. "Our high school teams are some of the best in the country, and I think that's due in large part to the strength of our Optimists."

Campbell, the same guy some in the mainstream liked to view as a modern-day Caligula, cofounded Optimist football in 1990 after he was approached to sponsor a baseball team run by Sam Johnson, a bus driver, who had felt compelled to help local kids after spying the despair and hopelessness along Bus Route 21, the line that weaves through riot-torn Overtown and Liberty City. Johnson called his program MTUNDU, an African word for community. With Campbell's help (he donated over $50,000 the first year for uniforms and equipment for the 750 boys who signed up for the program), the Liberty City Warriors won city championships in seven of eight weight divisions in the organization's first year in Pop Warner football. The Warriors' success sparked startup programs in a handful of other black neighborhoods. In 1998, Liberty City even won the Pop Warner national championship. The next year, one of Liberty City's sister programs, the Gwen Cherry Bulls, won the title, and then won it again in 2001.

Antonio Bryant was one of the first products of Sam Johnson and Luther Campbell's Pee Wee football program in Liberty City. "Antonio was just this little skinny stick," remembered Johnson. "But he was a fiery thing. He gave you everything he got in that little body of his. He had some pizzazz in him.

Down here, they all got that pizzazz. I think that comes from them seeing the UM. I got one kid now. I call him 'Tic-tac.' He's eight years old, but, man, you should see him. He's got so much confidence. He thinks he's a little Ray Lewis." Tic-tac, Johnson said, weighs sixty-seven pounds.

Most college coaches don't like to brag about things like that, but great football teams need that swagger, that edge. These coaches learned it the hard way, from getting stomped by the Miamis and Florida States. (The Seminoles learned it after years of getting beaten by the 'Canes.) "You don't want a team full of assholes," said one Big Ten assistant, "but you need guys with that 'Florida attitude.' Miami was winning championships with it, and this is a copycat business, so that's what you need to bring into your team. Like they say, nice guys finish last. We do believe that. Football is a game of attitude, and these kids know all about playing on the edge. Sometimes they tend to go over it, and that's a risk, 'cause this is a team sport, but that's a risk we need to take. This ain't golf we're playing."

"We are different," boasted former UCLA all-American wide receiver Freddie Mitchell, who grew up 250 miles northwest of Miami in Lakeland, Florida, as a Seminole fan. "I can definitely pick out who the Florida boys are in the Pac-10 just by the way they carry themselves," he said. "Florida players have got bigger heart. We're hungry and there's a certain swagger in our step."

Walt Harris rolled the dice with Bryant and won big, although it wasn't easy. In 2000, Bryant, as a sophomore, led the nation in receiving yardage and won the Biletnikoff Award. He also may have led the nation in tantrums thrown. Getting Bryant to think before he reacts was a challenge, Harris conceded. "He grew up in an area where they're taught to react first, and it's not the same here," Harris said. "This isn't Miami. We believe the most disciplined team usually wins, and the team with the greatest chemistry always wins."

Coaches all over the country got a good lesson on New Year's Day, 1994, about what bad chemistry can do to a football team. Not so coincidentally, that was the day pundits started celebrating the end of the 'Cane dynasty. The eulogies started rolling in before the clock ran out during the 'Canes' Fiesta Bowl matchup against upstart Arizona on the first day of 1994. The number sixteen Wildcats, a program that had never even won its conference championship, crushed number ten Miami 29–0. It was the first time UM had been shut out in fifteen years. The rout knocked UM down to number fifteen in the final Associated Press poll, ending a streak of seven straight seasons among the top three. The 'Canes finished the season 9-3, a record that would've been great at most schools, but not at UM. "They just kicked the living tar out of us," coach Dennis Erickson said. "They dominated the line of scrimmage, and their defense proved that it was everything they said."

Arizona's Desert Swarm defense pushed the 'Canes around, bottling up Miami's high-powered offense, collecting four sacks, three interceptions, and a fumble recovery. "The Hurricane tradition made us think everyone will lay down for us," said true freshman linebacker Ray Lewis. "It backfired on us. The fire the Hurricanes used to have—it wasn't there."

"Before, everybody we played respected us," junior running back Larry Jones told *Sports Illustrated*. "But from the first play, they weren't intimidated at all. I don't know why they don't respect us anymore. . . ."

The Wildcats' dismantling of Miami could be distilled into one play. It happened with 3:39 remaining in the first half. Arizona was leading 9–0, and then Wildcat tailback Chuck Levy took a handoff, ducked under some UM defensive linemen, burst up the middle, cut to the corner, and then did something no one had seemed to be able to do for a decade: he sprinted right past the Miami defense. Miami cornerbacks Paul White and Dexter Seigler gave chase, but they couldn't catch Levy— although through the tail fumes, they did get a good view of Levy's duckwalk as he strutted into the end zone. "You just don't see that!" wailed NBC announcer Cris Collinsworth. The referees, of course, flagged Levy for excessive celebration, not that it mattered much by then; the game was over.

"That game . . . everybody was like, 'Is this us? Is this really the 'Canes?'" Lewis said. "You sit and you're saying, 'This can't be happening.' But in reality, it is."

As the Erickson era wore on, the 'Canes had become a caricature of themselves. His governing-by-democracy approach had deteriorated into anarchy. The pressure was clearly wearing on him. Erickson started vomiting before big games and got fever blisters on his face. Anyone wondering whether the coach had lost his grip on the team needed only to watch the pregame coin flip. Before the 1992 home opener against Florida A&M, one of the game captains, Darren Krein, a junior defensive end, was told by Erickson to shake hands with the captains of the Rattlers. However, after a players-only meeting, the team voted against it. And sure enough, there was no handshake. Foote, still sick about UM's bad-boy image, told Erickson he wanted his players to honor the tradition. The 'Canes told Erickson, "With all due respect, no, thanks." They were starting their own tradition.

"I guess it goes back to what Jerome Brown said about not sitting down with the enemy at Pearl Harbor," said former UM all-American defensive end Kevin Patrick. "That was our whole attitude. It's a very physical sport, and if you go in with one ounce of weakness in your mind or in your body, you're gonna get hurt and you're gonna lose."

According to the *Orlando Sentinel,* Erickson said, "You just can't make rules anymore without having some flexibility, or at least listening to the other side of it. In the old days, the coach drew a line and, if you crossed that line, you were in trouble. Well, that's not how it is."

Erickson's words would come back to haunt him. The 'Canes machine started to show signs that it was indeed leaking oil. Before the '94 Fiesta Bowl, the first indicator came in the 1993 Sugar Bowl, when the number one–ranked 'Canes were dumped from the top of the college football heap by number two Alabama, 34–13. That loss had its own humiliating highlight when Alabama's George Teague tracked down UM's main mouthpiece Lamar Thomas as the 'Canes star was headed for what appeared to be a sure touchdown. Thomas, a member of Miami's four-hundred-meter relay team, had hauled in a sideline pass from Heisman Trophy–winning QB Gino Torretta and had a clear path to the end zone. But Teague, the Tide's strong safety, ran him down, catching Thomas at the Alabama 15. Teague, however, was not content just to make a tackle. Reaching over Thomas's right shoulder with his right hand, he wrestled the ball from Thomas, making one of the most amazing fumble recoveries in football history. The symbolism was perfect for the way the night went. So what if the play didn't technically happen, since an offside penalty against the Tide meant that Miami kept the ball—albeit seventy-seven yards farther back? UM's spirit was broken, and the 'Canes ended the possession three plays later with a punt. "That game was the turning point," said former UM defensive line coach Ed Orgeron. "Those kids were so used to winning, I think they forgot how they got there."

Then, in late October, Florida State, the eventual national champions, smacked the 'Canes, 28–10—Miami's worst regular-season loss in ten years. A month later, the 'Canes lost at West Virginia, their first Big East loss ever.

Quarterback Frank Costa privately predicted before the Fiesta Bowl that the 'Canes would be beaten badly. "That twenty-nine-zero score typified everything last year," Costa told reporters. "We could have played anybody and got beat that bad in that game. It was like, 'Why are we here?' There wasn't the intensity. I could have told anybody we were going to lose that game." The powerhouse that had been built on its "us against the world" mentality had taken on an "us against us" attitude.

Everyone on the team knew the 'Canes had too many cliques to win, Costa said. The tough, olive-skinned Philadelphian who had been dubbed "Costaverde" when he arrived at UM was at the center of one of the team's main rifts. A tall, Italian kid with a powerful arm, Costa—evoking visions of Testaverde—had been groomed as the 'Canes' next great quarterback. But he struggled making his reads and his throws were seldom accurate. His teammates never developed any confidence in him. Instead, many of them favored fleet-footed Ryan Collins, a lightly recruited African-American prospect from nearby Miami Lakes, who came amid whispers that the coaches would probably rather have him as wide receiver or defensive back. Collins rose up from fifth on the depth chart and wowed his teammates with his scrambling ability and his unflappable demeanor in the huddle. During the season, Erickson flip-flopped his two QBs as if he were driving a sports car, constantly shifting gears. The team was split along racial lines by who supported which quarterback. Other cracks, though, soon developed. The next biggest was between a brazen group of underclassmen and the seniors. Two days after the West Virginia loss, the 'Canes' locker room bubbled over with dissension. Players blamed each other and coaches for the loss. Frustrated backups whined. Many more groused that the season's final two games were irrelevant, since a national title was out of the question. Some players deemed it "an uprising." The seniors went to Erickson, who scrapped a Monday workout and attempted to clear the air with a team meeting. "Players didn't respect the program anymore," senior defensive end Kevin Patrick said.

After the 'Canes got blown out by Arizona, the dissension cut so deep that Rohan Marley, UM's leading tackler, told a teammate on the flight home from the Fiesta Bowl that he couldn't take it anymore; he was quitting the team.

"I've never seen anything like what was going on," Marley told *SI*, "not in high school, never. Guys started going their separate ways, the intensity level toned down. It was everybody on everybody: 'Screw you.' 'You're sorry.' 'You ain't in shape.' There was no positive vibe. We were always fighting."

The realization had sunk in that the 'Canes no longer intimidated opponents merely by walking on the field. Instead, their foes were now emboldened by getting a crack at mighty Miami. "We fell off one of the highest cliffs in Arizona," Patrick told the *Fort Lauderdale Sun-Sentinel*. "And we fell straight down. It was a devastating blow. . . . We thought we could walk on the field and we'd win off the bat because we are Miami. That's not going to happen. We lost our work ethic."

The problem was twofold. First, there was a talent dropoff, some of the blue chips never panned out, and it carried over to the practice field, where egos often went unchecked. "When we were there, the competition factor was so friggin' high that if you chose to go 'the wrong route' there was no way the next day you could do what you needed to do at practice, so you wouldn't play," said Orgeron, who left UM after the '92 season. "It weeded itself out, but then the competition factor went down a little bit, so guys could get away with it and guys were able to cut corners."

The other factor was that the dynamics of Erickson's staff also had changed. The chemistry between players and coaches had suffered. On Erickson's first two national title teams, he had four strong, hard-assed coaches—Art Kehoe, the offensive line coach; Sonny Lubick, the defensive coordinator; Orgeron; and strength coach Brad Roll. But by 1993, after Lubick became the head coach at Colorado State, Orgeron returned home to Louisiana and Roll moved on to the NFL; only Kehoe remained. "They lost guys that were real close to the team and they brought in some new guys," said Orgeron. "Now I'm not saying there was nothing wrong with the new guys, but they just didn't know those types of kids. I mean, you gotta know 'em well—how they were brought up, how they act, how they respond to you—and you had to respect them. That was a big key, and they had to respect you back. Sapp respected me and I respected him, but there was a fine line."

Back home in Miami on the same day that the 'Canes were self-destructing in the Fiesta Bowl, Bobby Bowden's Florida State Seminoles were celebrating their first national title after winning the Orange Bowl. One month later, Florida State emerged with two of the top prospects from Miami—cornerback Samari Rolle and Lamont Green, the nation's top-rated linebacker recruit. "I can't ever remember doing so well in Miami," Bowden gloated.

The 'Canes' dynasty was indeed crumbling. It turned out it had been rotting from the inside. Its greatest strengths—its swagger and rage—would prove its biggest weaknesses. And soon it would all come crashing down in one big, thunderous heap.

THE DIRTY SOUTH

When the eagles are silent, the parrots begin to jabber.
— SIR WINSTON CHURCHILL

The chaos around Coral Gables was rampant. Players were battling players. Players were jabbing at Foote. Erickson was butting heads with Foote. Dee, the new AD, was trying to referee it all. Meanwhile, inside the Miami athletic department there was fear of impending NCAA sanctions from a Pell Grant scandal that resulted in the jailing of Tony Russell, a former UM academic adviser.

Russell, whose son Twan arrived in 1993 as a freshman linebacker, pleaded guilty in March 1994 to helping students falsify Pell Grant applications (Department of Education grant money earmarked for students of families earning less than $25,000 a year) and was sentenced to three years in prison. Russell admitted conspiring with eighty-five student athletes in nine different sports at Miami, including fifty-seven football players, bilking the federal government out of $220,000 from 1989 to 1991.

For kickbacks totaling about $8,000—an average of $85 per application—Russell falsified information on hundreds of documents. The students involved in the scandal were put into a pretrial diversion program and received no criminal penalties in exchange for their cooperation and agreements to make restitution. Former Miami all-American defensive end Rusty Medearis said knowledge of Pell Grant fraud was widespread around UM's campus. He testified that falsification of the Pell Grant applications was a common topic of discussion among players. He said people connected with the team would have been "blind or ignorant" to not recognize what was transpiring. "I knew it was illegal, but I rationalized it by telling myself that a lot of people knew what was going on," Medearis said. "We decided we wouldn't get into trouble because [Russell] was so close . . . to the athletic director's office."

Medearis testified that he learned about the scam in 1989 from roommates Jason Marucci, a fullback, and quarterback Bryan Fortay. "They walked into the dorm room one day elated about something," said Medearis. "They were slapping high fives and singing and dancing. They kept on saying, 'measy-oney.'"

Measy-oney, Medearis soon learned, was the code for *easy money*. Medearis said he was encouraged by Marucci to meet with Russell to obtain a Pell Grant. Medearis said he was charged $85 by Russell (money that he borrowed from Gino Torretta). "Eighty-five dollars turned into fifteen hundred dollars, and I thought that was a pretty good deal," Medearis said.

Costa testified that he was recruited by Russell in 1991,

when he was a freshman. "He came up to me in the locker room and said, 'Why haven't you got your Pell Grant yet?' "

Costa claimed he ignored Russell, but was approached by him again two weeks later saying, "This is your money and you're entitled to it."

Costa further testified: "I thought it was wrong. I had heard other players were doing it, that it had been going on for a couple of years and nobody got caught. I figured if everybody else was doing it, I wanted to take advantage of it, too."

Players didn't seem to mind that Russell often got their parents' information labeled incorrectly, as long as he got them money. Medearis said he knew there were numerous falsifications on his Pell application form, filled in by Russell, including his parents' marital status (they were actually divorced), their income, their Social Security numbers, even the spelling of his mother Nancy Huff's last name.

Medearis said Russell was "like a hero" to the football players because of his ability to get them money. Prior to his arrival at Miami, Russell had been fired from his job as offensive coordinator at West Virginia State, according to the *Sun-Sentinel*, for his role in a telephone scam.

The stench from the Pell Grant scandal would not only send Russell to prison; it would ultimately expose Erickson's cavalier attitude toward disciplining his players and trigger a series of investigations that would paint a picture of a program totally out of control. In a May 1995 story by the *Miami Herald*, then UM athletic director Dave Maggard recounted an exchange he had with Erickson in 1992, in which he wanted the coach to suspend his star wideout for the season opener against Iowa after the federal government accused Lamar Thomas of lying about his family income to get $2,300 in Pell Grant aid.

ERICKSON: I need him to play.

MAGGARD: You need to pull him. He isn't going to play.

ERICKSON: Let him practice at least.

MAGGARD: No. No way. It's never going to stop around here.

ERICKSON: The guy hasn't been convicted of anything.

MAGGARD: Dennis, he has been indicted.

The *Herald* investigation detailed incidents ranging from one UM student's allegation that she was assaulted by several players in 1990 and subsequently talked out of going to the police by Erickson, to widespread drug use. According to the *Herald*, "Beth Samartino, the secretary to UM's assistant coaches from 1989–94, said she often bought marijuana for players and smoked it with them in their rooms, including the night before the 1994 Fiesta Bowl." The story alleged that Erickson pulled numerous end runs around Miami athletic director Paul Dee to avoid sidelining players who failed drug tests.

"Dennis was too lenient," Maggard told the *Herald*. "He needed some backbone behind him . . . Dennis is a really good Xs-and-Os coach. He has a big problem disciplining the team." Jankovich, the man who hired Erickson, echoed Maggard's comments. "At times he let some players intimidate him. You could say he could have been firmer."

The players also intimidated campus cops, according to the story, saying UM police clashed so often with players that it became commonplace for Erickson to receive after-midnight calls to come to the dorms to try to control his team. "Once or twice a week, we'd get some call regarding a player," a former campus police officer who worked two years during the Erickson era told the *Herald*. "Anything from drunk players throwing bottles to allegations of rape, theft, assault, battery, and drugs."

"The guys of that era delighted in the fact that the administration was mortified by them," said Dan Le Batard, a columnist for the *Miami Herald*. "I remember all the stories we got in the late eighties and early nineties were a product of these guys enjoying seeing their rebellion in print. If they beat up the pizza guy, I'd get a call from one of them saying, 'We beat up the pizza guy.' They all thought it was funny that the administration was horrified by their existence and needed them all at once because of the publicity that they brought."

The allegations were added onto a laundry list of sordid accusations that had been heaped on the program. One year earlier the *Herald* reported on a pay-for-play system that was bankrolled, in part, through Luther Campbell. From 1986 to 1992, a span that covers three Miami national titles, players received cash for big hits, interceptions, or touchdowns.

Former players told the *Herald* that they competed for two separate pools of cash. One was a player-generated pot that went to the 'Cane who made the biggest hit in a game. Players contributed $5 to $10 each to the pot, which could grow to more than $200 for big games. And former 'Canes sometimes added money to the big-game pots.

The second pool of money was an NFL players fund, supplied by old 'Canes, that went to players for momentum-changing plays such as sacks and interceptions returned for touchdowns.

Game-day bounties also were reportedly offered. The going rate? Fifty dollars for a caused fumble or fumble recovery; $100 for a quarterback sack, a block that flattens an opponent, an interception, or a touchdown; $200 for an interception returned for a touchdown. The catch was that if the 'Canes lost, nobody collected.

Before the 1989 Notre Dame game in the Orange Bowl, the story alleges that the pot was sweetened: "A slew" of former UM players gathered with Campbell on the sideline and added new incentives that were passed along to the team. The 'Cane who knocked Notre Dame quarterback Tony Rice out of the game with a clean hit would get $1,500. The one who KO'd receiver/returnman Rocket Ismail would get $1,000.

The heaviest charges in the story came from two former players—Perriman and tight end Randy Bethel. Both admitted that they gave players cash. "When we come back to school, we'll give them a hundred or two hundred dollars in the clubs," Perriman was quoted as saying. "They say they'll pay us back when they get to the pros. We say, no, don't give it back to us. Help somebody else on the team who is struggling. Keep the tradition going."

The story added that thirty hours after Perriman made those quotes he phoned the paper and retracted all he had said. "I ain't never given no money. Never. Never. Never. I'm taking all that back."

Bethel, then an assistant coach at North Carolina's Johnson C. Smith College, a Division II school in Charlotte, not only acknowledged that he often gave money to players; he added that he would do it the next time he saw a player too. "If they [the NCAA] think I'm wrong, then they have to do what they have to do," Bethel told the *Herald*.

"Aha!" was the reaction all across the country as newspapers and TV jumped on the story. This was proof that not only were the 'Canes crass and cocky, but, finally, there was some level of validation that they were cheaters too. Having it all link back to

Campbell, the bad boy of rap, only made it even sweeter for UM's critics. Here was the icon for what many perceived were all the ills of street culture, stoking the crew who seemed to be dragging down the game that was made famous by the likes of Joe Pa, the Bear, and the sons of Knute Rockne. Sounded like a marriage made in hell, right? "Something Stinks, and Surprise, It's Miami" was the headline of a column from South Bend.

The reality that most of America wouldn't—and, in many cases, doesn't want to—hear is that the 'Canes believed they were playing by a different set of rules. The myth of modern-day college amateurism—or shamateurism, as some have dubbed it—was being thrown in their faces at every turn. "We go into the bookstore and half the stuff is football memorabilia," Miami safety Charles Pharms said. "A Hurricane sweatshirt is thirty or forty dollars. I helped make that shirt popular, but I can't even afford it."

Their school president, Tad Foote, was scolding them at every turn, yet showing up and celebrating with all his cronies on the 'Canes' bowl trips—and also building a new library and giving a face-lift to an entire campus thanks not only to the millions that his blasphemous bunch brought in but also to the exposure they generated.

Bernard Clark made seventeen tackles and had an interception when the 'Canes routed top-ranked Notre Dame and ended the Irish's twenty-three-game winning streak. Clark said he didn't remember how much Campbell gave him for the interception, just that it was "in a big wad and I spent it." What he does have a clearer recollection of was how his stomach growled on some weekends because he couldn't afford to eat. "I'm two hundred and fifty pounds. And I don't think thirty dollars is going to feed me for two days, but that's where all the problems stem from," Clark said. "The training table is closed after lunch on Friday until dinner on Sunday. We got thirty dollars to eat Friday and Saturday, and that doesn't include going to a movie or hanging out. Usually you wound up staying home with a video."

Clark lamented that the NCAA just puts too many restrictions on athletes, and this—the pay-for-play approach—was the way around it. "There are just too many restrictions," Clark said. "This wouldn't even be news if guys were allowed to get jobs. During the season I can understand it, but during the spring when a guy has time to get a job, why is it a problem?"

"They want us to be like regular students," Bethel told the *Herald*. "But regular students don't generate revenue like we do. . . . I don't remember the last time that seventy thousand people packed into the Orange Bowl to watch a chemistry experiment."

Luther Campbell had been a diehard UM fan ever since he was seven years old. That was when his big brother, Stanley, started bringing him to games at the Orange Bowl. "Miami really sucked back then," Luther said. He remembered watching Notre Dame run it up on the Hurricanes 44–0 back in '73. "They were getting killed by everybody," he says. "But I still had this love for this sorry-assed team."

Campbell dreamed of someday playing linebacker for the Dallas Cowboys, and despite weighing only 170 pounds, he says he grew to become a decent defensive end for Miami Beach High, the school he was bused to from his Liberty City home. Campbell couldn't have explained his love for the game back then, but he knew it was more than just escapism.

Football, he felt, meant something to him—it was about becoming a man—just as it did to all his boys in Liberty City. He'd fantasize for the most of that forty-minute bus ride each morning about playing pro football, about hitting running backs so hard their helmets popped off. But in his senior year, he got booted off the football team because, Campbell said, he had a bit of an attitude problem. A John Wayne type, he said, fighting all the time. "I thought I was big shit. I thought I was the baddest thing to ever hit the field. Then I got introduced to some other issues—drinking, partying, women—and that was it."

Music was the one thing that seemed to keep him out of trouble. He started using his mom's new stereo, took the name Luke Skyywalker, and formed a seven-man band, the Ghetto Style DJs, and soon they began playing at local parties. The group developed into such a hit they began renting out a skating rink and charging fans $7 to hear their shows.

Campbell graduated from Miami Beach High in 1978 and took on another job: washing dishes at Mount Sinai Medical Center. He soon worked his way up to cook. Football, though, remained his first love, and his passion for the 'Canes grew even stronger in 1983, when UM signed Bratton and Bain, two of his homeboys. "The class that changed the program," Campbell said. "At the time UM wasn't really recruiting people from the inner city. There was always this perception that they were afraid of having these kids from Miami in there."

Campbell knew the 'Canes were on the brink of something huge. Coincidentally, so was he. 2 Live Crew, a southern California rap tandem featuring two U.S. servicemen, Chris Wong Won and David Hobbs, had made their way to Miami and performed at a local show. Campbell, then moonlighting as a concert promoter, joined up with the West Coast act. They cut their first track, "Throw the D," in 1984 and created what is now known as the Miami bass sound. "Throw the D" was a tribute to a part of the male anatomy, and was fueled by a monstrous, reggae-style bass line. It was also a tribute to bawdy Redd Foxx–style comic Rudy Ray Moore, who starred as Dolemite, king of all pimps in the blaxploitation cult classic of the same name.

Campbell pressed three thousand copies of the record and hawked it from the trunk of his car, and a year later it was an underground smash, selling 250,000 copies. The band's first album, *Is What We Are,* featured the breakout cut "We Want Some Pussy" that made the Crew a national name. The song offered up some of the raunchiest lyrics ever heard, including one line referencing Campbell's "long hard dick for all of the ladies."

2 Live Crew hit a nerve. Their music not only had a butt-shaking sound, but it was different from any other music playing on the radio or even in the clubs—it was laugh-out-loud funny. Just like the Richard Pryor records Campbell grew up listening to. Two years later, 2 Live Crew made headlines across every newspaper in America. Campbell and one bandmate were arrested on obscenity charges in 1990 after their appearance at a Hollywood, Florida, nightclub. A judge had previously ruled the band's 1989 album, *As Nasty as They Wanna Be,* obscene after tallying up eighty-seven references to oral sex. The record's hit song, "Me So Horny," sampled the groaning of a Vietnamese hooker from the Stanley Kubrick film *Full Metal Jacket* for its hook. An appellate court judge, though, later overturned that ruling. Fueled by the controversy, the album reached double platinum, selling more than

two million copies. Meanwhile, Campbell, fancying himself the black Hugh Hefner, was building an empire around Miami, owning music publishing, development, and mortgage companies; a recording studio; and a nightclub. In 1993, his companies grossed $14 million. He became the first rapper ever profiled on *Lifestyles of the Rich and Famous* and was featured in a sympathetic *60 Minutes* portrait. He also packed his SUV and handed out turkeys and gifts during Christmastime, sponsored educational programs and athletic programs for inner-city children around Miami, and in 1992, he and Reverend Jesse Jackson flew a planeload of food and supplies to Haitian refugees in Guantánamo Bay. "A lot of people associate him with the bad rap image, but the man does a tremendous amount of good in the community," said Joe Zaccheo, the football coach at Miami's Pace High School and former director of youth football in Miami in the eighties. "A lot of guys go on to success and forget where they come from, but you have to have respect for this man because he reaches into his pockets and gives back. It's really too bad that people only see the one side of him."

Campbell had become a friend of the UM football program in the mid-eighties. Players started to hang out at his club, Strawberries. He said he soon realized he could act as a needed big brother for inner-city kids trying to adjust to life in Coral Gables. "I knew I could talk to these cats, who were up there wilding and didn't know what kind of opportunity they had," Campbell said. "And they listened to me because they looked up to me."

He was "Uncle Luke," and he had street cred. He was Miami's ghetto superstar, the Don, as he refers to himself, and he had made it "out" without ever leaving. Campbell prided himself on being able to deal with "the crazy ones." They were his *patients,* as he liked to call them. Cornerback Darrell Fullington and Jerome Brown were his first. Later it would be Mark Caesar and Warren Sapp, a pair of loquacious three-hundred-pound defensive tackles. There were times—shocking as this may sound—when even Erickson himself felt one of his guys was straying and he'd call Campbell to rein him in. "Coach E was my man," Campbell said. "I got no problem saying that. If he ever had a problem with somebody, he'd say, 'Luke, this motherfucker right here, talk to him,' and I would talk to him.

"I was hard-core, but at the same time I could talk to them about how to 'flip it,' and it's really about flipping it." By "flipping it" Campbell means channeling, or redirecting, their rage. Campbell became an honorary 'Cane. When his group, 2 Live Crew, started wearing 'do rags on their heads, so did many of the 'Canes. Whenever 2 Live Crew performed in concert, they wore UM gear, and when most of the older 'Canes returned to the sidelines for games, Campbell, with his all-access pass, was right there alongside them, whooping it up and talking the most shit. "He was on the way up when we met him, but he was still the same Luke," said Bain. "One of the boys from the 'hood. Never changed. And he was a hero to a lot of guys from the neighborhood." Campbell even had Bain and Bratton rap on one of his records.

Sometimes players would bring recruits by to "see the Don," as Campbell put it. "It was like dangling a scarf," Campbell said. "Only the real players get to wear the scarf. 'If you're soft, go somewhere else, dawg. We don't want you.' I'd talk to them and give 'em that big rah-rah speech—'If you wanna go play football in the bushes at Florida, you're probably gonna end up being an alcoholic 'cause you're gonna get so damn bored.'

"People always thought it was Luke paying them kids. I ain't paying no kids to be recruited. I just give it to 'em real, like a father figure, and then say, 'If you need to talk to somebody, I'm here. You ain't gonna have that nowhere else.'"

Campbell said he was misquoted about his role in the pay-for-play scheme, although he said through a chuckle that he has a *recollection* of how it worked. "It's like if [David] Klingler, the Houston quarterback, gets in the newspaper and they're hyping him up, from what I understand somebody—and I don't quite remember his name—would let the players know that if they knocked his ass out of the game, they might get a hundred dollars," Campbell said. "Now, I don't know no specifics, but that's how I heard it was."

Campbell paused a few moments, and conceded he did what he thought he should do, and he encouraged the older 'Canes in the NFL to take care of the guys who were in the program because most of them didn't have anyone at home who could send them $50 to go out to eat, get into a club, or take a girl out. Besides, Campbell said, "I don't think I helped them in a way that when I went to sleep at night I did things that I think were wrong. To me, though, what the NCAA does to basketball and football players really isn't right."

A short but stoutly built man, Paul Dee has gray hair, an over-stuffed, fleshy face, and is slightly cross-eyed. He breathes heavy even after completing a sentence or cracking a joke. He is in his late fifties, but looks much older. He appears to be the complete opposite of his players. UM staffers think he may have narcolepsy because he tends to fall asleep so often. Dee, who oversaw the UM investigation, is used to having to defend his program. In fact, he is so whipped he often answers questions that haven't even been asked yet. But maybe that's what two decades at UM can do to a lawyer. Dee said a lot of the incidents were "just individual indiscretions. I refer to it as our period of misunderstanding," he said with a nervous laugh. "We were simply being too misunderstood.

"There was a time when no matter what happened it became like another log on the fire and then it just kept getting to be a bigger and bigger fire. Every time something happened, the media wanted to string it all together like it was a pattern, like it was organized to be that way, but it wasn't; it was just a series of unfortunate independent events that became the picture of the 'old Miami.' We had to break that string, and you can't just announce you're breaking the string. You have to have some good leadership and some good fortune—and be a in position where you don't have these kinds of incidents for a while. We had to break away from that image."

With the black cloud of probable NCAA sanctions hanging over the program from a host of questionable incidents, most notably the Pell Grant scandal, the pressure started to wear Erickson down. Rumors of Erickson's drinking were running wild. One day while visiting one of the south Florida PGA Tour stops in the spring, a spectator spotted Erickson in front of one of the mirrors in a men's room. Erickson, wobbly and glassy-eyed, clearly had been drinking. The fan said, "Hey, Coach, hope you win another title," and smacked Erickson on the back. The coach hunched forward and then proceeded to vomit on the floor.

Not surprisingly, his relationship with the local media, particularly the *Herald*, had become nasty. He said the paper was as reputable as the *National Enquirer*. Reports of Erickson's flirtation with NFL teams seemed to be coming on a weekly basis. One day he would say he would consider an NFL offer. The next he'd talk about hoping to become a fixture at Miami.

The 1994 'Canes were talented, led by Sapp, the Lombardi Award–winning defensive tackle, and fierce sophomore middle linebacker Ray Lewis, but the offense was young and inconsistent. They came into the Orange Bowl ranked fourth and with an outside shot at another national title. Top-ranked Nebraska was waiting for them. But for the third year in a row, the 'Canes would come away empty in a bowl game, losing 24–17. After the game, an embattled Erickson stormed past his assistants to challenge a UM fan who had been heckling him. Ironically, it seemed Erickson had taken on the personality of his players. But in reality, Erickson had had enough of the fight. It was time to throw in the towel. He had compiled the best coaching record in UM history—a 63-9 mark—won two national titles, graduated three-fourths of his players, but by now the heat was too high. The NCAA hammer was ready to drop on their heads and the Seattle Seahawks, from his old stomping ground in the Pacific Northwest, were dangling a $5 million offer in front of him.

Less than one month after Erickson said his goal was to be like Joe Paterno and Bobby Bowden and be a guy who stayed in college "a long time," he bolted to the NFL.

"I just wasn't appreciated down there," Erickson said on January 12, 1995, the day he was announced as the Seahawks' new coach. "You can only take so much. I came there six years ago and never did anything to hurt anyone. You've got to be happy at the place, and I wasn't lately. I wasn't treated well." He went on to say the previous thirteen months in Miami had been "pure hell."

In truth, the administration was glad to see him go. Dee said that he was looking for a man of character, a man with a backbone who would take Miami in "a different direction." Preferably that man would also have head coaching experience, Dee announced. But as the search began, finding those qualities in a coach wasn't the difficult part. Finding a man who wanted to take the job was.

Former UM offensive coordinator Gary Stevens got the first interview with Dee. Stevens, who was bypassed for Erickson in a bid to replace Johnson six years earlier, was loved by UM players and the community. But word was that Stevens never really had a shot because he scared Foote and some of the UM brass, who believed he wasn't polished enough.

The next day Dee met with the man most figured was on top of UM's list—Colorado State's Sonny Lubick. A UM former defensive coordinator, Lubick had a grandfatherly way about him and was well respected for turning the Rams into a legit top-twenty-five team. Even many of Lubick's CSU players thought it was a no-brainer and wished him well, and joked that they wanted him to take them along. Erickson recommended Lubick for the job, although he didn't necessarily recommend that Lubick, his close friend, take it. Erickson warned Lubick that no matter what he did at UM, it still wouldn't be good enough to please the Miami people.

Meanwhile, Wisconsin's Barry Alvarez, South Carolina's Brad Scott, and Duke's Fred Goldsmith all piped up that they had been contacted and were not interested in the job. Two other coaches—Kansas's Glen Mason and Bill Snyder of Kansas State, a guy who speaks to the media about as often as Roman Polanski—both announced they had not been contacted and they were not interested. The day after interviewing

Lubick, Dee met with Jim Tressel, the head coach at Division 1-AA powerhouse Youngstown State. Tressel, who had won three national titles in the previous four seasons, wowed Dee in the interview. "You could tell this guy was gonna do some great things," said Dee, who was so moved he phoned Auburn coach Terry Bowden to discuss the challenges of making the move from 1-AA to 1-A. (Bowden had made a similar move from Samford to Auburn.)

The next day, Lubick took himself out of the running, opting to remain at a job that would pay him $200,000 less and afford him no real shot at a national title. Tressel removed his name from consideration too. Just like that, Dee was down to Stevens and another former Jimmy Johnson assistant, Butch Davis, the Dallas Cowboys' forty-three-year-old defensive coordinator. Dee met with Davis on the eighth day of his interview process. Immediately Dee realized he was *the* guy, the "sheriff" he was looking for to swoop in and clean up town. So what if the only head coaching experience Davis had came at Tulsa's Will Rogers High School, when as a twenty-six-year-old he went 3-6? Forty-eight hours after the interview, Davis's agent, Steve Endicott, and Dee were negotiating the contract. "Butch was very determined, very focused, and very organized," Dee said. "He was very strong and very straightforward and he was just what we needed."

9

THE RESURRECTION

Butch Davis was relaxing with some of his pals at a lakefront home in northern Arkansas enjoying the piece and quiet of life in the country when the phone rang. It was late June 1995, and Davis, after a whirlwind first six months on the job as Miami's new head coach, was back home for a short vacation. The man on the other end of the phone was Pete Garcia, UM's director of football operations. Davis's heart sank. He loved Garcia, but dreaded hearing his voice sometimes. Like now. He knew Garcia wouldn't have bothered him just to see how the fish were biting.

"Coach, we have a problem," said Garcia. Linebacker James Burgess, the 'Canes' second-leading tackler, got arrested for a fight outside a Miami dance club, Garcia told Davis. Burgess was charged with battery on a police officer and resisting arrest. The vacation ended right there.

The next day the coach made sure word got out. Davis was

suspending Burgess for UM's first two games of the season, which meant the hard-hitting linebacker wouldn't be available for the 'Canes' opener against UCLA. It didn't seem to matter that the details of Burgess's arrest were sketchy.

The police report had said that the linebacker shoved Officer Melissa Rietmann while she was trying to break up an altercation at Lime Key, a Kendall dance club. Burgess left the club and went across the street, where Rietmann found him, and he resisted arrest. The linebacker denied shoving the officer, saying he accidentally bumped into Rietmann and that she pushed him twice. Burgess had witnesses, he said, who would corroborate his story. (He was later acquitted on all charges.)

Davis, however, wasn't waiting for any judge to make a decision. He determined that Burgess was guilty of not taking care of UM's beleaguered reputation, and for that he had to be punished. Immediately.

Clearly, the days of Dennis Erickson were gone. "It's much different than last year," linebacker Ray Lewis told the *Herald*. "Everyone listens to Coach Davis. He's going to lead us down the right path." Lewis's words spoke volumes of the respect Davis had commanded, since the star linebacker was with Burgess when the incident happened and he could vouch for his buddy's story.

"I'm impressed by Coach Davis," Lewis said. "He gets down deep under your skin and into your heart. He came down on James in a respectable manner. Coach Davis had to take care of business. I respect him for that. James will suck it up. We have no power over the coach."

Davis said his decision had more to do with team policies than the actual arrest and that the suspension was in the best interests of the football program. "I thought it was a very important message to send to the football team and everybody else that there are some things that we just are not going to allow to compromise the integrity of the football program," Davis said. "We don't even want the perception here that you can do anything you want to do and there won't be any ramifications."

"That sent a message to the team," UM center K. C. Jones said. "That let people know that if you want to play here, you've got to keep clean on and off the field. Coach Davis isn't going to put up with any shit."

Leadership was in Davis's blood. Paul Hilton Davis Jr., the son of a football coach, was born in Tahlequah, Oklahoma, in 1951. (His mom, Pat, started calling him Butch so people wouldn't call him Junior or Little Paul.) One of his grandfathers was a sheriff and the other a Nazarene minister. His great-great-grandfather was Ezekiel Proctor, the legendary Cherokee warrior. When Butch was seven, his dad left coaching and moved to Springdale, Arkansas, to work with his brothers in the real-estate business. Davis grew up idolizing all-American types Mickey Mantle, Vince Lombardi, and Roger Staubach. His toughness and sense of responsibility were forged in a blue-collar poultry-farming town. By the time he was twelve, Davis was loading up the family tractor in the back of their pickup and driving all over the neighborhood to mow lawns. A few years later he got a crash course in overcoming adversity. His mother died of lung cancer when he was seventeen. Shortly after, he blew out his knee as a freshman defensive end at the University of Arkansas. He underwent five knee operations in eighteen months, but never was able to regain his agility again. He never played a down of varsity football. The Hogs' coach, Frank Broyles, let Davis help out as a volunteer assistant. Davis got to learn from Broyles's energetic staff;

one of his mentors was a bright young Arkansas coach named Joe Gibbs. Davis, who had pondered a law career, was hooked.

Like another one of his mentors, Jimmy Johnson, Davis was a big believer in the power of positive thinking. His instinct was as much about understanding as about winning. He would read every *New York Times* best seller he could get his hands on. One of his mottos was "Maintain a positive attitude at all costs; don't let negative things permeate." One of his closest friends was Zig Ziglar, the onetime door-to-door aluminum pan salesman turned world-renowned motivational speaker.

Davis was something of an enigmatic figure too. He had an imposing six-foot-four frame with a soft aw-shucks voice. He had lots of freckles across a ruddy-faced complexion. He once compared his mission statement for UM's regeneration process to that of Alcoholics Anonymous: "It's one day at a time. We can't change it in a week. It's going to be a series of ongoing events—how we practice, how we play, how we dress, how we behave. It's not going to happen just because I want it. Players are going to have to want it, too."

The first challenge waiting for Davis when he returned to Coral Gables in 1995 was trying to put together a recruiting class. Davis was fortunate in that Dee had named Art Kehoe, the 'Canes' buzzsaw of an offensive line coach, as the interim head coach. Kehoe was the one guy who had been at UM throughout the 'Canes' entire run of dominance. He also wasn't the kind of guy bashful about reminding recruits that Florida no longer wanted to play UM or that the archrival Seminoles were 2-8 against Miami in the last ten years. Still, Davis had just eight days to evaluate, woo, and sell prospects on the future of Miami football, something that, with the threat of NCAA sanctions looming, wasn't going to be easy.

Davis had a plan: They weren't going to go the junior-college route. They stressed character because he knew he couldn't risk wasting a scholarship on a problem player. All recruits would get cross-checked with three or four coaches. And then Davis, armed with his Dallas Cowboys Super Bowl rings, hit the road. "Those first six or seven days, I think the staff averaged three hours of sleep a night," said Pete Garcia, UM's recruiting coordinator. "It was a very hectic time."

Inside recruits' homes, Davis painted a picture of a new day dawning in south Florida. Miami would return to the mountaintop, he affirmed, but he promised the 'Canes would do it "the right way," with class. Davis realized rival coaches would engage in negative recruiting tactics, so he explained the circumstances to prospects and outlined both best- and worst-case scenarios and then left it to the kids to decide. His vision and charisma wowed high school kids and their families. He was able to convince five players who had committed to other schools to sign with UM. In all, the 'Canes landed seventeen recruits on signing day, eight of whom would go on to play in the NFL, including cornerback Duane Starks, a sleeper recruit who developed into a first-round pick.

"As a relief pitcher, [Davis] is as good as Bruce Sutter or Dennis Eckersley," cracked Garcia. "He can close."

Davis conducted spring ball at a similar pace. Tempo was key. His practices were run like military drills. Players hustled back to the huddle instead of strolling. He hammered his team about conditioning. "Even stretching is intense now," UM punter Mike Crissy said. "There used to be guys laughing and goofing around out there during stretching. Not anymore."

Davis instituted a dress code for road trips, requiring coats and ties, and he demanded that players treat flight attendants and waitresses as they would treat their mothers. Unlike Erickson, who made players who skipped class run extra laps, Davis would sit them out of games. Extra laps, he reasoned, weren't changing their behavior. They would run laps regardless.

The 'Canes' attitude adjustment would be more than just philosophically oriented. Davis believed in a more physical brand of football, and to instill that, Erickson's pass-happy, one-back offense had to go. Davis announced that he expected the 'Canes to produce a thousand-yard rusher every season. (In its history, UM had had just one thousand-yard back, Ottis Anderson, who ran for 1,266 yards in 1978.)

But before spring practice was over, the 'Canes would again have to deal with more disturbing news. Luther Campbell, in another bombshell story in the *Herald,* threatened to "tell all" about possible wrongdoing in the University of Miami football program if quarterback Ryan Collins wasn't named the team's starter.

"If he were white, being from Miami, he'd be God's gift to America," Campbell said. "If they don't start Ryan Collins, the University of Miami will get the death penalty. I will tell all. I will tell everything I know to the NCAA. If he doesn't go out there for the first play versus UCLA, I'll give you all the violations from 1986 to last year. As of now, I don't know anything. I'm stupid. But if Ryan doesn't start, [Coach] Butch [Davis] is going to wish he never took that job."

Davis balked at Campbell's suggestion that he would choose UM's starting quarterback based on the player's race. "Whether it's Luther Campbell or whether it's the guy that pumps my gas down at the Mobil station, they are people who have no impact on the program," Davis said. "They're not going to make the decisions as to who plays and what kind of team we're going to have."

Collins tried to laugh off Campbell's comments. "It's nice for someone to think highly of me," Collins said. "I'm glad he supports me."

As it turned out, Campbell's ultimatum was never tested. Through the spring, Collins clearly beat out his two younger competitors for the starting job, Scott Covington and Ryan Clement.

Just two months after Campbell's well-publicized threats, the 'Canes would have to battle through yet another heap of bad press. *Sports Illustrated*, jumping the gun on the NCAA, came out with a cover story, "Broken Beyond Repair," with its own take on what should happen to Hurricane football—the UM administration should kill it. "The revelations of the past few months make it clear that the University of Miami football program has become a disease, a cancer that is steadily devouring an institution that you have worked so hard to rid of its image as Suntan U," wrote *SI*'s Alexander Wolff. "It is time, President Foote, to fire the program."

SI also advised Foote to fire Paul Dee. To further its point in a seven-page story, the magazine cited numerous examples of misconduct dating to 1980, ranging from player arrests to drug use to improper cash payments to sexual assault.

"Well, obviously the story affected me personally, since its first suggestion was that I be fired," said Dee. "Institutionally, though, rather than take it as a suggestion, we took it as a challenge."

"When I read the article in *Sports Illustrated*, I was sad," Davis said, "because for every one negative incident that *SI* mentioned, I can give you ten examples of guys who are great people, the Steve Walshes, the Bernie Kosars, the Russell

Marylands, the Darrin Smiths. The list is endless of quality, good kids who have gone through that program, and the public perception of one article that spanned seventeen years of the program was momentarily tarnished for that one week."

Davis, with Dee's blessing, used the story as a mandate to revamp the Miami program to fit his clean-cut image. With UM having had advance warning about the story, Davis spent a good portion of May crisscrossing the country meeting face-to-face with all eighteen of UM's signees. He warned them about the upcoming *SI* article and assured them not to worry about the future of the program. He also got on the phone and called every returning player to brief them. "It's like I told the players, 'This thing reads like a history book, not like a crystal ball foretelling what's going to happen in the future,'" Davis said. "I want this to be the classiest program in Division One. There are some things that need to be addressed and I may need to weed out some guys. It's going to take some time, but we'll get there in the foreseeable future."

Davis's debut on the field was ugly. UCLA mauled the 'Canes 31–8, as Bruin tailback Karim Abdul-Jabbar ran all over the Miami defense for 180 yards. In the locker room after the game, some Miami players lamented the face-lift Davis had given the team. "Five years I've been around here, and I've never felt anything like this," UM offensive guard Alan Symonette said. "It's like we were afraid of that damn celebration rule, so we didn't get excited or emotional. You can't play this game without emotion." After UM lost at previously winless Virginia Tech, emotions spilled over in the 'Canes locker room, leading to a couple of bizarre scenes, including one in which Father Leo Armbrust, UM's team chaplain, yelled at one player: "You think I have a [bleeping] attitude?"

Armbrust then railed at 354-pound offensive tackle Freeman Brown at the postgame meal. "You don't like it, go pick up the [bleeping] sandwiches yourself!" the chaplain screamed at Brown. "Like you need another sandwich!"

Davis, however, wouldn't let up. He preached patience, that this makeover would take years, not weeks.

The 'Canes got off to a 1-3 start, their worst since 1976, but they battled their way to finish the season on a seven-game winning streak. Class attendance rose. So did the team's focus. Davis repeatedly made it known that no one on the team was above reproach. On the eve of Miami's game at Boston College, Tremain Mack, the 'Canes' star safety, was a few minutes late for the team bus to the airport. Davis's secretary called him at the airport to ask if he would hold the charter. "No," Davis answered. "He missed the bus. He stays home." The 'Canes went on to win 17–14. Then on December 1, word came in from the NCAA. The verdict: a three-year probation that included a one-year ban from postseason bowls and the loss of thirty-one football scholarships stemming from the Pell Grant scandal. The coaching staff winced when it heard the news. Aside from SMU getting the death penalty, there might not have been a harsher penalty handed down by the NCAA. Apparently, the organization wasn't thrilled with how quickly Auburn bounced back from its probation, so they took away the one thing a program must have to play football—players. The NCAA, though, didn't make a finding on Luther Campbell's involvement. "It was nothing," said Dee. "They said he wasn't a booster, and even though he had been very close to the team, the NCAA Committee on Infractions found that he wasn't acting as a representative of the university."

Nonetheless, it was now official: Miami was on probation, and nobody could say for sure just how long it would take to shake off the effects of the scholarship restrictions. Some said UM might never be able to get back. "Eighty-five wins and seven losses in eight years," Kehoe huffed, "and to see it all go down because of Pell Grants? Makes you want to throw up twenty-four hours a day. The greatest program in history? God, I wanted to run around hitting my eyes with pitchforks every day." On the bright side, Miami wasn't prohibited from playing on television, which was essential to keep recruiting hopes alive. Davis and the rest of the program took a deep breath. "It was the period and the exclamation point," Davis says. "Now we could go forward."

That winter UM had only thirteen scholarships to offer. Davis, playing up his rep from his days as a Dallas Cowboy, emphasized Texas. The approach worked. He not only landed Sulphur Springs' Damione Lewis, the nation's top defensive tackle recruit, he also nabbed Daniel "Bubba" Franks, a raw but promising six-foot-six, 235-pound tight end prospect. Both would later become first-round draft choices. Davis also signed hard-hitting middle linebacker Nate Webster, the top recruit in Miami. The class had a more-than-respectable 2.7 GPA and 920 SAT average. "I'm not taking any recruiting risks," Davis said. "We are not recruiting any high-maintenance people. A million guys can run forty yards in 4.5 seconds. You have to ask, What does he bring? Academic problems? Police problems? Training room problems? Or is he the kind who goes on automatic pilot and stays out of trouble and keeps on achieving? That's what we're after."

Even though UM couldn't spare a single washout, Davis kept one scholarship open. Three months later his gamble paid off. A Parade All-American running back, who had fallen off most recruiters' radar, finally passed his ACT test on his fourth try.

Anyone who ever saw Edgerrin James play knew he was special. He was quick, he could cut, he had soft hands, and the kid never allowed the first tackler or even first two tacklers to bring him down. Trouble was, James missed all but five games of his senior high school year in Immokalee, Florida, with an elbow injury. Still, the six-foot-one, 220-pounder rushed for 1,252 yards and ten touchdowns. James always had a soft spot for UM, but got spooked by the sanctions. Florida and Ohio State were high on his list, but both lost interest when it appeared James had no shot at qualifying. Miami, though, never gave up on James. It wasn't the first time Miami struck gold long after everyone else finished taking their bows after signing day. The 'Canes landed Ray Lewis and Russell Maryland late as well. (A few years later, in 2000, UM held three spots open. Those scholarships ended up going to tight end Jeremy Shockey, defensive end Jerome McDougle—both eventual first-round picks—and defensive tackle Santonio Thomas.)

Credit Pete Garcia for doing a lot of the grunt work. Garcia was insane about details. He kept files on ninth graders. He interviewed guidance counselors, church pastors, stadium attendants. "Anyone," he says, "who didn't really care that these guys were football players."

Born in Cuba, Garcia grew up in Miami and had become a huge Hurricanes fan in his days as a UM student in the early eighties. He was working for Eastern Airlines on the ramp helping to load planes when one day in 1989, while listening to his car radio, he heard Tom Heckert, the Dolphins' new director of college scouting, talking about the draft. Garcia drove straight to the Dolphins offices, knocked on Heckert's door, and asked for a job. Heckert was so impressed by Garcia's determination, he kept him around. Garcia eventually worked his way back to UM and became one of Davis's right-hand men. During Davis's first week on the job, Garcia came into the coach's office with an NCAA rule book dripping with more than two dozen yellow Post-its sticking out of it, raving, "Here's some things that we can do." Garcia's keen understanding of the rules would later enable UM to find creative ways to stretch their scholarship limit. (He got speedy receiver Santana Moss on a track scholarship and feisty offensive lineman Joaquin Gonzalez on an academic scholarship. He also plucked wideout Andre King out of minor-league baseball and got the Atlanta Braves to pay his tuition. All three would become NFL players.)

But just as things were perking up around UM, tragedy struck. On the morning of April 13, 1996, 'Canes defensive back Earl Little opened the door to apartment 36C, the on-campus place he shared with tailback Trent Jones and linebackers Marlin Barnes and Ray Lewis. Little looked down and spotted Barnes, his best friend since the second grade, lying on the floor in a pool of blood that was so large and so deep red, he thought it was fruit punch. Little thought his buddy was playing a joke, but Barnes could barely move. The linebacker turned his head and Little couldn't believe his eyes. Barnes' face was gone. All the skin and bones were shredded. Barnes's girlfriend, Timwanika Lumpkins, also bludgeoned, was found in one of the bedrooms.

No one could be sure how long the bodies had been there, only that at three thirty a.m., a tow truck had driven Barnes and Lumpkins home from a club after the linebacker had discovered that the tires on the car he had borrowed from Little had been slashed.

Labrant Dennis, Lumpkins's ex-boyfriend, was arrested a

few weeks later and sentenced to death for the double murder. Police had determined that Barnes had taken twenty-two blows to the face with the butt of a shotgun. "Although this is just one step in bringing this to closure, I am hopeful that this may be the beginning of a process which will result in a sense of peace and comfort to the families and friends of Marlin Barnes and Timwanika Lumpkins," Davis said after Dennis's arrest.

Dee called it the hardest thing that UM has ever had to deal with. Barnes may have been the most popular player on the team. He was a muscular six-foot, 210-pound junior who had just been voted the team's most improved player in spring football. Davis liked that other players looked up to Barnes because of the guy's resiliency. Barnes was a battler. When he was two, his father, Mackey, was shot and killed. He was a solid student, who along with a bunch of his high school buddies—Little, Nate Brooks (a cornerback at UM), Lawrence Wright (a Florida DB), and Florida State running back Rock Preston—founded the Right Track, a privately funded program for at-risk kids in Miami.

UM brought crisis counselors in to speak with the players. They also spoke to Davis and the UM coaches. They warned Davis there would be trouble—fear and frustration and sorrow that would manifest itself in rage and anger. Still, Davis didn't expect what happened that summer. Five UM players—three starters—were suspended in one June week, all of them close to Barnes. "That clearly gripped our football team," Davis told *ESPN the Magazine.* "It shocked our players, scared them. It affected the team for more than a year. We had team meetings for the grief, but guys erupted anyway."

Davis said he was also hamstrung by not having recruited

many of these kids. Because of that, he had never been in their homes, met their parents, or talked to their Little League coaches or guidance counselors. So it made it that much tougher to figure out who came from the dysfunctional homes and who were the potential high-maintenance guys who needed to be eyeballed extra closely.

Davis was on vacation back in Arkansas later that summer when he got another call from Garcia. Jammi German, UM's leading receiver, had been involved in an altercation. He was already in jail, and other players might have been involved, Garcia said. Davis, again, cut short his vacation and hopped on the next flight to Miami. He conducted his own investigation, interviewing witnesses and police officers to learn that German and a half dozen others, including UM linebackers Jeffrey Taylor and James Burgess, went to the campus apartment of Maxwell Voce, a former captain of the UM track team. German was enraged because he heard Voce had been spreading word on campus that he was gay. The police report said German entered his apartment "without permission" and assaulted him. German was arrested on charges of burglary and simple battery. Davis didn't need to hear German's side. Davis's sources (Taylor and Burgess) had informed him that German provoked the confrontation and threw the first punch. Davis suspended the star wideout for the '96 season, because regardless of the outcome of the criminal charges (he later pleaded no contest and got two years' probation), German had violated a team rule by instigating a fight. Davis also suspended Burgess and Taylor two games for not intervening.

In the classroom, though, Davis's stern approach was paying off. The team's grade-point average had jumped almost a full point in a year, from 1.9 to 2.8. Its class attendance had improved 30 percent. UM also had graduated 83 percent of its players, marking the sixth straight year the graduation rate was among the handful in major college football to top 70 percent.

The 'Canes began the '96 season still woozy from the Barnes tragedy. Davis had suspended ten players from the opener for misdeeds that ranged from assault and battery to being treated to a limo ride by an agent. UM routed four cream puffs to open the season 4-0, but was jerked back to reality by blowout losses at home to FSU (34–16) and underdog East Carolina (31–6). "Our intensity wasn't there; we weren't hyped," Burgess said after the East Carolina game. "It used to be, regardless of who we played, we'd be fired up. Not everyone was tonight."

Said Twan Russell, another UM linebacker, "I could look into the eyes of some guys before the game and tell they weren't ready to play."

Many former 'Canes players attributed that to Davis's crackdown on UM's notorious swagger. They said whether it was intentional or not, in his drive to cleanse the program and its image, Davis also stomped out that spirit that made the 'Canes special. To be or not to be 'Canes; it is the issue that is the great paradox around Miami. In some ways the place is like Germany, proud of its strong heritage, yet embarrassed and afraid of it all at the same time. When things are going good, there is always suspicion that something evil is lurking, and when things are down, it is because the place has gone soft.

To many of the former 'Canes, Davis had already been out of line when he limited their access to the program. Instead of sideline passes, they were now put into a section in the upper deck of the Orange Bowl. "It was a slap in the face," said Tolbert Bain, a former cornerback in the mid-eighties. "Butch closed practice to the former players too. The worst part of it was Butch was on that staff with Jimmy and he knew we didn't have bad guys."

"We were pissed," said Melvin Bratton. "We knew how we felt when we were players there and saw Jim Kelly on the sidelines when they made it back if their teams had an off week or a Monday night game. You'd see them and you'd be like, 'Man, I got to play.'

"I was in the stands for the Florida State game and I had to fight recruits for seats. They had me in the fucking nosebleeds. I'm watching [UM tailback] Danyell Ferguson opening his foot toward the hole he's going to. And he's doing it on every play. I saw it, and I'm quite sure Florida State saw it too, because they would slant and go that way. I guess they must've saw something on tape, and I'm up in the stands, thinking, 'Holy shit!' I jump over the railing and try to go into the locker room at halftime to grab him, but the security guard stops me. I said, 'What? I need to go tell this kid something.' And the guard just says, 'Butch does not want any of the former players in the locker room.' It hurt me."

"I couldn't understand that," Lamar Thomas said. "It was an awful time for Miami, some real dark years for Miami. I remember going down there to work out and he made me sign some stupid waiver. I have no idea what it said. I was like, 'Come on, Butch, give me a break. Why don't you win some games before you start telling people what to do, buddy.'"

In truth, those restrictions were part of an edict passed down from Dee and the UM administration. "A lot of that was part of the fallout of things that had happened before with people on the sidelines that the *Miami Herald* wrote about and the program got a lot of flak for," said Garcia. "When Butch came in, it was pointed out that those kinds of things can't continue."

Regardless, the 'Canes' reputation as thugs in many people's eyes still lingered. Even when they weren't being bad, most people still didn't give them the benefit of the doubt. In the Temple game late in the '96 season, Earl Little returned a blocked field goal seventy-four yards for a touchdown. When he finally reached the end zone, he dropped to one knee in prayer and pointed a finger toward heaven out of respect to Barnes, his best friend, and his recently deceased grandfather. Excessive celebration, the referees ruled. Fifteen yards! "It's just the University of Miami," Little observed. "They just throw that yellow rag."

Quietly though, there were some genuine visions of the old Miami sparking up. After that Temple game, UM receiver Magic Benton was ribbing tailback Dyral McMillan in the locker room. Benton was telling anyone who would listen that McMillan's playing days were over at Miami. His job now belonged to Edgerrin James, the true freshman, who jumped into action after McMillan left the game with a sprained ankle. All James did was run for a game-high 105 yards and take a swing pass sixty-nine yards, busting seven tackles along the way. Benton, of course, was right. James became a superstar, the centerpiece of Miami's rebuilding plan, and McMillan transferred to South Florida.

James's toughness, competitive fire, and charisma charged up the program. He commanded respect. That presence was especially apparent in "the Hole," the ersatz no-holds-barred wrestling pit formed by three couches in the shape of a U inside the team's locker room. The Hole was a proving ground of sorts. Defensive backs would challenge wide receivers. Fullbacks would challenge linebackers, and Edgerrin James would challenge everyone. "E.J. was so powerful and so quick, he'd take on linemen and still nobody could beat him," said former UM wide receiver Daryl Jones.

UM finished the season going 9-3, beating Virginia in the Carquest Bowl, 31–21. But the coaches knew the team was going to get worse before it got any better. The numbers game was going to catch up with them. Miami lost twenty seniors plus three underclassmen to the NFL. They simply didn't have enough players. Thanks to some ingenious bookkeeping, Miami—despite having only fifteen scholarships available, signed nineteen players—six of whom decided to either delay enrolling until December or walk on and receive scholarships during the spring semester. Even more impressively, UM's haul came in the face of some intense negative recruiting. One FSU assistant coach had even been showing recruits a newspaper account of Marlin Barnes's murder, suggesting to parents their kids might not be safe in south Florida. Signing day, though, occurred within a week of Davis's inking a seven-year extension that would keep him at UM through 2003—and temper suspicion that he was flirting with an NFL head-coaching job.

The numbers crunch caught up to Miami in '97, when Davis had twenty-nine freshmen on his forty-four-man depth chart. After beginning the season with a win at hapless Baylor, UM came home and got outmuscled by Arizona State. Sun Devil players—and a few of their coaches—even paraded around the west end zone of the Orange Bowl and taunted the Miami fans. UM then lost at Pittsburgh and then again against West Virginia, making it an unthinkable stretch: The 'Canes, a team that just two years ago set an NCAA record for consecutive home victories, had dropped five of their last six games at the Orange Bowl. Banners flew over the Orange Bowl that read, *From national champs to national chumps. Thanks, Butch.* Players were embarrassed to wear UM shirts in public, where a community spoiled by success labeled them losers. "You would walk down the streets of Miami, and you would rather wear a Florida State shirt than a Miami shirt, because everybody is asking you what is going on," said offensive tackle Joaquin Gonzalez.

Ryan Clement, UM's senior quarterback, lashed out at the former players. "To point fingers at Coach Davis is ridiculous. If you're going to point fingers, point them at the NCAA or at the '87 national champs and the '91 national champs," Clement said. "Those teams put us in this state right now. Those guys, especially the ones with the Pell Grant thing, broke rules. And later, with no thought of what might happen, they told the NCAA everything, knowing there would be probation coming down. They lived fat for a long time down here, won lots of national titles, but they didn't do it the right way and now we, who had nothing to do with it, are paying for it."

The next weekend, the 'Canes bottomed out at FSU, losing 47–0—UM's worst loss in fifty-three years. The effects of the probation, of having just fifty-three scholarship players in the program, were never more evident than that day. "I think they had sixteen starters from our area," Kehoe remarked. UM's patchwork team couldn't even run normal practices. "Our numbers were so far down that [Miami defensive line coach] Greg Mark and I wouldn't go one-on-one anymore," Kehoe said. "Greg would coach his guys and I'd look for Butch, and then vice versa. I didn't want Butch coming over to see us do nothing. But we simply couldn't hit each other."

That brittleness was obvious. Eleven players rushed for a hundred or more yards against UM, including three Syracuse players in a 33–13 loss to the Orangemen at the Orange Bowl, ending the nightmarish '97 season. UM's record: 5-6, its first losing season since 1977. "This is the season we had to pay for," Davis said after the Syracuse game. "This is the season we had to suffer." As Davis exited the locker room that day, he spoke of being in a transition mood. "I'm eager for Monday to come, so I can start convincing kids this is where they want to be. Because this is where the national championship is going to be won before they leave."

Not too many people gave Davis's words any credence, especially after the 66–13 beating Syracuse put on UM late in the following season. But then the Hurricanes caught a break. Actually the Hurricanes caught a break from a hurricane. Their matchup with UCLA was supposed to take place on September 26, but due to Hurricane Georges the game was delayed till December 5. The additional time gave the young talented 'Canes more time to mature. Of course, with the unbeaten Bruins coming to town with a national title game ticket hanging in the balance, few gave UM a shot. Miami was a ten-point underdog. Some 'Canes, paying homage to the old days, wore fatigues to the game. Feeding off that spirit, linebacker Dan Morgan played every defensive down and on special teams despite a badly broken thumb. Leonard Myers, cornerback, played through with a strained knee while fullback Nick Williams played with a strained groin and broken finger. No one, though, epitomized UM's resilient attitude better than Edgerrin James, who continued to pound away at the Bruins. By the time he was done, James carried the ball thirty-nine times for a school-record 299 yards and led the 'Canes back from a seventeen-point second-half deficit to a 49–45 upset. Davis used the momentum to put together an unmatched recruiting class. In it he got a quarterback (Ken Dorsey) who would become the winningest QB in school history; a tailback (Clinton Portis) who would become the NFL Rookie of the Year; a wideout (Andre Johnson) who would get taken with the third-overall pick in the NFL draft; an offensive tackle (Bryant McKinnie) who never allowed a sack during college; and a cornerback (Philip Buchanon) who would become a first-round pick—and those were just the sleepers. Miami's two headline recruits, mammoth offensive lineman Vernon Carey and tailback Jarrett Payton, the son of Hall of Famer Walter Payton, also grew into stardom. Added to the nucleus of Santana Moss, Reggie Wayne, Gonzalez, Dan Morgan, Damione Lewis, and Ed Reed, all guys who blossomed underneath the wreckage, UM was clearly poised to jump back into the college football landscape.

The '99 recruiting class should go down as one of the smartest jobs of scouting any staff has ever done in college football. Dorsey, a beanpole from northern California, was overlooked by most schools out west; however, Davis was intrigued with him based on one key stat. Not his size, speed, or the velocity of a fastball; it was because in Dorsey's senior year at Miramonte High, he didn't get sacked once. "That either means he has a great offensive line or is something really special," Davis said. UM also scored with Portis, a Gainesville native who the hometown Gators believed was too small to play tailback, and the six-foot-ten, 330-pound McKinnie, a guy who was in the high school band and unearthed by Kehoe at Pennsylvania's Lackawanna Junior College.

It also didn't hurt the 'Canes' talent level that after three or four years, Davis had loosened the grip a little on his screening process. "That meant we might be able to take one or two kids that might be a little rough around the edges because we knew the other eighty kids in the locker room were gonna try and keep them in line," said Garcia. "We had some great kids and they policed their own locker room."

With a deeper, more talented roster, UM went 9-4 and reached its goal of winning a New Year's Day bowl, beating Georgia Tech in the Gator Bowl. In 2000, the year Davis's undermanned probation class became seniors, the 'Canes reemerged as a national powerhouse. UM, thanks to a dramatic two-minute drive by Dorsey, beat the top-ranked 'Noles 27–24. Less than a month later, the 'Canes blew out second-ranked Virginia Tech 41–21. UM had done something it had never done before: they had beaten a number one and a number two team in the same season. The only thing keeping Miami from the national title game was an early season loss at Washington and some quirky BCS mathematics. (FSU, despite losing to UM, got the chance to play top-ranked Oklahoma in the Orange Bowl.) The 'Canes still figured they had an outside shot at the title if they could beat number seven Florida and FSU beat Oklahoma.

The Sugar Bowl served as UM's reintroduction to America. The funny thing was, now they were the darlings of the sport (at least for the moment). The media fawned all over Davis's cleanup job. None of his marquee men had arrived in Coral Gables with any fanfare. They were underdogs again. Morgan—the only player ever to win the Butkus, Nagurski, and Bednarik awards in the same season—was perceived by many colleges as "the typical slow, white running back." Safety Ed Reed's next best offer was from Tulane, while UM only had to beat out the football powers of the Ivy Leagues to get right tackle Joaquin Gonzalez. "What Butch was able to do that Jimmy and Dennis couldn't or didn't care to was discern character," *Miami Herald* columnist Dan Le Batard said. "Butch could see that Edgerrin James, even though he comes from an awful area, even though his family has a history of legal problems, even though he looks like something that you don't associate with higher education, he's a good kid. He's got good character. Edgerrin James isn't going to do stuff that is going to embarrass you or your program. He's just grateful for the opportunity to be there."

Reed, though, said it wasn't so much the types of people UM brought in as much as the way Miami's staff nurtured them. "If they weren't as strict with regulations on uniforms and celebrations, we'd probably be doing the same thing," Reed said. "We wouldn't be running with agents and all that, but we'd probably be taking our helmets off, celebrating.

"It was a different game then. Back then, it was football. Now, it's more of a business. But I think it's a lot better now. You can't do all that, but we try to sneak our little things in, maybe on a wristband or something. We all make sure we don't get any penalties."

The reality of the situation was that the culture of football had changed too. The level of theatrics and performance on the field shifted toward what the 'Canes had been doing years before. Kids who grew up watching and imitating were now playing, and the NFL may not have embraced the likes of Deion Sanders and Michael Irvin, but they really couldn't muzzle them anymore either. The game evolved into a highlight game, and with the boom of the ESPN generation, sack dances and end zone celebrations were just that—celebrated. Football was an extension of the video games many of the players were addicted to. Tennis star Andre Agassi defined the new generation with three simple words: "Image is everything." Away from the field, mainstream society was suddenly embracing the antihero. The Rock, a hulking pro wrestler, built an on-stage persona around cutting put-downs and sizzling bravado, and became a pop culture icon and would soon market himself into a Hollywood sensation. Not so coincidentally, the Rock, aka Dwayne Johnson, honed his act while toiling as a reserve defensive lineman behind all-American Warren Sapp. The "Miami vice" actually provided Johnson with a blueprint for his larger-than-life character. "Funny thing is, Dewey was actually pretty quiet back then," said former UM defensive end Kevin Patrick. "He loved country music and he'd sit on the bus to games singing. He had a great voice." That voice grew in some sense into a generation's voice, and his rise coincided with UM's rebirth. Surely the 'Canes had toned down their act, but as Miami rose back up it became apparent that success wouldn't make it any easier to keep the cap on their emotions.

Six nights before the Sugar Bowl a brawl broke out when groups of Florida and Miami players battled in the middle of Bourbon Street. Gators defensive end Alex Brown was punched in the eye during the melee, which ended with two Florida players being handcuffed and briefly detained by police. Gators players insisted that the fracas had been instigated by a group of Hurricanes players, led by senior safety Al Blades, who were mocking them for their 30–7 loss to Florida State on November 18. "They set the tone for the game right there on Bourbon Street," said Florida wide receiver Jabar Gaffney. "Al Blades was telling us the Gators aren't anything anymore and they're going to mop the floor with us. That's what made this a rivalry again, right there."

The incident underscored what a narrow line Davis had had to tightrope in rebuilding UM. Miami, at its best, reveled in its bad-boy persona. "That's Miami, always will be," senior defensive tackle Damione Lewis said proudly.

In the 'Canes' final four games of the regular season—games UM won by a combined 154–34—UM started to resemble, for better and worse, the great Miami teams coached by Jimmy Johnson and Dennis Erickson. Tackles led to gyrations, touchdowns to dances. Reed and Moss yanked off their helmets after scoring touchdowns, drawing penalties. Most of it was harmless, and Davis didn't rein down on any of his players. "I don't want to say I turned guys loose to behave any way they wanted to," he explained, "but we've got a bunch of kids who have started forty games in their careers. You let those guys go a little bit."

Miami's once-ragged crew of freshmen closed out their UM careers beating UF 37–20. Dorsey, who threw three touchdown passes, was named game MVP. Miami was indeed all the way back. UM's national title claims, however, would ring hollow after Oklahoma beat FSU, 13–2. Meanwhile, Davis continued to downplay the increasing speculation that he was interested in a possible head-coaching job in the NFL. When asked what there was left to prove after this year, Davis simply said, "I'd like to keep doing it over and over again."

His agent, Marvin Demoff, continued to work with Dee on a contract extension while his staff worked on putting together a recruiting class. Then Davis recruited two of his juniors—McKinnie and Reed—who were toying with the idea of jumping to the NFL themselves. Reed was an easy sell, but McKinnie was teetering. A few days before the January 12 deadline for underclassmen to declare their intentions, McKinnie announced he was staying at UM. A few days after the deadline passed, Davis sidled up to McKinnie, a lock first-rounder, to thank him for coming back. Davis told McKinnie—Dorsey's insurance policy—that he was "the final piece to the puzzle," a reference no doubt to a national championship in 2001. But then on January 29, less than twenty-four hours after UM hosted ten recruits and Davis pledged that he would be at Miami, one of those pieces would disappear. The news broke on an early Monday morning and shock waves ran through the Miami football office: Butch Davis was taking the Cleveland Browns job. Players still thought someone was pulling a fast one on them. But by late morning, they realized that this was no joke. Garcia told every UM player there would be a team meeting in the locker room at eleven thirty a.m. and to show up even if they had a class scheduled at that time. Davis dropped his bombshell and broke down crying before exiting the room. Many players, recalling Davis's "If I leave now, that makes me a deadbeat dad, because this is my family" speech on the eve of the Sugar Bowl, were close to tears too, feeling jilted and betrayed. "He should have done it a different way," Gonzalez said. "He shouldn't have gotten our hopes up and had meetings telling us not to worry about it.

"Instead of leading us on and telling us, 'I really want to be here. Don't worry about me. I'm going to retire here. I don't want an NFL job. I'm a family man. I want to spend time with my kid.' That's what he sold us on. It's a shock. It baffles me."

UM, again, was looking for another head coach. Only this time, Dee had even less time to make a hire.

10

THE GOODFATHER

"What now?"

It was both the most innocent and the most frightening thought any of them could conjure up as they sat there stewing that Monday morning in late January. Butch Davis had been gone from their lives for sixty seconds and that was what each of them, all hundred or so UM players, kept asking themselves.

"What now?"

For Paul Dee, the frumpy old UM athletic director, tipped back in his chair, gazing at the ceiling of his office, that same god-awful question had an entirely different context. Dee, of course, had just slogged through, along with Davis, a miraculous rebuilding project that had battled hit after hit and still took his football team right to the brink of a national title, but . . .

After Davis told the players he was leaving, many of them

held their own meeting. "We were pissed off," said Ed Reed, UM's all-American safety. "We were *pii-iiissssed* off. 'There it goes,' we said. 'Our national championship. Gone.' " The feeling was that they were close to a national title, and nobody wanted to start over, not with a new coach, not with a new system or one that would require their learning somebody else's terminology. "They should make Coker the head coach," Ken Dorsey told the room. "Yeah, they need to make Coker the guy," echoed Clinton Portis, UM's flashy star tailback. Coker was Larry Coker, the 'Canes' soft-spoken, jug-eared offensive coordinator. The same guy many UM fans wanted fired after the 'Canes' early season 34–29 loss to Washington in 2000. (They were chaffed because Miami scored only three first-half points.)

Everyone on the team liked Coach Coker. He was easygoing and understanding and had a dry, often self-effacing sense of humor. But Dorsey, who had worked closely with Coker for three years, also knew that he had great attention to detail and that he related to people well. And it didn't hurt that if Coker was named head coach, he wouldn't clean house and force players to get acquainted with new position coaches or new schemes. The players decided a group of team leaders should march up to Dee's office and state their case. "We're gonna tell him, we won't play at UM unless they hire Coker," Brett Romberg, Miami's free-spirited center, announced.

As Dee sat in his office, mulling over possible candidates, bouncing between Miami Dolphins head coach Dave Wannstedt, a former UM assistant, and Wisconsin's Barry Alvarez, a close friend of Miami's incoming president, Donna Shalala, he spotted the cluster of players approaching. There was Romberg, the quick-witted three-hundred-pound Canadian with the devilish eyebrows and messy goatee; Reed, the gritty Bayou kid with the unruly dreads; Dorsey, the spindly Heisman hopeful with the Harry Potter haircut; Bryant McKinnie, the towering left tackle; and a few other seniors. Dee waved them in.

Reed said they represented the rest of the players. "The team wants Coach Coker to be Miami's next head coach," Reed said. Dee leaned back in his chair, thought about it for a moment, and then asked, "Why?"

"I wanted to know from them if this was a case about them not wanting to have to prove themselves to a new coach," Dee explained later, "and not wanting change because they're comfortable. Or is this about not wanting change because we don't need it? I asked them, 'Are you telling me it's because this is the right person?' Because it's two different issues."

The players said it was, indeed, because Larry Coker was the right man to lead them. Dorsey explained what a great teacher Coker was. Reed talked about how the players would respond to Coker. But they knew Dee wasn't convinced of that. They were well aware Dee probably wanted someone with a bigger name and head-coaching experience. And even when Reed brought up how well Davis had done even though he didn't have that prior experience, it was apparent Dee was leaning toward another direction. After all, they were touting a career assistant who had been passed over for the head-coaching job at Tulsa and who couldn't even get an interview for Baylor's vacancy.

"We didn't want Barry Alvarez coming in trying to change us," Reed said. "Guys weren't gonna play for him, at all. Nobody would've played for him I don't think."

Reed asked if Dee would address a team meeting Wednesday morning in the locker room to try to explain the search process to the players. Dee agreed. Then at midweek he offered Wannstedt a ten-year, $20 million deal to come south to Coral Gables. But Wannstedt declined. Dee then offered the job to Alvarez—the contract was for $1.4 million for five years—but again the Miami AD got rebuked.

Rival recruiters were licking their chops, hoping to poach some UM recruits. "Miami's in a tight spot," said one ACC coach. "Just when it looked like they were gonna finish with a huge kick, Davis leaves and now we're all trying to pull everything apart. Kids get frustrated pretty fast. We know the longer they wait to name a coach, the better it is for us to get a player who's sick of hanging on."

It was Friday, just five days before national signing day, and UM still didn't have a replacement for Davis. Dee thought about the looks on Reed's and Dorsey's faces when they were in his office lobbying for Coker. He also worried about the feeling he got when he had met with the entire team that Wednesday in the 'Canes' locker room, wondering if they would take coaching and embrace some outsider if he didn't "keep it inside the family," as they kept pleading. Coker, meanwhile, was recruiting in Arkansas. He was at a fast-food restaurant when Dee called to ask if he wanted to travel to Washington, D.C., Saturday morning to interview with Shalala, the former secretary of health and human services to President Clinton.

In the interview Coker came across as sincere and charming, a real people person—both folksy and focused. But what ultimately sold Shalala and Dee was when Coker showed them his plan to run a powerhouse program—his philosophy and the kind of staff he'd use to orchestrate a top team. Dee then asked Coker if he could save Miami's recruiting class in the eleventh hour. Coker looked him in the eye and said, "Yes, I can do that. I think we can save ninety percent of it."

"The new coach had to understand this was going to be an extention of what Butch had done," said Dee. "And having been a coordinator here for five years, Larry understood the importance of that."

The official announcement was made on a Saturday afternoon, less than twenty-four hours after Coker had been summoned to D.C. Dee knew the local media was ready to pounce, saying UM could've done much better. After the press conference introducing Coker as the 'Canes' new head coach, Dee approached Reed and Dorsey in the hallway. He patted Reed on the shoulder and said through a smirk, "Well, I've done my part."

Reed, without missing a beat, winked and replied, "Now we'll take care of the rest."

Coker's first big test was patching back together UM's recruiting class. Brooklyn's Leon Williams, the nation's top prospect at linebacker who committed to Miami over Penn State just a few days before Davis bolted, was getting pressure from Nittany Lion icon Joe Paterno, while cornerback Antrel Rolle, the most coveted recruit in the Miami area, was targeted by Ohio State and Notre Dame. Thomas Carroll, the best player in New Jersey, said he started hearing from Kansas State and Alabama—two schools that had never even tried to recruit him before. Wide receiver Cro Thorpe, a speedster from Tallahassee, was so distraught with the hounding he was getting from fellow students, teachers, and even guidance counselors that he left school at eleven a.m. just so he could go home and escape the madness. Only there he would have to listen to the answering-machine-recorded calls from his mom's family—

Seminole fans—about the Davis departure. "I kept hearing, 'We can't wait till you get to FSU,'" he said. Chris Murray, a rangy six-foot-four receiver from Tampa, bailed from his commitment to Miami and announced he was headed to North Carolina State. Coker, however, did even better than he told Dee he would. He not only saved Davis's recruiting class; he made it stronger. UM ended up losing Murray to NC State (Murray wanted a promise that he would start right away and Coker wouldn't commit) and Thorpe to Florida State, but instead got three recruits that they never figured they'd nab, linebacker Rocky McIntosh away from Clemson, tight end Kevin Everett from Texas, and Frank Gore, the top tailback in the South, who appeared headed to Ole Miss. "We had some very positive surprises at the thirteenth hour," Coker said. He also opted to sign local hero Roscoe Parrish, a diminutive blazer who Davis had felt was too small for UM.

Recruiting analysts hailed it as a top-ten class. One week later, it got even better when Kellen Winslow II, a tight end from San Diego, announced he was headed to Miami too. "Saving that class was like the eighth wonder of the world," Coker said. "When Butch left, everybody was down in the dumps. But I told my assistants, 'I'm going to get this job. I'm going to be the next head coach at the University of Miami, and we need to recruit that way.'"

Coker's upbeat energy isn't quite what you'd expect from the slender, bald man with those deep-set basset hound eyes. At first glance he seems like the most unlikely man to be leading college football's most dynamic program. He grew up in tiny Okemah, Oklahoma (population 2,500), in the land of John Steinbeck books and Woody Guthrie ballads. Coker's father, Edgar, scrapped for seventy-five cents a day as a pumper on an oil rig. His mom, Vera, worked at a sewing machine plant and a five-and-dime to help make ends meet. Every Sunday the family attended the Last Chance Baptist Church.

Coker was just a kid when Bud Wilkinson's Oklahoma Sooner squads were trampling opponents, winning forty-seven consecutive games from 1953 through 1957. "Bud Wilkinson was my idol," Coker said. "Coach Wilkinson gave the people in our state something to identify with. They were so down, and to see a Bud Wilkinson team go and defeat a Notre Dame or a Southern Cal gave people a lift."

When Coker's fourth-grade teacher had her students write down their dream job, Coker wrote "football coach." Good thing because even though he was a two-way star at Okemah High—playing as a 140-pound quarterback/defensive back—his playing career wasn't going to take him too far. The Sooners weren't interested, so he decided to walk on at Northwestern (Oklahoma) State, an NAIA school. His coaching career started at twenty-two, when he took a job on an Osage Indian Reservation in Fairfax, Oklahoma, where he was the freshman football coach, the sixth-grade boys basketball coach, the junior high girls' basketball coach, and head track coach—he also taught five science classes, all for $7,000. Coker spent six years in Fairfax winning two state titles before taking over as the head coach of the Claremore High Zebras in a suburb of Tulsa. Coker pumped life into a downtrodden program before leaving after two seasons to take a pay cut so he could become the running backs coach for John Cooper at the University of Tulsa. One year later Coker was the team's offensive coordinator. He eventually became the offensive coordinator at OU, then Oklahoma State, Ohio State (where he also coached the defensive backs for a couple of seasons), and Miami, building a reputation for nurturing talents such as Barry Sanders, Thurman Thomas, Eddie George, and Edgerrin James. The key thing about him was that although he was as unassuming as a picture in a hotel room, Coker related well to star talent. He had a Will Rogers–like charm. "He's a really tremendous human being," said Dee. "Nice family. Low-key. There are people who, it's about them. Not him. It's not about him."

It never was. That was because rule number one in Coker's world was never to take himself too seriously. "The thing about Larry," said Rob Chudzinski, whom Coker hired as his offensive coordintor, "when you watch him on a day-to-day basis, is that he just enjoys what he is doing. You see head coaches who are stressed out. Whenever you see him, he's enjoying it."

After quieting some skeptics with his first recruiting class, Coker made a few more converts by hiring Chudzinski and Randy Shannon to be his offensive and defensive coordinators. Both were rising stars on the coaching scene and both were former 'Cane standouts in the late eighties. Chudzinski would continue to rely on a balanced pro-set system, but with added emphasis on the tight end, his old position. Shannon, who had been working as the Miami Dolphins linebacker coach, planned on keeping things simple. The 'Canes were so dominant up front they didn't need to gimmick anyone, he believed. It was the same philosophy employed during Jimmy Johnson's days with Jerome Brown or Cortez Kennedy or Russell Maryland anchoring the middle. Shannon just wanted his playmakers to make plays and run to the football. The influx of new blood suddenly had the locals thinking Dee might've found the right guy after all.

Still, not everyone was sold as Miami headed to State College, Pennsylvania, to kick off the season against Penn State in a nationally televised night game before 109,313. Emotions in Happy Valley were sky-high that night. Former Nittany Lion safety Adam Taliaferro, who had made a miraculous recovery after being paralyzed nine months earlier while making a tackle, was planning on leading Penn State out of the tunnel. Miami was a fourteen-point favorite, but many of the experts were predicting an upset. Most first-time coaches, they said, should open up with West New Mexico State or South Dakota A&M, not the Penn State Nittany Lions on national TV. They said ol' Joe Pa was hiding in the weeds. The home team would have emotion all on their side because of Taliaferro, and because the school also was honoring State's 1986 national championship team (the one that upset UM in the Fiesta Bowl), and because Paterno was bidding to tie Bear Bryant as the all-time winningest coach in major college football, and because it was a night game. Of course, the pundits were right—for about two minutes. That was about how long Penn State seemed to have an emotional edge. Then Miami, behind McKinnie—the towering left tackle—ran right over the hapless Penn State defense. UM scored on its first five possessions and built a 30–0 halftime lead, outgaining the Nittany Lions 372 yards to 67. UM won 33–7, but the 'Canes probably could've scored twice that many points. Dorsey carved up an overmatched Penn State secondary, completing twenty of twenty-seven passes for a career-high 344 yards and three touchdowns, while Portis—who a few days before the game had said UM might score seventy points on Penn State—danced his way to 164 rushing yards in a little more than two quarters of action. Miami did all that despite getting flagged fourteen times, one of them for a personal foul when Portis chucked the ball into the stands after what he thought was a touchdown run. After that play, which had been nullified by a holding penalty, Coker did not let Portis have the ball again. "I wanted to make a point with Clinton," Coker explained. The message apparently was received. The following week reporters failed to goad Portis into saying anything. "I can't make those predictions anymore," he chuckled.

After the demolition of Penn State, the 'Canes went on to beat their next three opponents, Rutgers, Pittsburgh, and Troy State, by a combined score of 142–28. From there, they headed up to Tallahassee, where Florida State was riding a fifty-four-game unbeaten streak at home (dating back to 1991, when UM beat FSU). Najeh Davenport, UM's senior fullback, tried to set the tone for the game during Miami's walk-through practice at Doak Campbell Stadium Friday afternoon. As the Hurricanes walked onto Florida State's sacred sod, Davenport came upon a soft spot at midfield on the logo of FSU's mascot, Chief Osceola, and carved out the letters UM in the turf, just below the chief's chin. In the 'Canes' locker room before the game, UM's fifth-year seniors—seven of whom were redshirt freshmen during that humiliating 47–0 stomping in Tallahassee back in '97—told the team to huddle up and join hands. Reed, the defense's emotional leader, a guy who tended to say things twice for dramatic effect and who often got so worked up in his speeches he got teary-eyed, implored his teammates to recognize just how far the program had come. "We came here and got beat, forty-seven to nuthin'," Reed yelled out. *"Fo-tee-say-vin to NU-THIN'!*

"Don't be the weak link out there," Reed continued. "Go out there and give it your all and when you come to the sideline, you gotta be throwin' up. But that's okay, because everything else will take care of itself."

Keeping those emotions in check was impossible. The 'Canes committed fifteen penalties for 125 yards against FSU that day, but it didn't matter. UM's mission to "break history and make history" was accomplished with a 49–27 romp. UM got more payback later in the season, beating Syracuse 59–0 (the Orangemen had routed probation-ravaged Miami 66–13 in '98) and Washington 65–7 (the Huskies had been the last team to beat the 'Canes, a 34–29 win in Seattle). Those back-to-back whippings were the largest consecutive blowouts over ranked teams in modern NCAA history.

Coker, the rookie coach, had UM headed for the national title game. The 'Canes had also been reshaped in his image, and it was an ideal transition of coaching style. He had maintained Davis's commitment to keeping the 'Canes' high jinks down while still lightening the mood around the team. Whereas Davis had the presence of a military man, Coker was more like a favorite uncle coming for a visit. He'd mingle during practice and tell his goofy jokes. He did away with the full-contact practices that Davis loved to run on Tuesdays and Wednesdays. "He gives us freedom as players and as people," Romberg said. "Before, it was kind of like a dictatorship. Every decision Coach Coker makes, he kind of gives us a say. There's a mutual respect there.

"We thought he would get all tight, play the big-boss role. I think he had a big advantage being a coordinator in the program. He got to hear what all the players had been hearing about [Coach Davis]. The first practice, he yelled a little bit, and we all thought, 'Oh, man, here we go.' But a few seconds later, he was giggling and laughing with us. He knows where to draw the line. If you do your job, everything's okay."

"Coach Coker is like one of the brothers," said Reed. "He was just all fun. The best coach I ever played for."

UM still had its share of characters, particularly Portis and tight end Jeremy Shockey, but Coker didn't have to worry about the 'Canes showing out too much because now his players were policing themselves. "We still had guys who would say 'We need to do this' or 'We need to do that,'" Romberg said, "but anytime they would, we'd just tell them to sit down and shut up. We do enough."

If anyone showed just how far the new revamped 'Canes had come, it was Portis. The guy had a neon wardrobe, drove a lime-green Cadillac, and could outyap Chris Tucker. In high school, he took his mom to his senior prom, clearly a move only a kid with such deep self-confidence could pull off. When running backs coach Don Soldinger came to Gainesville High to recruit him, the UM assistant walked into the football office and found Portis in the coach's seat, with his feet up on the desk. Portis smiled and then tossed Soldinger his highlight tape and said, "Take a look at that and tell me what you think."

"That's Clinton," said Soldinger. "He'll walk in a room of running backs and say, 'Which one of you guys is going to be my fullback?' But the funny part is, he's serious." Portis wasn't kidding that first day he showed up at UM either, when he noticed he was listed as fifth on the depth chart. He promptly walked right up to the starter, James Jackson. "I'm better than you," Portis said. "And you'll see that."

Art Kehoe, the UM line coach, once yelled to Portis that he registered 99.9 percent on the ego index. Portis responded, "I'm as high as you can go."

Portis carried himself with a chip on his shoulder, always feeling as if he were being snubbed. Yet it never became a huge problem with this star-studded squad, and for that, credit had to go to Coker and his team leaders. Portis would practice his end-zone dances and run them by Coker, who would always laugh and give the thumbs-down sign with a wink. But just as with the old-school 'Canes, Portis always backed his bravado. At Boston College, the 'Canes, with a 7-0 record at the time, were in their tightest game. Dorsey was struggling with BC's pass defense. Portis told Coker, "Give me the ball. Put it on my shoulders." The coach did. Portis wound up with a career-high thirty-six carries for 160 yards, his second-highest rushing total of the season behind 164 yards against Penn State in the season opener. UM, despite committing a season-high five turnovers, beat the Eagles 18–7. Afterward, Portis was less ebullient than his usual peacock self. Instead, he would just shrug his shoulders and say, "Dorsey can't be an all-American every week." In a different environment, he might've overtaken his team.

In truth, it is all about the spotlight—and it's not, and therein lies the delicate balance of the ego of today's elite athlete. Portis was as brash as any 'Cane from any era, totting around a sackful of resentment for all the doubters and haters out there. He even had a bit of venom stored up for Miami's sports information people because he felt that they were constantly pushing the milquetoast Dorsey for Heisman honors (instead of him), or at least not giving him the push he felt he was due. Yet Portis never resented Dorsey. It had become that type of environment around UM. "We realized when you're at the University of Miami, you gotta give yourself up," Portis said. "You gotta sacrifice. One player's not going to be bigger than the team. That's not happening. You had Shockey, Ed Reed, Bryant McKinnie, Phil Buchanon, Ken Dorsey. Man, we were loaded, and the leaders wouldn't allow us to get big-headed. That carried us a long way.

"It could get frustrating, but you just got to understand that it is a team game and our ultimate goal was the national championship. Not many guys win the Heisman and the national championship in the same year. Just look it up." He was right: Only Florida's Danny Wuerffel and Michigan's Charles Woodson did both in the previous twenty years.

Under the leadership of Reed, McKinnie, Joaquin Gonzalez, and Dorsey, these 'Canes had more of a playful charm to them, a mischievous innocence. They took on the personality of Reed, a wonderful athlete who happened to own the UM record in the javelin, yet would be remembered by UM coaches as the closest thing to perfect from the neck up they'd seen in terms of his maturity and spirit. Teammates dubbed him "Eddiecane." Following Reed's lead, the 'Canes got up before dawn to do off-season conditioning drills; they studied more film and pushed each other harder. But they also would cut up and do silly imitations at practice, like mimicking screaming teenage girls on MTV's *TRL*. They goofed around with their new president, the diminutive Donna Shalala. On the team flight up to Tallahassee for the Florida State game, UM safety James Lewis brought Shalala into the front of the cabin and taught her how the 'Canes shake hands, to the howls and laughter of the team. "Miss Shalala was the coolest," Reed said. "We all love her." Lewis even rolled up her pants leg so she could "style" her way off the plane, something that never would've happened with her predecessor, Thaddeus Foote. Back in the day, Jimmy Johnson's boys probably were more likely to give Foote a wedgie.

Reed and his teammates were right. Larry Coker was the perfect man at the perfect time. Dee, extolling the virtues of Coker's coaching genius, said whipping kids into a frenzy, yelling, and kicking them in the butt simply doesn't work with today's players. "Today's youth is not about that," Dee said. "It's about setting standards. Reward performance. Encouragement. Direction. They react well to Larry. That's the way he is, and it works with these kids. They are looking for someone to give them direction, leadership, the plan, but not cram it down their throats. That's Larry. That's what he was when we hired him. His personality, his temperament, his way of dealing with people. He has flourished in his persona but it hasn't overwhelmed him."

Most "experts" around the country, though, clung to the belief that Coker was just a caretaker, a yes-man who was winning with Butch Davis's players. After all, Coker did have the luxury of coaching a roster that had what one NFL scout sized up as four *dozen* future NFL players. "Could somebody else have stepped in and done it? I don't know. Maybe, but in reality, I don't think so," Coker mused on the eve of UM's national title game against number two Nebraska. "There would've been a new system, new numbering, not knowing the players; I think it would've been very difficult."

Regardless, it would've been hard to imagine that Davis could've had the 'Canes playing any better. Coker's pregame locker room speech was vintage: "Just let's be who we are. Don't try and play outside the lines. Let's be as good as we can be. But don't try to be more than we are." For Larry Coker, that finally appeared to be enough to get the job done—although, an hour before kickoff, Coker didn't seem too convinced. "Coach Coker probably won't like this story, but he was scared," said Curtis Johnson, UM's receivers coach. "He was like, 'I was at Oklahoma State. Nebraska used to put sixty on us.' Well, Ed Reed happened to be standing near by, and Ed turns around and goes 'Nebraska? Nebraska? We Miami! Coach, don't be scared. We got this.' And he patted him on the shoulder and walked off."

Reed was right. Coker's 'Canes blew number two Nebraska off the Rose Bowl field. UM led 34–0 before the first half was over and had people discussing whether this Miami team was the best college squad ever. The offense set the school record for points (475), and the defense led the nation in interceptions, forced turnovers, and gave up a paltry 9.3 points per game. "Offense, defense, special teams, this team is loaded," said Kehoe, the lone link to all five Miami national title teams. "It's the best one I've ever seen, and I think we could line up and play with any college team that's ever been."

Coker became the first rookie coach in half a century to win the national championship. (The last was Bennie Oosterbaan at Michigan in 1948.) "He's a conductor, a great maestro," Dee said. "And he's got some good oboe players."

After the 2001 season, the 'Canes lost eleven players who were drafted by the NFL, three of whom—Portis, Shockey, and cornerback Philip Buchanon—passed up their final season of eligibility. Five of those players were taken in the first round. But Coker challenged his players to do something no Miami team had ever done—repeat.

11

THE HIGH-WIRE ACT

Winter—as in the *off*-season—lasts all of two weeks at Miami. This is what life has become in the world of big-time college football. It's mid-January, 2002, classes start in six days, but inside UM's Hecht Athletic Center, a different kind of schooling is already in session. Three muscular men sit at the back of a windowless twelve-by-sixteen-foot classroom, staring at a projection screen. Today's subject: advanced linebacking. The pupils are redshirt freshmen Leon Williams and Rocky McIntosh; the teacher is junior Jon Vilma, the team's stud middle 'backer. They marvel as they watch Miami Dolphin Zach Thomas reading blocks, staying low, shooting gaps. He's pure textbook. Next up, Vilma pops in a tape of the Tampa Bay Buccaneers to check out Derrick Brooks to see how he maneuvers in space. After that, it's Ray Lewis. Truth be told, the Ravens scheme isn't that similar to what the 'Canes are running, but for eager young linebackers, watching Lewis work is akin to budding jazzmen listening to Miles Davis. Surely they won't reach that level of artistry, but it's always a good motivational tool. The room fills with oohs and aahs as the Ravens star flies sideline to sideline, leveling ball carriers. Suddenly spring can't come quickly enough.

Halfway across the country, Larry Coker is undergoing his own skull session. The UM coach has traveled to Denver to meet with Broncos coach Mike Shanahan about how he orchestrated their back-to-back Super Bowl wins. "There were some parallels because when you're a champion your schedule gets tougher, and that happened with us too," said Coker. "I just wanted to get his thoughts on how he approached the season."

Fast-forward to late February. It's five fifty on a Wednesday morning, and freshman TE Kellen Winslow II—the son of the Hall of Fame tight end—adjusts his orange 'do rag as he hustles into the sprawling twelve-thousand-square-foot weight room that overlooks Miami's Greentree practice fields. K2 (nobody calls him Junior) joins a dozen of his teammates, each wearing identical dark green shorts and gray T-shirts with a cartoon of a fierce-looking bird surrounded by the words, *Power, Strength, Speed, Miami.* They could pass for a marine platoon as they flank out in lines of three to begin warming up. Strength coach Andreu Swasey plays drill sergeant. After the players break off into smaller groups, Winslow loads two forty-five-pound plates on a bar and cuddles it across his shoulders as if he's about to do a squat. Instead he closes his eyes for a moment, then raises his right leg off the floor, bringing his knee to his waist. He holds it for a for a few seconds—the sweat sneaking out from under his rag, his left calf starting to quiver—then gently lowers his foot and catches his breath before lifting his left leg. The principle is to train unilaterally, because if much of the game is played off one foot then the athlete should train off one foot, so honing balance is a premium.

Swasey's program is heavy on developing explosiveness and core strength via Olympic-style lifting, not the machine training UM used to do. "That way doesn't strengthen joints and tendons," he says. "And I'm all about first-step quickness."

Swasey ("Swaay-*zee*") is a mythical figure around the UM program. In college football, the strength coach can mean as much as any high-priced coordinator, because due to NCAA restrictions these are the only guys who have access to the players in the off-season. The rule allows only eight hours of work a week, and no coach is any better at it than Swasey. Whenever Miami players are asked for their take on why the 'Canes seem so much faster than everyone else, they always give the same answer—"Swasey."

Unlike most strength coaches he doesn't have a power lifter's girth. Instead he has the lithe, muscular build of a defensive back, which is what he was in the early nineties for Baylor. Despite his modest frame, Swasey has a commanding presence. He has narrow eyes, a wide nose, and a knock-off-the-bullshit glare that could make a glass of iced tea boil. Players rave about how the guy knows exactly which different button to push on each guy and when. "He just knows how to get inside people's heads," said Vilma. Swasey also has one big edge over most guys in his position in that he actually was a football coach, having worked as Houston's defensive backs coach before taking over at Miami. Just as important, Swasey knows where most of these kids come from. He grew up in Liberty City not far from Randy Shannon, and he starred at Carol City High School playing for Coach Walt Frazier, one of Florida's legendary prep coaches.

Before Swasey puts his guys through his program, he does the same sprints and lifts starting at five a.m. He had learned a valuable lesson one day when Edgerrin James asked if Swasey would work out with him. Swasey agreed. "During the run, James said, 'Whatever you do, don't ever stop.' I said, 'What are you talking about?' And he said, 'Training with the guys and staying in the trenches with them.' I took that to heart."

Swasey worked out with all the players, often going through the training regimen three or four times a morning. "He definitely earned the players' trust and respect," Clinton Portis said.

What is exposed in his weight room and on his practice field is, in a word, real. Most kids cloak themselves in bravado, but in Swasey's "lab," true character is revealed. Pain and pressure have a great way of peeling away layers. "The armor of your character doesn't fall too far from you," said Swasey, "especially in the weight room. You just can't hide it." Swasey loves to call players out as a way to test them so he can get a read on their personalities. "The world doesn't like to be called out, least of all in front of their peers, but when you do that to them, something's coming out of them, good or bad—and that's what we want."

For Swasey, the weight room during wintertime is one big crystal ball. "Before even the coaches know who's gonna do well," he says, "I know." His first tip of the 2002 off-season: "Watch out for Kellen and [redshirt freshman corner] Kelly Jennings," he predicts in early March, the day before spring practice begins. As a speedy six-foot-five, 210-pound wideout and special teamer, Winslow was one of only four true freshmen to play in 2001. He even made a hellacious hit on special teams in the Sugar Bowl against Nebraska. Now he's weighing in at a sculpted 232. "He's gonna shock the coaches," Swasey says. "He's so much stronger and much more disciplined and focused."

It's a few minutes past eleven a.m. on the first Saturday of April, and small clusters of fans in tank tops and sunglasses mill about the stands inside the Orange Bowl as Miami's final spring scrimmage gets under way. "Spring game" is a misnomer at most schools. It's actually one of three scrimmages that dot fifteen practices stretching over a five-week span. And it's as much for the fans as anyone else—a gridiron dress rehearsal with position coaches littering the field like overbearing parents at a Little League game. Just as Swasey promised, Winslow makes his presence known, snaring three passes for fifty-seven yards. In fact, K2 and redshirt wideout Roscoe Parrish, the speedy Smurf whom Davis didn't want to recruit, have been turning heads for the past month. Likewise, the bobcat-quick Jennings is rocketing up the depth chart. Good thing, because the other new DBs—the 'Canes had to replace their entire secondary—have been shaky all spring. Coach Larry Coker is encouraged by his young linebackers, though, and the defensive line is deeper than ever. Taking it all in from the sideline is freshman Frank Gore. He slouches over a pair of metal crutches, looking like the kid whose mom forgot to pick him up after school. Three weeks ago, the starting tailback—a guy one rival coach called Miami's most talented player—tore his right ACL in practice. Now rehab is starting to take an emotional toll. "Frank's never had to deal with any physical setbacks," says trainer Scott Bruce, "and there is a huge psychological barrier." Doctors project a mid-September return for Gore, but it is later pushed back to October 1. Without Gore, the 'Canes will have to rely on redshirt sophomore Willis McGahee. A sculpted six-foot-one, 224-pound Adonis with 4.28 speed, McGahee is the most impressive specimen in the program. Trouble is, the coaches are keeping their fingers crossed that McGahee isn't also a broken horse. In 2002, he let Portis get inside his head and the brash former UM standout did all kinds of damage, wrecking McGahee's confidence.

As if that's not bad enough, star WR Andre Johnson gets dragged into the headlines in March for allegedly cheating on a sociology test last fall. A three-member UM judicial board suspends him for the summer, meaning he can't train at the school's facilities. Just like that, Miami's stellar spring has gone sour.

Stomping across a crowded parking lot on an eighty-five-degree May night, Brett Romberg looks like a giant Fred Durst, what with his scruffy goatee, devilish grin and air of pure mischief. Romberg, a center, is the leader of Miami's offensive line; trailing a few feet behind him is his sidekick, an Iranian-born, Canadian-bred, 325-pound guard named Sherko Haji-Rasouli. They're fifteen minutes late for dinner at Monty's, a trendy Coral Gables seafood spot where three of their linemates are waiting. But Romberg knows nothing starts without him. A fifth-year senior, he's the main holdover from last year's line, maybe the best in college football history. Nowhere is chemistry more of a must than up front, which explains these weekly binges at various area restaurants. As the crew strut to their table, they turn more heads than the busty brunette staking out the bar. They range in mass from six-foot-five, 369-

pound right tackle Vernon "Bigfatvern" Carey to the six-foot-three, 290-pound Romberg. Here, nothing is off-limits. Well, except for the fries—Swasey has the guys running before dawn tomorrow. They make fun of Carey's ample gut, Sherko's back hair ("the sweater") and his penchant for wearing shirts two sizes too small, and feisty line coach Art Kehoe's poor dating record. It's all good-natured, but make no mistake: This is serious business for a unit replacing three starters. Losing Dorsey, who was sacked just four times in 2001, would mean losing another ring. And that's not something Romberg would joke about.

Just like Kehoe, their leader, they are scrappers. Only Carey came to UM as a big-name recruit—although, Romberg is quick to point out he was number one in Canada. Last year's offensive line—which also included dominating left tackle Bryant McKinnie; Joaquin Gonzalez, the scholarly right tackle; and Martin Bibla, the pugnacious guard—had great chemistry. As the group exits the restaurant, Romberg explains how he hopes this O line will develop the same. But suddenly his tone isn't quite so confident. That's the tricky part about chemistry: The equation changes and so often the ingredients have to change with it.

Jon Vilma is standing at the center of Miami's practice field with his fists clenched at his waist. He looks like he's ready to go twelve rounds with Tyson. It's seven fifteen on a Wednesday morning in June, and it's already so sticky-hot that the only things moving in south Florida are the mosquitoes and about eighty Hurricanes. Coaches are an NCAA no-no during off-season workouts, so Vilma plays ringmaster, firing up his defense and yapping at the receivers. He hardly resembles the guy his school trots out as the new, freshly scrubbed face of Miami football: a 3.7-junior finance major fluent in German and so analytical that former 'Canes great Micheal Barrow once got pissed at him for picking his brain too often. Off the field, Vilma is soft-spoken, witty, and polite. He even finds time to go home and do the chores at his family's place down the road in Coral Gables. On the field he could pass for Barrow, Ray Lewis, or any other 'Cane spit from the image of Michael Irvin. Vilma earned a national rep in the Rose Bowl by delivering two vicious hits and emerging as Miami's latest linebacking terror. And when it comes to seven-on-seven in the summer, the dawg in him comes out again. As the sun ascends, Vilma and junior outside linebacker D. J. Williams battle the raw receiving corps, turning every pattern into a personal challenge of their manhood. Think "Showdown at the OK Corral" meets "Rucker Park." For sixty minutes they taunt, chase, and roughhouse, hoping that the attitude will rub off on the pups working into the mix. At the other end of the field, 320-pounders do bear crawls and engage in hand-to-hand combat. Carlos Joseph, a six-foot-six, 334-pound sophomore expected to replace monster left tackle Bryant McKinnie, is off to the side practicing his footwork. Head up, hips back, hands out, he tries to make each stride of his massive left leg identical. Not too long. Not too steep. Keeping your balance is key when you have to protect Dorsey's narrow backside. Joseph occasionally checks his size-sixteen footprints in the dewy turf; after ten minutes, he stops to admire his work, just as a golfer would smile down at a divot after a perfect chip shot. A sheepish grin creeps across his moon-shaped face. Kehoe would be proud. On the last play of the morning, D. J. Williams—Vilma's devilish alter ego—

swoops down on sophomore tight end David Williams and swats away a pass, then playfully shoves him to the ground. Standing over his victim, he looks back at Vilma as both do their best Dikembe Mutombo finger wag. Dorsey's workday, meanwhile, is far from done. The senior QB still has to meet Johnson, the suspended receiver, at Coral Gables High, where they hook up three or four times a week to keep their timing. A half dozen incoming freshmen are getting their first gulp of college football. They arrived a few months early to get a jump on conditioning and terminology. Johnson's absence means more reps for wideouts Akieem Jolla and Sinorice Moss, kid brother of ex-'Canes star Santana Moss. Both rookies have almost held their own, but their heads are spinning and their bodies are sore. Swasey, keeping a watchful eye over all the proceedings, is wary. He says that motivating this team is much different from last year's championship squad because most of these guys did not experience that 5-6 season of 1997. "You're talking to these young guys about fire and many never have been burned," he says.

Miami opened the 2002 season with a tune-up, blowing out Florida A&M, 63–17. The 'Canes' real first test would come in Gainesville, where the number six Gators had lost only five times in the previous twelve years. Miami entered the game a 2.5–point underdog. The 'Canes' all-new secondary was supposed to be fodder for Rex Grossman, Florida's strong-armed Heisman hopeful. Instead, Miami's D line mauled Grossman, and UM safety Mo Sikes picked off two passes, returning one for a ninety-seven-yard touchdown. The 'Canes rolled 41–16, the twenty-five-point margin Florida's worst defeat in twenty-three years. The better news for Miami was the way McGahee attacked the Gators, gashing them for 204 yards on twenty-four carries. Not bad for a guy who had once thought of fleeing the UM program.

McGahee's psyche had been squeezed by Portis's ribbing, by the constant "You'll never be better than me" chirping. "He got in my head," McGahee said. "Just Portis being Portis." But McGahee's family wouldn't let him transfer. His older brother, Eugene Poole, who owned a gym in nearby Opa Locka, forced him to train harder. So McGahee had spent his mornings working out with Swasey and his evenings at Eugene's place, Muscles 'n' Curves, pushing more iron. Some nights Eugene even had his baby brother push his truck around for an entire block to build up his legs. The results were eye-opening. McGahee followed up his performance in the Florida game with three more hundred-yard efforts. Then he bailed out UM against Florida State. The 'Canes were down six with less than six minutes remaining when McGahee sprinted sixty-eight yards on a screen pass to set up the game-winning touchdown. The blinding burst shot McGahee into the Heisman race. McGahee's emergence—at least in the spotlight—came at the expense of Ken Dorsey.

Dorsey, the spindly Californian, was smart, polite, and had seemingly been at UM forever. Dorsey's critics said he had a rag arm and was a product of the system. The guy wasn't even the best player in his own backfield, they said. All he did was lead UM to victory after victory and pilot amazing fourth-quarter, game-winning touchdown drives. Dorsey's numbers were down, but the 'Canes' offense was still thriving. In their first eight games, UM was held below thirty-nine points once (the 28–27 victory over Florida State). However, unlike the 2001 juggernaut, this team was showing signs of weakness. The Seminoles hammered at the 'Canes, rushing for 296 yards, with powerhouse tailback Greg Jones getting 189. Questions about whether UM might have gone soft only increased after West Virginia piled up 363 rushing yards in the 'Canes' next game. Miami's winning streak had swelled to twenty-nine games, but heading into their November 2 game against Big East cellar dweller Rutgers, there was friction within the UM program. Coker didn't start Sikes in the West Virginia game for skipping a team meeting, and a few weeks earlier he had benched Winslow, free safety Sean Taylor, and cornerback Al Marshall for academic reasons. Romberg and Haji-Rasouli mused that this squad wasn't as close as last year's team and its underclassmen weren't as hungry. "With the young guys, it's not confidence," Haji-Rasouli said. "There's a lack of understanding of what it takes to win."

"I'm very concerned," Romberg said. "I know what the attitude was in the past. It was confident but humble. Guys around here now are bred on championships and winning football games. It's a sad day when you're on a plane for five hours after losing a football game. Your body hurts so bad you don't want to talk."

West Virginia exposed a flaw in UM's defense. The Mountaineers, sensing that the 'Canes' front seven had the tendency to freewheel a bit too much, had spread Miami out with their four-wide sets, then let fleet-footed quarterback Rasheed Marshall take off. Rutgers couldn't take advantage of it though, and Miami beat them 42–17. Virginia Tech followed the West Virginia model, and once again Miami's defenders struggled to play assignment football, allowing Hokies QB Bryan Randall to run for 132 yards as Tech almost knocked off UM 56–45.

Still, few gave Miami's Fiesta Bowl opponent, 13-0 Ohio State, much shot at upsetting the 'Canes. The second-ranked Buckeyes, coached by former Youngstown State boss Jim Tressel—the same guy whom Dee interviewed seven years earlier before hiring Butch Davis—were the nation's other unbeaten team, but they had a penchant for eeking out 12–7 victories. They were installed as an eleven-and-a-half-point underdog. In reality, though, they weren't the typical plodding Big Ten team. They had ten players from speed-rich Florida, including two-way stud Chris Gamble and ace wide receiver Michael Jenkins. But their best offensive player, freshman tailback Maurice Clarett, had been slowed down by a shoulder injury, and it appeared Ohio State had limped its way across the finish line. Skeptics dubbed them the Luckeyes, carping about how they never blew anyone out; instead OSU seemingly was doing it with mirrors.

The Yale Club was buzzing. A few hours earlier, former Yalie and *Sex and the City* star Chris Noth, aka Big, entertained his fellow Elis in a production of *What Didn't Happen*. But after the sun disappeared, five hundred guys with ketchup stains on their blazers descended on the Yale Club to see some history. It was Heisman night. Normally the crowd conducts its business in the run-down, plaster-peeling-off-the-walls Downtown Athletic Club, but due to renovations, the show was moved uptown. Word around the Yale was that Miami tailback Willis McGahee might become the first sophomore in the award's sixty-eight-year history to win the prized statuette. McGahee, the soft-spoken mama's boy, had made quite a case for himself in 2002, rushing for seventeen hundred yards and leading the nation in touchdowns, with twenty-eight. He even scored six

TDs against the vaunted Virginia Tech defense. The biggest thing going for McGahee? He was the only one of the five Heisman finalists who had excelled in every game his team played that season.

The biggest thing going against him? Ken Dorsey, the quarterback who had led Miami to its ridiculous thirty-four-game winning streak. Dorsey was the guy everyone at Miami thought deserved it. He was, after all, 38-1 as a starter, and a senior—the team's leader and most recognizable star. But critics called him the second coming of Gino Torretta, the 'Cane quarterback who won the Heisman in 1992, then floundered in the NFL. Some just said he was flat-out boring. Inside the program, Miami was seething over the way the media had attacked Dorsey. The truth was, the guy was an honor student and about as squeaky-clean as Richie Cunningham. He once waited two hours inside the Miami sports information office for a reporter whose plane got delayed. Dorsey, they'll tell you, is everything that the typical Hurricane wasn't supposed to be.

Doug Walker, Miami's sports information director, a stocky Texan with a buzz cut and a short fuse, had become very close to Dorsey in his three years at Miami. Walker came on board toward the end of Butch Davis's "Let them eat crap" approach to the media and immediately found a go-to guy in Dorsey to navigate through the fickle Miami press. Walker woke up with a bad feeling that day. He was in Orlando when every 'Cane nominee (including Romberg, Dorsey's roommate) got shut out of the other major awards, going zero-for-five in the Outland, O'Brien, Maxwell, Walker, and Camp awards. Walker thought the voters had fallen for USC's Carson Palmer, who torched Notre Dame over Thanksgiving weekend, and that there could be a Miami backlash brewing. Palmer was the trendy pick. So what if he was mediocre till midseason? The NFL scouts loved him.

As it turned out, the voting wasn't as close as everyone predicted. Walker was right: Palmer cruised to the podium. McGahee was fourth. Dorsey was fifth, or as he called it, "dead last." As for those who figured McGahee and Dorsey would split each other's chances? Their combined points total didn't even add up to Palmer's. "I almost feel like there's a very big lack of respect for the University of Miami that we want to earn back," Dorsey said, as he sat with his mother and his girlfriend, Jordan, an hour after the presentation. He and McGahee would get that chance in Tempe.

Bowl run-up time is all about story lines. In many ways the BCS title game has taken on a Super Bowl air of weeklong hype. For the 2003 Fiesta Bowl, three subplots surfaced—the magnitude of the Miami dynasty and its thirty-four-game winning streak; Clarett, the mercurial Buckeyes star; and the return of Vince Wilfork, Miami's mammoth young defensive tackle.

In Clarett, there was a soap opera unfolding each day in the desert. The six-foot, 230-pound freshman became a national name midway through his rookie season when in an *ESPN the Magazine* cover story titled "One and Done?" he contemplated leaving school after one year for the NFL. Then in the middle of bowl week, he stirred up more controversy when he said Ohio State officials lied about why he couldn't go home to Youngstown for his buddy Juan Bell's funeral.

Someone reminded Clarett what he had said when he signed with Ohio State out of Warren Harding High, something about restoring Buckeye pride. "That was cool to say at the time," Clarett answered. "[Ohio State media relations stooge] Steve Snapp told me the right things to say to make the program look good. He's got a job. I've got a job. As a person, I've got to look at myself in the mirror."

Wilfork's drama had a completely different tone. Conversely, his was the story about why college football can still represent something larger; it was the talc of a chubby manchild who was once so broken he was ashamed to walk to his mailbox, and about how he became the most powerful man in college football, literally and figuratively.

Most people never thought Vince Wilfork would be in Arizona, ready to lead Miami to another national title. Not just a few weeks after his mama passed. Not just a few months after his daddy passed. But, really, there is nowhere else Big Vince could be. At least not in early January.

The story actually started ten years earlier. That was when the kidney failure started to gut his old man. In just two months back in 1992, David Wilfork lost 140 pounds, dropping from 285 to 145. But he kept battling. Then he lost an eye and had to have a toe amputated, and as his body kept betraying him, he vowed he wouldn't let diabetes or anything else get the best of him. He promised himself that as long as there was air in his lungs he would be there for his boys—David Junior and Vince—even if that meant showing up at the kids' football practices hobbling around on crutches or with a cane, battling heat and humidity.

And Vince would be there for the old man too. He bathed his father, fed him, even carried him to the bathroom. The old man did whatever he could to make it to Vince's games as the chubby kid grew into a dominating defensive lineman. But the kid's path wouldn't be easy, either. He failed to get his eligibility after signing with Miami. He stayed home in Boynton

Beach, Florida, and kept prepping to pass his test scores—and piling on pounds while his self-esteem shriveled up and his weight ballooned from 315 to 380. "We couldn't talk to him at all," his father, David Wilfork, had said in 2002. "He just wanted to be alone, but we pressured him more than ever. People around here kept telling him he'd never do anything more than high school, so me and my wife kept saying, 'Prove them wrong. Make 'em liars.' But he was so humiliated. He just didn't want to be seen. He wouldn't even walk to the mailbox."

"I was like, 'Vince, you gotta get out of the house. This is ridiculous,'" recalled Ray Berger, Wilfork's coach at Santaluces High, who eventually—with the old man's prodding—got Vince out to his alma mater's practices, where he became a de facto assistant. The old man couldn't have been happier when his boy made it to UM and emerged as a star. He was right there to be a water boy to Vince and his teammates, even though his own battles were getting tougher. After the kidneys went and his eyesight vanished, his hearing disappeared, and then, finally, in June of '02, Big Vince knew it was time to say good-bye. He placed his national championship ring on his father and then his dad was gone. David Wilfork was forty-eight.

"I thought that would be the worst of it this year, my father passing," Wilfork explained at the Fiesta Bowl's media session. "I mean, what are the odds of something else?"

As Wilfork shared his story he said he realized he was not alone. That he not only had his older brother, David, but an entire family to support him and keep his mind right, he said as he gazed up at fifty or sixty Hurricanes goofing around in the bleachers at Sun Devil Stadium. "I don't have a dad anymore. But I have twelve dads here, all the coaches. The only thing I'm missing is my mom."

At Wilfork's father's funeral, Vince's prep coach, the guy the old man had affectionately referred to as his boys' white godfather, stood up and spoke. Berger explained how in his faith, as a Jew, boys were believed to become men at thirteen, but he admitted he really didn't become a man till he was twenty-four, when his father passed away. "Today," he said as he looked at the Wilfork boys, "you guys are men."

"Honestly," Berger said later, "I don't know if I could even deal with all they've had to endure this year." A big reason was "all these guys up there," Wilfork said, pointing to the players in the stands. "They saved me."

When all his teammates showed up at his father's funeral, Wilfork realized he wasn't alone. Then, as the season kicked off and Miami made its drive to become the first Miami team to repeat as national champs, his brothers were still there for Wilfork, making sure he was okay, playing games with him, watching movies with him, or just teasing him. Then, the week of the big game at Tennessee on November 9, his mom suffered a stroke. He rushed home to be by her side. But he called UM coaches and told them he still wanted to play. They needed him to shut down that Vol ground attack, right?

"Vince, this is just football," Coker told him. "Stay home. Be with your mother. She needs you."

After Miami's romp in Knoxville, defensive line coach Greg Mark called from the team bus, asked how Vince was, and then passed the phone to a player seated next to him. Who passed it to another player. Who passed it to another. And the phone snaked its way around the whole bus. "I talked to everyone on the bus besides the driver," Wilfork said. "You can't imagine how things like that helped."

Things then seemed to steady with his mom. Her condition

appeared to get better. Vince made the ninety-minute drive back to campus and returned to the team. He was all excited that his mom was coming home and was about to begin therapy. David Junior was there at the hospital the night before her release. "Go home so you can get ready for work," she told him. So he did, and then, just like that, her body stopped working and she was gone too—before Vince could get back to her. Gone at forty-six.

At her funeral, two buses pulled up. Hurricane players and coaches piled out, went to the service, and heard stories about what a sweet woman and loving mother Vince's mom was. And one by one, they hugged their brother. For the next ten days or so, Wilfork didn't want to do anything, not even turn on the television. He was tired of hearing about how this was going to induce him into bolting Miami for the NFL. He wasn't sure if he'd make the trip to the Fiesta Bowl. Then Vince realized something. He needed to go to Tempe, but not for the team. Not because the Hurricanes needed him to freight-train some poor Buckeye linemen or gobble up Clarett. No, Big Vince needed to come to Tempe for himself. "Playing football, being around these guys, that makes me happy," he said.

Teammates missed Wilfork's enthusiasm and jovial, joking personality. They missed the guy who always seemed to be able to calm the coaches down, UM defensive coordinator Randy Shannon said. Besides, they figured no one would be playing with more steam than Wilfork. "He is so ready to play and take out all that anger and negativity and stuff out on somebody," said Miami defensive end Jerome McDougle.

Privately, the Buckeyes were licking their chops. They felt their D line, led by future first-rounders Kenny Peterson and Will Smith, would overmatch what they believed was an overrated Miami offensive line. Buckeye defensive coordinator Mark Dantonio's game plan was to disrupt the Miami offense by sending players at unexpected angles. They'd slant, cross-blitz, zone-blitz, and turn loose their linebackers and defensive backs on Dorsey while dropping D linemen back into coverage. It was similar to the scheme Boston College had utilized two years before to befuddle Dorsey and throw off his timing, only the Buckeyes would attack much more and do it with better personnel.

Not that the 'Canes didn't expect it. Rob Chudzinski, UM's offensive coordinator, stressed that it was vital for Miami to take care of the backside pressure, meaning the heat was on Carlos Joseph. That worried some of the Miami coaches, since the massive left tackle had been sluggish in practice after letting his weight get out of control. Sure enough, the Buckeyes' defense attacked, but the 'Canes' O line acted as if it didn't know what it was seeing. Smith sacked Dorsey on UM's first play from scrimmage. Ohio State sacked him three more times and knocked him down on ten other occasions, even knocking Dorsey out of the game temporarily.

Even though UM scored first, on a twenty-five-yard pass play from Dorsey to Roscoe Parrish, the Buckeyes' defense continued to swarm. McGahee couldn't find any room, and by the midway point of the second quarter, the 'Canes abandoned their man-blocking system and switched to slide-protection in hopes of giving Dorsey more time. The pressure got to the UM quarterback and forced two turnovers in the second quarter that the Buckeyes promptly turned into fourteen points. It all happened in a seventy-eight-second span. The only weapon the 'Canes had working was Winslow, the sophomore tight end. The truth was, he wasn't someone Ohio State had worried much about going into the game. That was because they felt Cie Grant, a former cornerback, was the best coverage linebacker in the country. Still, before the first half was over the Buckeye coaches realized Winslow was too big and too fast for Grant. "Winslow was eating him up," said Buckeye linebackers coach Mark Snyder. "We couldn't believe it."

With Winslow emerging as UM's go-to guy, the 'Canes rallied late in the second half, but then, just as McGahee was getting warmed up (having gained twenty-nine yards on his last four carries), he took a swing pass from Dorsey, headed up the field, and was blasted by Will Allen just above his left knee. The joint exploded upon impact, leaving McGahee a crumpled heap on the field.

"That was crucial," Allen said. "We needed to take him out. We needed to eliminate that part of their offense. I came in with a big shot. When I saw him down, holding his knee, I got hyped. Then I thought about it, and I prayed to God. I prayed for him."

McGahee was carted off the field sobbing with a torn anterior cruciate ligament, posterior cruciate ligament, and medial collateral ligament. Despite the loss of their star, the 'Canes—trailing 17–14—still had a chance to win. The Miami sideline was chaotic. Everyone sensed something amazing was about to happen as UM's defense forced a punt. Warren Sapp, Jessie Armstead, Clinton Portis, and two dozen other former 'Canes all smacked at each other. This was the time when the U always made its move. Baseball star Gary Sheffield—who was there because . . . well, these were the 'Canes, the team that had become synonymous, even among superstar athletes, with excellence—just soaked it all up. Sheffield was there for much the same reason that Charles Barkley had come out to Miami's practice seventy-two hours earlier. It was the same reason that Michael Jordan and Mario Lemieux golf together or that Ken Griffey Jr. and Tiger Woods hang out. It's the velvet-rope club among elite athletes that stretches beyond just winning. The looks on Sapp's and Portis's faces were a testimony about what true belief and confidence really were from the program that hardly ever lost games. And damned if they weren't right. With just over two minutes left in the fourth quarter, Andy Groom, Ohio State's all-league punter, angled a kick left. Tiny Roscoe Parrish faded over, caught the ball at the UM twenty-four-yard-line, paused for a split second as the entire stadium took a deep breath, and then Parrish dodged a Buckeye tackler, found a wall of blockers, and shot up the right sideline, going fifty yards down to the Ohio State 26. But this time UM couldn't convert on a game-winning touchdown. Instead, the 'Canes called time-out with three seconds to go to set up for the game-tying field goal from forty yards. Kicker Todd Sievers had been only three for six from forty yards and beyond on the year, and none of those six were anywhere near as big as this one. Just to lump even more dramatic effect on the situation, Ohio State called time-out. Then one minute later, the Buckeyes called their final time-out just to give Sievers even more time to ponder the magnitude of the kick. Surely the program that had won so many big games on the other teams' kickers' failure was due for some payback from fate, no? As Sievers paced off his steps, Miami players held hands on the sidelines. Former UM standout Lamar Thomas, decked out in a lime-green suit, couldn't bear to watch. He folded a white hand towel on the ground and took a knee with his back to the field. When he heard the crowd gasp and then all his buddies roar, he knew Sievers had come through. The kick sailed just inside the right upright. On to overtime.

The Buckeyes won the toss and chose to start OT on defense. On second down from the 7, Dorsey threw a pass over the middle. Winslow jumped and reached back over a defender to make perhaps the best of his eleven catches and give UM a 24–17 lead.

A penalty and a sack put Ohio State in trouble. The Buckeyes faced a fourth-and-14 from the 29, but quarterback Craig Krenzel, who had completed only five passes in regulation, converted a seventeen-yard pass for a first down. But after a Krenzel run down to the UM 5 yard line, Ohio State again faced a fourth down. Krenzel dropped back, looking for Chris Gamble running a fade-stop in the right corner of the end zone, but the pass fell to the ground and officials waved incomplete. The stadium shot off its fireworks. The 'Canes had won another title, their sixth in twenty magical years. Miami's Sean Taylor flung his helmet in the air; the UM sideline rushed the field, and Armstead and a bunch of other former 'Canes did too. Sapp jumped up so high, a chunk of dip flopped out of his mouth and off the belly of his hideous Coogi sweater. This was always the way Miami won, right?

But wait. Field judge Terry Porter threw his flag five seconds after the ball dropped and signaled interference on Glenn Sharpe. "I saw the guy holding the guy prior to the ball being put in the air," Porter said in a statement afterward. "He was still holding him, pulling him down while the ball was in the air. I gave the signal for holding. Then I realized it should be pass interference because the ball was in the air."

Porter, part of a Big Twelve officiating crew, said the call was delayed because he replayed it in his mind: "I wanted to make double sure it was the right call."

"He definitely hesitated," said Gamble. "I didn't think he

was going to pull it out. I thought the game was over. Then, hallelujah, out it came."

With new life, Ohio State scored three plays later on a Krenzel QB sneak from inside the 1 to make the score 24–24, and instead of celebrating their second national title, the 'Canes were back on defense in a second OT. "I really thought that game was over," said UM secondary coach Mark Stoops. "Just like everybody else. And there's not another official in the history of the game that would make that call."

Sharpe said he didn't think he interfered. He was only being aggressive. Just as Stoops instructed him to do. "We were blitzing," Stoops explained. "I didn't want them to catch a little slant or a little hitch. I told 'em to get in the receiver's face because there's not an official that's gonna make that call.

"They'd been letting us play all day, so let us play. A couple of plays before, they pushed off to create some separation, so if you're gonna let us play, well, let us play.

"I wanna see the replay, and if that's as bad a call as I think it was, something ought to be done. That was a joke. That's all I can really say."

But the 'Canes did have a chance to answer. However, a huge momentum shift had taken place. The teams switched ends and Clarett capped a five-play drive with a five-yard TD run to give the Buckeyes a 31–24 lead. On second down, Dorsey was hammered by linebacker Matt Wilhelm with such force that he stumbled to the sideline. Backup quarterback Derrick Crudup came in and completed an eight-yard pass on third-and-11 before Dorsey returned. Still wobbly, Dorsey found Winslow for seven yards on the third successful fourth-down conversion of overtime. Miami then had a first down at the 2, but the Buckeyes didn't bend.

Without McGahee, UM turned to Jarrett Payton, the son of

football legend Walter Payton. On first down Payton banged ahead, but managed only one yard. On second down Dorsey had huge freshman tight end Eric Winston open in the end zone, but, feeling pressure from his left, the quarterback rushed the throw. Incomplete. On third down Miami ran full- · back Quadtrine Hill into the line, but he was snuffed by Wilhelm just outside the goal line, setting up another fourth down.

Dorsey dropped back and was immediately pressured by an unblocked Grant, who was blitzing. Before being dragged down, Dorsey threw a desperation pass that Wilhelm knocked down, setting off a second celebration—this one for good. This time it was the Buckeyes storming the field.

"We shocked the world!" Shane Olivea, Ohio State's enormous offensive lineman, screamed. "We shocked the world!"

The 'Canes in uniform didn't quite know how to react to defeat. Many of them had never lost a college game. So some just stood there in disbelief as they watched wide-eyed Buckeyes jump all over each other at midfield. Other 'Canes sulked and stomped off the field. Jon Vilma, the affable academic all-American middle linebacker, chased after a photographer who tried to snap a picture, before being restrained by Walker, the UM sports information guy. Sievers's eyes filled up as he shook his head before Kellen Winslow Sr. consoled him and told him how proud they should be about the effort they gave.

"Here's your headline," Winslow Senior told reporters, "'Miami Robbed!'"

Inside the Miami locker room, McDougle, the senior defensive end, spoke up. He glanced around the room. He saw most of his teammates with their heads bowed between their knees and remembered something like this. Only this pain felt ten times worse. That last loss, three years ago up at Washington, was before the Hurricane Machine had gotten truly revved up. Losing occasionally happened back then, just as it did to Oklahoma and Florida and Tennessee. But Miami wasn't like that anymore.

They had taken the program even higher than the old guys had had it.

McDougle looked at all the freshmen wide receivers and all the freshmen DBs, the guys redshirting and the guys who were warned earlier this season by Romberg and the other upperclassmen about not knowing what it was like to lose. Not knowing how much it burned. "Remember this feeling," McDougle began. "You don't ever wanna feel like this again. We win as a team and we lose as a team. Don't point any fingers at no one. Just remember how terrible this feeling is. You can't do nothing about it. Just suck it up."

For some, like Kellen Winslow II, one of the kids who had never lost as a 'Cane, the taste was especially bitter. "They didn't beat us," he said, shaking his head. "We beat ourselves. We're the best team in the country. They're not. We just beat ourselves. We didn't execute."

"Right now, I feel numb inside," said linebacker D. J. Williams, a guy who, dating back to his high school days at California's De La Salle High, had lost only once in seven years.

Payton confessed that at Miami, losing really wasn't an option. It may sound clichéd, he said, but it never happened. Never. "So nobody really thinks about it," he said softly, pondering both the gravity of the streak and its ending. "I think it probably does hurt a lot more being that it happened in the big dance. That wasn't just another Big East game. This was for all the marbles. I think that's what makes it hurt the most. And this will make us work harder."

Time to start working toward starting a new streak.

12

THE SEND-OFF

The greatest embodiment of the power of Hurricane football stands five feet tall, wears pastel-colored dresses, and once had aspirations to be a journalist. Donna Shalala didn't have the deep voice of Howard Schnellenberger, the scowl of Jimmy Johnson, or the girth of Jerome Brown, but she could rival any of them when it came to pure grit and gumption. And it sure didn't take long to realize that she had no problem flexing her ample muscle. Although when she proclaimed, "I am going to shake things up," a few days before she officially took over as the University of Miami's fifth president, no one could've known that would've included shaking up the entire college sports world. The funny thing was, Shalala's bold statement sounded a whole lot like something one of the guys from her school's football team might've said.

Shalala came to UM in 2001 after having served seven-plus

years as President Clinton's secretary of health and human services, and brought with her a rep as a dogged trailblazer full of pep and spunk. Her nickname was "Boom Boom." As a college undergraduate, Shalala spent two years in Iran in the Peace Corps, living in a mud house. She got her Ph.D. from Syracuse. Then, in 1980, Shalala became the youngest woman, at thirty-nine, to run an American university when she was named president of Hunter College. Seven years later she moved on to Wisconsin and became the first woman to run a Big Ten university. When she arrived in Madison, Shalala found an athletic department awash in debt and a football program that had become a laughingstock. She recruited former Badger great Pat Richter to take over as her athletic director, and recruited Notre Dame assistant Barry Alvarez to coach the football team. Five years later, Wisconsin won its first Rose Bowl, but by then Shalala had already moved on to bigger things. She went on to hold her cabinet post longer than any HHS secretary in history, a term in which she presided over sweeping welfare reform and made health insurance available to some 3.3 million children and was called by the *Washington Post*, "one of the most successful government managers of modern times."

However, when the *New York Daily News* broke a story on April 16, 2003, about Big East Commissioner Mike Tranghese's alleging that the Atlantic Coast Conference was tampering with his schools, it would trigger a three-month saga of he-said, she-said that would ultimately cast Shalala as a selfish, money-hungry tyrant and place her at the epicenter of what some were hyping as the end of college athletics as it was then known. Once again the Hurricanes were portrayed as the bad-boy mercenaries out to screw the rest of college sports.

The bombshell of Miami's possibly moving to the ACC was the sports story of the 2003 off-season because it had such widespread ramifications. Any move the 'Canes made would set off a huge domino effect, forcing the Big East to turn around and raid other conferences in hopes of keeping itself alive. Huge television dollars were kicked around. Lawsuits against UM were filed. Some college presidents, like Tulane's Scott Cowan, opined that their schools could get unfairly squeezed out of sports entirely.

As the ACC's courtship with Miami played out, the normally even-tempered Tranghese got more venomous each time he found himself in front of a microphone. "A move by the Hurricanes to the Atlantic Coast Conference will trigger the most disastrous blow to intercollegiate athletics in my lifetime," Tranghese said. He hammered the ACC, calling them "a bunch of hypocrites" for trying to lure, among others, UM, his marquee school, and he assailed Shalala for going back on her pledge from November 2001, when she told other league presidents, "We're committed to the Big East. You have our word. We're not going anywhere." Tranghese said Shalala needed to "look at the integrity issues" and "the irreparable harm" she would cause the conference. (Shalala claimed she made her statements of 2001 in good faith, but owed it to her school to explore the merits of switching conferences after the idea was first broached with her by Georgia Tech president Dr. Wayne Clough in mid-February.)

Tranghese had been responsible for the arranged marriage of the Big East and Miami. The relationship had worked nicely for both parts. Miami, which had been an independent, needed a conference that it could dominate in football, but also needed one that could nurture the school's listless basketball program. The Big East, a one-dimensional basketball conference founded in 1979, faced with an exodus of football-playing colleges, needed a high-profile football program to keep the league intact. Tranghese also brought in West Virginia, Virginia Tech, Rutgers, and Temple and created a Big East football conference.

Inside UM there was much debate over what the 'Canes should do. Many on the board worried about the increased level in competition that UM would face in the deeper ACC. Others celebrated the ACC's appeal toward broadening UM's other sports programs, particularly its women's sports, which would have a much better chance to flourish in the new league. Some even said UM had attained such a level the 'Canes should consider forming their own league, just as Notre Dame would do. The one thing everyone seemed to agree on was the money, especially since just a year earlier, when UM won a national title in football and its men's basketball team qualified for the NCAA tournament, the school's athletic department still came in $1 million in the hole.

On July 1, Shalala made the announcement everyone expected: Miami—despite a last-ditch Big East offer guaranteeing UM $45 million over five years—was accepting the ACC's invitation. She called it a "bizarre, strange, goofy process" and expounded about the Hurricanes' desire to define "who we are, where we are, and where we want to be."

The bottom line was that it was all about the bottom line. Money talked and the 'Canes jumped. Shalala wasn't fazed by lawsuits filed by ticked-off college presidents and ambitious attorneys general. She saw an opportunity to pump up non-revenue sports, pay smaller travel bills, and profit from a two Bowl Championship Series (BCS) bid conference that figured to get its own lucrative league championship football game, one way or another. Just like that, the ACC, the conference of Dean Smith, Coach K, and Tobacco Road unofficially became a football conference.

Meanwhile, the 'Canes were struggling to come to terms with their own identity suddenly. How would Coker handle losing? How would UM deal with life after Ken Dorsey? The first signs weren't good. Just a little more than one week after the Miami-to-the-ACC talk heated up, the real buzz around Coral Gables was about allegations that race may have played a part in UM's quarterback derby.

In a *Fort Lauderdale Sun-Sentinel* story that came out just two days after Larry Coker had named Florida transfer Brock Berlin as his starter, Derrick Crudup Sr., the father of the QB who was announced as the backup, claimed that race played a role in his son's not getting the starting job. The elder Crudup, a former Oakland Raider safety who had transferred from Florida to Oklahoma after allegedly being told by Gators coach Charley Pell that he couldn't play quarterback because he was black, said Miami QB coach Dan Werner used terms like "redneck" and "cracker" in quarterback meetings. Crudup Senior added that Werner "can't be trusted. He hasn't been in my son's corner from day one. . . ." Even though the *Sun-Sentinel* curiously chose to bury the story in the back of its sports section and the reporter who wrote the story, Omar Kelly, later went on local talk radio and contradicted himself repeatedly, the charge ripped through the UM program. Coaches worried that after the media got hold of the issue it could split the team apart. Hurricane coaches and players knew all about one of college football's worst-kept secrets: that archrival Florida State had been turned inside out when its quarterback controversy between the white Chris Rix and the black Adrian McPherson had divided some players along racial lines the previous season.

Coker acted fast. He called a meeting with the Crudups and Werner. Less than seventy-two hours after the allegations, a statement—signed off on by the Crudups after they met for seventy-five minutes—was released to the media. "We are all in agreement that race was not an issue in deciding the quarterback competition," the statement said. "The Crudups regret that Coach Werner was unfairly labeled. Derrick Junior does not believe Coach Werner is a racially biased person, nor does anyone else involved in this situation. . . . Sometimes when there are issues that are raised, it can make each of us more sensitive to individual differences, and that can be a positive."

Still, everyone around the program knew that once those ugly allegations were heaved out into the open, they were, no doubt, sure to fester if Berlin, the onetime national prep player of the year, didn't shine. It evoked memories of Luther Campbell's threats to Coach Butch Davis to start Ryan Collins or else.

As the team prepared for two-a-days, UM had more delicate PR matters bubble to the surface that also had the potential to wreck team chemistry. Kellen Winslow II, Miami's all-American tight end, created a stir all on his own, bringing back memories of the cocky, old-school 'Canes by making some outlandish comments that, thanks in large part to the Internet and a more wired media, showed up everywhere. He had dubbed himself "the Chosen One." The title actually had innocent enough origins. Earlier in the summer during a routinely fierce seven-on-seven workout, Winslow beat all-American linebacker Jon Vilma by snagging a pass thrown behind him with one hand. "Man, I must be the Chosen One, Vilma, 'cause nobody can catch like me," Winslow proclaimed. It was just some good-natured yapping, probably not much different from anything said from one college buddy to another while competing at X-Box. Only most college kids don't have reporters around asking them if they think they're ready to live up to someone else's image. So Winslow let a reporter in on the joke, and as it came out of his mouth, he liked the sound of it: "I don't think anyone has my ability. . . . I make catches nobody else can make. . . . I am the tight end of the new millennium. . . ."

Heady? Sure. Off base? Not if you ask a rival coach. "He is *that* good," said Buckeyes linebackers coach Mark Snyder. Still, within a week, "the Chosen One" was all over the Web, literally and figuratively. Winslow began scouring newspaper sites every day for his own name. He became addicted to the hype. He stopped watching film every day. Didn't need to, he thought. That's how it is when the beast that is ego starts feeding; you say something often enough, you can make yourself believe anything.

Meanwhile, the 'Canes' other most dynamic player, super-size free safety Sean Taylor, was doing all he could to dodge the spotlight. Taylor had angered the UM sports information people when he no-showed on a junket to Arizona for the Playboy All-American team weekend, becoming the first player to opt out of the trip and do so *not* for religious reasons. Taylor later said he just wasn't in the mood. Privately, the 'Cane football people, particularly Miami defensive backs coach Mark Stoops, had been trying to raise Taylor's national profile.

Stoops, the kid brother of head coaches Bob Stoops (Oklahoma) and Mike Stoops (Arizona), knew that it wouldn't hurt his cause any if his star player went on to win the Thorpe as the nation's top DB. Taylor clearly merited that consideration. Some scouts believed that if the six-foot-three, 230-pound defensive back had been eligible for the NFL draft after his sophomore season, he would've been a top-ten pick. He had uncommon size and range (he was fast enough to be a sprinter on the UM track team), and he could hit like a freight train. He had the look of an icon player, one who, when he got to the NFL, would become a breakout talent, and do for his position what Ray Lewis, Warren Sapp, and Jeremy Shockey did for theirs. Not bad for a guy most recruiting "experts" had never heard of during his high school career.

Taylor was typical of the kid UM always seemed to unearth in its own backyard. He arrived as a six-foot-three, 208-pounder ("a kinda soft, floppy thing," defensive coordinator Randy Shannon said) from tiny Gulliver Prep in Miami. Despite his linebacker size, 4.45 speed, and the fact that he scored a state-record forty-four touchdowns his senior year, Taylor was off most people's radar. He was labeled a three-star prospect (on a scale of five). The truth was that it was because Taylor missed most of his junior year due to a hip injury, and that was the time when recruiting reps tended to take stock. But UM knew better. The 'Cane coaches could spot Taylor's raw intensity and potential. "He was definitely rough around the edges, but supertalented," said Miami assistant head coach Art Kehoe. "I remember the first time we put pads on him, he hit everything that moved. It was scary. Still is. He's just a tough, nasty critter."

Around UM, Taylor had an aura. *ESPN the Magazine* wanted to celebrate Taylor's roughneck style as part of a photo essay on the game's toughest players for its college football preview issue. Taylor would be the cover boy. But one week after UM officials told Taylor about a potential photo shoot, ESPN phoned them to say they were going in a different direction. (The reason was because some magazine editors felt Taylor didn't have a big enough name nationally.) Instead, ESPN wanted to put Winslow on its cover. Miami's PR people, who had been trying to coax Taylor out of his shell, flipped. Stoops was irate. He lobbied Coker to not cooperate with the magazine. Coker, concerned over a potential chemistry issue within his team, agreed with Stoops and told Doug Walker, UM's sports information director, that the 'Canes were going to have to pass on ESPN's preview.

Despite the marquee talent of Taylor, Winslow, and a handful of other players (RB Frank Gore, OG Vernon Carey, LB D. J. Williams, MLB Jon Vilma, CB Antrel Rolle) earmarked as possible first-round picks, many pundits were predicting an end to Miami's run of dominance. ESPN football analysts Lee Corso and Kirk Herbstreit both predicted that UM wouldn't even win its conference title, with Corso touting Pittsburgh and Herbstreit picking Virginia Tech. The feeling was that finally UM would be slowed by a talent drain that, since the 2001 season, had seen the 'Canes lose an unprecedented twenty-six players to the NFL—thirteen of whom were first-round players. They also pointed to Miami's tough schedule (rated fourteenth most difficult among Division 1-A teams), featuring road games at Florida State, Virginia Tech, and Pittsburgh when the temperature figured to be below freezing. And, of course, they wouldn't have Dorsey to lead them.

It didn't help any that two-a-days were dogged by injuries. An already thin offensive line was decimated. Starting guard Joe McGrath was sidelined with a stress fracture, while Vernon Carey and Carlos Joseph, UM's two most experienced linemen, both went down with ankle injuries. Even the young receiving corps took their lumps when Roscoe Parrish and Jason Geathers both sustained leg injuries. On defense, Vilma hurt his hamstring; Rocky McIntosh, another returning starting linebacker, got dinged up too, with a knee injury. Worse still, Brandon Sebald, UM's best blocking tight end, missed camp because he had to return home to upstate New York to undergo medical exams that would later reveal "potentially cancerous polyps in his colon." (Sebald would return to the team at midseason, but have more tests scheduled for after the year.)

Winslow's persona notwithstanding, the focal point of Miami's season was Berlin. The son of a Shreveport preacher, Berlin was a high school legend, who had never lost a game while at Evangel Christian Academy. He was dating the reigning Miss Louisiana. Heck, he had already won three state title games in the Superdome, coincidentally, the same building where the national title game would be played. His father, Rickey, joked about how his boy "owns that house." Twenty-one-year-old Brock Sterling Berlin seemed to be leading a charmed life. His 'Cane debut even happened to be his homecoming game, since UM's opener at Louisiana Tech was being played at Independence Stadium, just minutes from where the quarterback grew up.

Berlin was a different type of quarterback from the cerebral Dorsey. Berlin sported a powerful arm and a cowboy's toughness, but in his stint at Florida, questions arose about his decision-making ability. That was one of the reasons he never overtook unheralded Rex Grossman as the Gators starter.

Berlin's coming out/coming home party was the main story line of a nationally televised Thursday-night game. The new QB shone on his first drive, connecting on two third-down throws to first-time starter Ryan Moore, and then he found him again for a twenty-four-yard touchdown throw to put UM up 7–0. However, as the game wore on, the rust showed. On Miami's next possession, Berlin had the 'Canes driving again. Then, on a first-and-goal from the Tech 4 yard line with reserve tight end Kevin Everett wide open for an easy touchdown, Berlin lost control of the ball and did a Garo Yepremian, fumbling and losing twenty-four yards on the play. Then he threw an interception on the ensuing snap. For the game, he completed only fourteen of twenty-eight passes, for 203 yards with an interception, although the Bulldogs dropped three other sure picks to bail him out. UM still rolled 48–9, with the game's lone highlight being Winslow's stylish six-yard touchdown snare on a fade pattern. The play itself wasn't all that spectacular, but Winslow's reaction was. Winslow caught the pass, tucked the ball under his arm, raised a bent knee, and extended a stiff arm—the mock Heisman pose. He didn't even hold it for a second. But that didn't stop all the highlight shows from airing it. Or from bashing him. Winslow's explanation was that he was only trying to have a little fun.

Miami's next game had even more emotional pull for Berlin. His old team, the Gators, was coming to the Orange Bowl. All week leading up to his showdown against Florida, Berlin heard all about how his ex-teammates were gonna hit him right in the mouth, make him bleed. He heard all the barbs about how he had never lived up to his National Prep Player of the Year status in his two years in Gainesville. "Flop Berlin" they nicknamed him. And, about three hours after kickoff, it looked like Berlin was living down to the Gators' expectations. He was showered with boos by the Orange Bowl crowd when he trotted out onto the field late in the third quarter after having just thrown two interceptions. The 'Canes—a fourteen-point favorite—were down 33–10. "Man, I don't think I ever heard them boo a 'Cane here," said former UM wideout Lamar Thomas.

The Orange Bowl crowd was begging coach Larry Coker to yank Berlin for backup Derrick Crudup. But Berlin had a response for them—and his former teammates. Playing in a no-huddle shotgun attack, similar to the system he had thrived in at Evangel, Berlin got hot, leading UM on a nine-play, eighty-five-yard TD drive in just under three minutes. "It kept them [Florida] off balance," said Miami offensive coordinator Rob Chudzinski of the hurry-up shotgun offense. "It was a good change of pace for them and for Brock." Just as important, his receivers started hanging on to the ball.

Berlin hit eighteen of his last twenty-one passes, including twelve in a row to lead UM to its four TD drives. He also converted a fourth-and-1 by scampering six yards on a bootleg to keep the game-winning drive alive. The manic second-half comeback from a 33–10 third-quarter deficit will go down as one of the greatest wins in Miami's storied history, equaling any of the Wide Right miracles against Florida State or Steve Walsh's dramatic 31–30 comeback at Michigan in 1988 when the 'Canes rallied from 30–14 with ten minutes left in the fourth quarter. The truth is, though, none of those other wins had the drama that Berlin's revenge had.

After the clock hit zeros, it was obvious just what the game meant to Berlin as he strutted toward the open end zone of the Orange Bowl, where a sea of orange-and-blue-clad Gator fans sat with their jaws on the floor. Berlin surveyed the scene for a second and then nodded his head at them, pointed both index fingers and broke into his own mock Gator chomp. "My emotions are sailing right now," a dehydrated Berlin said after the game. "I am grateful to be here in Miami."

"We are the Miami Hurricanes," John Square, Miami's soft-spoken defensive end, said from the back of the locker room while his teammates continued to celebrate. "We win games like this."

It seemed like that. Miami's Thursday-night game against West Virginia, October 2, only provided more evidence. Once again Berlin and the 'Canes dug themselves a deep hole, which started when Frank Gore, UM's leading rusher, crumpled to the turf after being tackled following a twelve-yard run midway through the first quarter. Gore, who had to be helped off the field, was later diagnosed with a torn ACL in his left knee.

Without Gore, Berlin continued to struggle, locking on receivers, forcing throws into coverage, and misfiring on intermediate-range passes. In the 'Canes' first four games, UM's offensive struggles had been masked by its defensive and special teams returning seven plays for touchdowns. This time, though, it appeared the offense's inefficiency would surely cost the 'Canes the game.

Just as in the Fiesta Bowl against Ohio State, Miami's only consistent weapon was Winslow. The big tight end also seemed to be the only 'Cane who came to play, although some were critical of his chest thumping and barking at West Virginia defenders. Herbstreit and Corso, the ESPN announcers calling the game, hammered Winslow for his behavior. Herbstreit later questioned the 'Canes' focus and whether Coker had lost control over his team when the cameras caught injured safety

Mo Sikes on the sidelines talking on a cell phone. (It turned out he was speaking with his mom to update her on his condition.) After Gore's understudy Jarrett Payton fumbled, it looked like the 1-3 Mountaineers were poised to pull off the biggest upset of the season. Then, with just two minutes remaining in the game, tailback Quincy Wilson took a screen pass from quarterback Rasheed Marshall on a third-and-13 from the Miami 33. Wilson juked Vince Wilfork behind the line of scrimmage, broke a tackle, outraced a linebacker down the left sideline, then bowled into and over safety Brandon Meriweather at the 10 and scored to give West Virginia a 20–19 lead. It was the first Mountaineers third-down conversion of the game.

West Virginia's defense shut down the 'Canes on their first three plays, forcing a fourth-and-13 situation from the Miami 25. The Mountaineers opted to send a linebacker blitz at Berlin, who lofted a pass over the middle in Winslow's direction. The toss looked like it was overthrown, but the six-foot-five-inch junior soared for the ball, snatching it out of the sky with his fingertips for an eighteen-yard gain. Three more Berlin completions and a pass interference penalty against the Mountaineers set up freshman Jon Peattie's game-winning twenty-three-yard field goal with eleven seconds remaining to give the 'Canes another miracle rally.

"It just gives you a sick feeling," Mountaineer secondary coach Tony Gibson said of the loss. "I mean, the kids played their asses off. To let it slip away like that is tough. We had everything set. We told them we would go back out, score, then go hold them. We got them to fourth-and-thirteen. Then Winslow made that catch. That's why he's the player of the year. No one else in the country makes that catch."

The victory, though, showed how vulnerable Miami was. It also illuminated the positives and the negatives of Winslow, who was now the country's most compelling figure. Winslow—aka the Chosen One, Junior, K2, or Diesel (as in the actor girls told him he looked like)—had gotten off to a slow start, catching just ten passes going into the West Virginia game. Defenses were targeting him with double and, in some cases, triple coverage. (When you call yourself the Chosen One, you do tend to draw a crowd.) Worse still, when Winslow did see the ball, he had a few drops, one a sure touchdown against Florida. He was overthinking. His sculpted, sinewy muscles were tightening.

The day after Miami rallied to beat Florida, the 'Canes assembled in a circle, as they do on Sundays, around the team's conditioning coach. Only this time an intervention of sorts was about to take place. Swasey, the modestly built man with a drill sergeant's voice and a sociology degree, called Winslow out. "See these hands?" Swasey said clasping Winslow's elongated mitts. "These are billion-dollar hands. But they aren't doing you—or this team—any good. You need to get your shit straight."

Swasey zeroed in on Winslow's "Chosen One" persona; the one Swasey said was doing all kinds of "retarded" stuff. "They are mocking you," Swasey railed. "They are making fun of you."

The admonition echoed in Winslow's head. He vowed he would change. No more interviews for a while. No more endless Web surfing. Every day he would be in the film room. "Swasey leveled me out pretty good," Winslow said. "I was pressing too much. I wanted to live up to this whoever-I-am thing."

As the 'Canes were scuffling to score points, their archrivals, the Seminoles, were blowing people out. It didn't seem to matter to the pundits that FSU had lost three in a row to Miami; the oddsmakers still made the 'Noles a six-point favorite for their October 11 game with UM in Tallahassee. With Gore out for the season, many figured the 'Canes would turn to converted wideout Jason Geathers, a former tailback, to save Miami. Or perhaps they would put the game in freshman Tyrone Moss's hands, or maybe the 'Canes would just stick Berlin in the shotgun and take their chances. The trouble was, when game day arrived, storm clouds hung over north Florida. The rain poured down, and Doak Campbell Stadium turned into a swampland, not exactly an ideal setting for an aerial show. UM's game plan: Ride Payton and let the 'Canes' defense win the game, meaning allow FSU's shaky quarterback, Chris Rix, to try to make things happen. It turned out to be a stroke of genius. Taylor, the great defensive back, was everywhere, blasting Seminole receivers, knocking down passes, intercepting two others. But the real story was the way Payton ran in the rain. The Son of Sweetness rushed for ninety-seven yards and also caught a touchdown pass in UM's 22–14 win.

Don Soldinger, Miami's grizzled old running backs coach, said he knew Payton was ready for his moment on the drive to the game. "I saw he was wearing his dad's game jersey, and that's when I knew," he said.

Credit Soldinger for planting the seed. He's the one who was always going on about Superman and about wanting his guys to think as though they had an S on their chests. Payton didn't own any Superman gear. Instead, he did the next best thing. He broke out old Bears number 34. "My favorite superhero was my dad," he said.

Miami leaned on its defense—and on Payton—and in turn, the kid leaned on his old man. Payton would look up above the skyboxes and talk to his dad whenever things felt tight. "Just be calm," "Don't rush things," "Be patient," were the things his old man kept whispering into Jarrett's ear. "Keep me focused," the younger Payton kept asking his father. "Keep me calm." He knew his teammates were going to think he was crazy, standing there talking to himself, but, hey, it was finally his time, so they would understand. He said he tried not to put too much pressure on himself, but still said he saw the game, this opportunity, as "life and death."

You couldn't have blamed Payton if he had sunk after almost fumbling away the West Virginia game. Especially considering that he was the same back who got stuffed near the goal line when Miami couldn't score in overtime against Ohio State in the national title game after Willis McGahee shredded his knee. But Payton never buckled. He hadn't buckled after being involved in a horrific car wreck on I-95 a few years earlier either. Or when he gashed open his foot on some coral while scuba diving. Or when he lost his father right at the start of his college career. He could've given up. Unlike most of the guys on the field that Saturday, Payton didn't need a football career to stabilize his family financially. Instead, he waited his turn, through Clinton Portis and Willis McGahee and Frank Gore. "I'm so proud of Jarrett," said UM's offensive coordinator, Rob Chudzinski, the guy who had recruited Payton out of Chicago. "That was big-time. That's what's been so great about this program over the years; when somebody gets hurt or guys graduated, other guys step up when they have their opportunity."

The 'Canes' next big hurdle, a trip to Virginia Tech, suddenly didn't seem so big after the Hokies got crushed by West Virginia, 28–7. Much was made about how the Hokies never won big games; fueled by that—and a prime-time television audience—tenth-ranked Tech ambushed number two Miami. The game turned on two plays. The first was when Hokie cornerback DeAngelo Hall snuffed out an end around to Roscoe Parrish, and in one motion the Tech cornerback corralled the tiny UM speedster and popped free the ball, gathered it in, and then raced twenty-eight yards for a touchdown. Hall's thievery left Miami fans with flashbacks. Nine months earlier, Ohio State's Maurice Clarett had snatched the ball from Sean Taylor's mitts after the UM safety had picked off a pass. A decade earlier, Alabama's George Teague had picked Lamar Thomas to cost Miami another national title.

A few moments later came more heartbreak for UM. Trailing just 7–0, the 'Canes lined up for a forty-five-yard field goal attempt by Peattie. But Miami's holder, backup punter Matt Carter, took the snap, rolled left, and heaved a pass toward the end zone, where reserve tight end Kevin Everett was alone near the goal line waiting for it. But Everett apparently had too much time to watch the ball float toward him. The ball hit him in the chest and then slipped through his fingers. He collapsed to the turf in horror. The Hokies, who completed only two passes, matching the number of passes they caught from Berlin, won 31–7, ending Miami's thirty-nine-game regular-season winning streak—college football's longest stretch in forty-six years. "This is a painful time for me and for us," Coker said. "The tough part now is going to be to regroup."

The coaches worried about talk that the 'Canes' diminished national title hopes might affect a team that has always had an all-or-nothing stance. There was also increasing heat on Berlin. Many in the media were championing a quarterback change, giving Crudup the starting job. On deck for UM was SEC powerhouse Tennessee. The Vols, a team UM had ripped 26–3 a year earlier in Knoxville, limped into the Orange Bowl having squeaked by lowly Duke a week earlier. But their game plan was to allow UM to self-destruct and, similar to UM's own strategy against FSU, force Berlin to beat them. It worked, and for the second consecutive week another long-standing UM streak went down. This time it was a twenty-six-game home winning streak, the longest in the country. The Vols were outgained 321 yards to 170, but they had no turnovers and committed only six penalties, while Miami was penalized twelve times for 121 yards and turned the ball over four times. UM, which during its Orange Bowl streak had outscored opponents by an average of 31.3 points, couldn't even manage one measly touchdown.

Most of the crowd blamed Berlin, although even UM's vaunted defense came unglued. Wilfork, the star defensive tackle, was called for jumping offsides three times and got a personal foul for ripping the helmet completely off UT quarterback Casey Clausen's head. "I saw the offense struggling," Wilfork said. "They can fault me if they want, but I'm just trying to get something going."

Some in the media lumped blame on Payton, the gutsy tailback, who on one play broke through a hole big enough to drive a Hummer through and had a clear path to the end zone, only to get caught from behind. It was the kind of play, the *Herald* wrote, that "Edgerrin James, Clinton Portis, and Willis McGahee would never, ever, ever have been caught from behind on."

But the real postgame fireworks came from Winslow, who was asked about a questionable unsportsmanlike conduct penalty he got and for his opinion of the Southeastern Conference officials. "They don't call nothing on them," Winslow said. "That one on me [a fourth-quarter personal foul after his twenty-two-yard reception] was bullshit. They said I took my helmet off. My helmet popped off. I picked it up, started celebrating, and they threw the flag.

"Bullshit, man! I hate refs. I only like our own. I like the Big East officials. They were looking at me the whole time. I can't even get hyped up after a play. I can't even hype my own crowd, our own crowd. 'Hey, watch it, Kellen! I'm going to throw a flag.'"

On UM's second possession of the second half, a devastating Winslow block of two defenders got him a warning. A reporter asked Winslow if he realized the Volunteer was injured on the play. "I don't give a hell. I don't give a flying you-know-what about a Vol. He'd do the same thing to me. It's war. They don't give a freaking you-know-what about you. They will kill you. So I'm going to kill them. You write that in your paper. You make money off that.

"I'm pissed. I'm pissed, man. We don't care about nobody except this U. If I didn't hurt him, he'd hurt me. They were gunning for my legs. I'm gonna come right back at him. Fuckin' soldier."

Clearly, UM was reeling. "No one has ever dealt with this before," UM offensive lineman Chris Myers said from the other side of the locker room. "No one knows how to handle it."

Footage of Winslow's tirade made all the national highlight shows. Every talking head in the country ripped Winslow for what they believed was his disrespecting of the United States Armed Forces. Winslow's rage was perfect for many national columnists to crawl onto their soapboxes again and drudge up their "See, it's the old Miami" barbs.

In truth, Winslow's comments—aside from the expletives—didn't rub too many coaches or players the wrong way. After all, most players—at all colleges—can't think of a pregame pep talk or practice where some coach doesn't try to inspire his team without using some war analogy. The UM coaches quickly jumped to Winslow's defense. Coker lauded his tight end's work ethic, saying he'd be troubled if Winslow acted that way only on game days. Instead Winslow brought a title-game intensity to a routine Monday and Tuesday practice, something Coker believed only made his team better. Coker was treading on a delicate path, though, because it wouldn't have been a stretch to think that much of the bravado and brash behavior that had been weeded out by Butch Davis had indeed seeped back into the program. Coker announced that he was benching Winslow for the start of the next game to hopefully teach him to keep his emotions in check. (He sat out a portion of the first quarter.)

Of course, the former 'Canes cheered their approval of Winslow. "He could play with us any day," said former UM running back Alonzo Highsmith. "He and Michael Irvin are identical. Mike got into fights every day at practice. They both are guys who always go a hundred miles per hour."

Winslow's father, an analyst for Fox Sports Net, scoffed at critics' bashing his son for showboating or getting caught up "in the extra" after a catch. "It just pisses me off," Winslow Senior said. Maybe, he continued, if those announcers had played at a level of some significance, he might consider their opinions. But did they really know what it took to be a star? If Junior didn't have a swagger, Winslow Senior said, he wouldn't get on the field at Miami: "The program will eat you alive. Ego is healthy. Lack of ego is what is dangerous." The issue reignited the old debate about what style and attitude brought out the best in players. "The problem with this team is they don't have more players playing like Winslow," said Bratton.

It's a delicate issue, especially given Miami's boisterous past, and it's one that most of the players can see right through. Still, the swagger issue has become a tightrope act. "Personally, I think we've cut back too much," said Eric Winston, a mammoth offensive tackle from Texas.

Coker concedes "the how much is too much" dilemma probably will always plague the UM coaches. "You have to wrestle with it because you don't want to cut back on the emotion and enthusiasm," said Coker. "Those things are so important to have in football. When Butch [Davis] first got here we really had a problem: guys with swagger that couldn't play. That's the worst kind of swagger. But honestly, we really don't talk about it unless there's a problem."

While the "soldier" incident was still being discussed nationally, another little drama hit the newspapers three days after the Tennessee game, when Winston, one of the team's better spokesmen, ripped the UM fans, calling them "idiots" for jeering the home team. "It's ridiculous," the big Texan said of fans booing early in the 'Canes' loss to UT. "It's stupid. It's pretty pathetic. . . . I'm tired of it. . . . I would rather have ten thousand loyal fans than sixty thousand who don't know what the heck is going on.

"If they're going to be like that, stay home. Don't come out there. Every time we came out for a drive, they booed. . . . After a while, it's like, 'What are we out here for?' "

While Dee winced at those words—especially with upcoming home dates against Rutgers and Syracuse, two struggling programs—a more pertinent issue around Miami was the brewing quarterback controversy. Coker announced that Crudup would start against Syracuse—news that didn't seem to bother some old 'Canes. "About time," said former UM star Melvin Bratton.

"Berlin sucks." Irvin also ripped Berlin. "He's just not a Miami QB," Irvin told the *Herald.* "Steve Walsh and Ken Dorsey didn't have the strongest of arms, but they had leadership abilities."

On the eve of the Syracuse game, the 'Canes would hear more from the alums. Only this time it came right into their faces, when former UM star Cortez Kennedy showed up at practice. "Hey, fellas, this is bullshit," the enormous former defensive tackle shouted at them. "This shit can't continue. This ain't Miami Hurricane football. And lemme tell y'all something—you ain't just playing for yourselves. This is about all of us," he said, poking his beefy index finger into his massive chest. "It's embarrassing, and it ain't gonna continue."

"He really showed us the intensity," said Winston. "This is a guy who hadn't played here in, like, twelve years and he was so passionate and so fired up about UM football, tears were coming to his eyes. It was unbelievable."

Kennedy's speech revved up the linemen and the defense, but still couldn't do anything for the quarterback play. Crudup floundered. In front of a season-low Orange Bowl crowd of 48,130, Crudup completed five of thirteen passes for eighty yards, a touchdown, and an interception. He also had a fumble. Both of his turnovers led to all of Syracuse's points as Miami slogged its way to a 17–14 win, thanks again to a nasty defense and the running of Payton and Moss. Coker, who said he thought it only fair to play Crudup most of the game against the Orangemen, gave Berlin one series. On that possession, Berlin was sacked and threw an incomplete pass that was caught out of bounds. But it was enough to convince Coker that Berlin gave his team a better chance of winning.

The 'Canes stuck to the same formula to beat Rutgers. Going to number twenty Pittsburgh, though, would be tougher.

Much was made about how the subfreezing temperature would be the coldest place UM had ever played. An even bigger obstacle would be Larry Fitzgerald, the Panthers' fantastic wide receiver, a huge target who had set an NCAA record with seventeen straight games with a touchdown catch. Fitzgerald had emerged as a Heisman Trophy favorite, and just in case the 'Canes somehow missed that point, they could see hundreds of "Fitz 4 Heisman" signs throughout the stadium. Coker had challenged his defense to try to hold the all-American to under fifty yards receiving, about a third of his average.

As Miami waited to come out of the tunnel, Panther fans—spotting Winslow near the front of the pack—serenaded him with chants of "Soldier! Soldier!" But it didn't take long to realize the 'Canes would be the ones making all the noise. Payton and Moss ran all over the Panthers, each topping the hundred-yard mark, while Antrel Rolle, UM's rangy cornerback, blanketed Fitzgerald, preventing him from catching any passes in the first half as Miami took a 21–7 halftime lead. The 'Canes' pass rush swarmed all–Big East QB Rod Rutherford, sacking him nine times in the game, and Fitzgerald was so beaten, he turned to Rolle and said, "Will you lay off the coverage and let me catch some?"

Rolle, in a statement of pure 'Cane spirit, later explained that he was actually disappointed he didn't get more balls thrown *his* way. "I just came into this game prepared," he said. "As good as he is as a receiver, I felt I'm even better as a defensive back. That's the confidence I came in with."

UM rolled 28–14 to clinch the Big East title, Miami's fourth in a row. In the game's biggest subplot, Fitzgerald managed just three catches for a paltry twenty-six yards. Fittingly, in their last Big East game ever, the 'Canes had destroyed another

Heisman candidate's hopes. "They're champions," Fitzgerald said. "You can see it in every aspect of the game. They don't get rattled, even when we scored early. It's like a machine with them. They're so conditioned to winning."

Unfortunately for the 'Canes, the rumors about a potential Orange Bowl showdown with Ohio State were untrue. There would be no Fiesta Bowl rematch. Instead, UM would face Florida State again, which would mean the two schools would end up playing three times in a ten-month stretch, since both teams were slated to kick off the '04 ACC season on a Monday-night game Labor Day weekend. The Orange Bowl wasn't a matchup the TV people wanted, and it wasn't one UM was too thrilled with either, although after hearing a lot of FSU people carping that the only reason Miami won October 11 was because of the conditions, the game again became a grudge match.

In the days leading up to the game, both coaching staffs downplayed the game's ramifications on recruiting. (Both schools were battling over a half dozen blue-chippers.) One, the nation's top linebacking recruit, Willie Williams from the Miami area, though, announced that the Orange Bowl's winner would have the upper hand in landing him. Just as important was the 'Canes' bid to send their seniors out unbeaten against FSU, and, as Rolle put it, to launch the off-season "the right way."

Payton, the star of the first meeting in Tallahassee, had his own motivation: to prove that his big game against the 'Noles wasn't a fluke. Through film study Payton knew he was going to have to change his approach for this game. Most of the season, he observed, he'd been staying inside. "But I noticed they spill like crazy, so I knew I had to bounce things outside," he said. Payton, who had given his beaten-up upper body a chance to rest over the break, also kept his legs sharp by running extra with Swasey. The difference was startling, and it all showed up on one crucial play midway through the second quarter with the 'Noles leading 14–3. FSU had momentum on its side and then Payton knifed into a gaping hole and darted outside, down the left sideline. Kendyll Pope, FSU's star linebacker, had the angle on Payton, but the 220-pound tailback burst past him for a forty-six-yard gain. Three plays later, the 'Canes scored. "Man, I never saw J.P. run like that before," said Winston.

Payton's sprint turned out to be one of three huge plays in the game.

The second was set up after Berlin was stripped of the football on a third-and-1 sneak play at the 30 yard line while the 'Canes were trying to protect their 16–14 lead. Following the fumble recovery, which gave the 'Noles their deepest possession in Miami territory in the second half, FSU offensive coordinator Jeff Bowden, leery of the Miami defense, opted to let the game come down to kicker Xavier Beitia's foot. Bowden called three consecutive running plays between the tackles to set up the field goal attempt.

Beitia's thirty-nine-yard field goal attempt was—what else?—wide right, marking the fifth time since 1991 that a missed field goal had cost FSU a chance at victory against the 'Canes. (It happened in 1991, 1992, 2000, and 2002. Beitia missed a forty-three-yarder wide left against UM as time expired in 2002.)

All Seminoles coach Bobby Bowden could do was shake his head. Only Charlie Brown had a harder time kicking field goals. "I might as well [believe in a curse]," Bowden said. "You know, I made the statement I don't know of any rivalry in the nation where so many games came down to a missed kick. I said that three kicks ago.

"I have a hard time understanding it."

Then Coker locked up the victory with a call as bold as any UM coach had ever made. With two minutes remaining, UM still nursed a 16–14 lead. The 'Canes had a fourth-and-1 from their own 32 and were in punt formation. The snap went to up-man D. J. Williams, who sprinted thirty-two yards up the middle for a first down. "I felt like if there was a crease he was going to make a first down," Coker said. "Besides, we didn't do too well punting. You have a gut feeling that things were going to work, and that one did."

After the game, the players mobbed Payton, the game's MVP, for his twenty-two-carry, 131-yard game while reporters scoured the UM locker room looking for Rolle, Sean Taylor, Winslow, and Wilfork, the four juniors everyone expected to be announcing their intentions to turn pro. It had been a crazy year, even by 'Cane standards. Yet they still beat their archrival twice, won another Big East crown, and produced, perhaps, six more first-round picks. Not a bad way to make an exit.

13

FREE WILLIE?

The nation's most coveted recruit was led into the courtroom with his hands cuffed behind his back. He wore a drab green jail smock, matching pants, and a wry smile. Outside the Broward County Courtroom in Fort Lauderdale, 150 supporters packed the lobby area. Many of them wore Carol City High School football jerseys; others wore T-shirts with a picture of the recruit smiling, the photo taken from Carol City's senior breakfast with the captions *Happier Times* and *Free Willie,* a play on the children's movie about a captured whale. Many wearing the T-shirts were classmates; some were teammates; others were coaches and teachers who had driven an hour from Dade County to show their support and love for Willie Williams at his bond hearing. The handsome nineteen-year-old, a strapping six-foot-two, 228-pounder whose chiseled muscles were even apparent under the loose-fitting prison garb, had been brought here after having just spent three god-awful nights in the Broward County Jail.

Inside the weathered old courtroom, the proceedings were watched by a gallery of thirty family members and friends, including Williams's aunt, uncle, mother, stepfather, two grandmothers, Carol City principal Albert Payne, Carol City coach Walt Frazier, and more Carol City teachers, as well as Williams's family reverend and pastor. The courthouse scene, a cross between a pep rally and *A Few Good Men,* was surreal. It was Friday the thirteenth, just a week after the most bizarre day in the history of college football recruiting, and no one here had any clue what could possibly come next.

Nine days earlier, the day hailed as national signing day, Williams was the toast of south Florida. By nine a.m. on February 5, television crews with their bulky cameras and bright klieg lights, and newspaper reporters, along with their photogs, had all descended upon Carol City High School, a ramshackle glob of buildings in northwest Miami, to learn Williams's latest move.

Around the South and in parts of the Southwest, national signing day has practically become a holiday. It is the first day high school football recruits can sign scholarship papers with a college, and it comes on the first Wednesday every February. Newspapers list 900-numbers, updated every fifteen minutes with the latest lists of "official" commitments to provide desperate college fans with a fix. Many TV stations even lead with it on the local news. Willie Arthur Williams, though, had bumped everyone into the background. College recruiters treated him like their Moby Dick.

Williams was a breathtaking talent. One of his former coaches, Joe Zaccheo, called him the best linebacker Dade County had produced in twenty years. Former Penn State star Mark D'Onofrio, a Virginia coach, said Williams was the best high school player he'd ever seen.

He was dubbed "Da Predator." He was an incredible blend of explosive power, closing speed, and gridiron savvy. But more than just his football skills, Williams also had an aura about him. A charisma. People were drawn to him. He seemed to be very comfortable in his own skin, and with his impending celebrity. "It was hard not to be sucked in by him," said Jorge Milian, the UM beat writer for the *Palm Beach Post.* "Almost a hundred percent of these kids lack social skills. Not him. He had it all down." Williams was also an honors student who had scored a 1070 on his SAT—about three hundred points higher than most other blue-chippers. "And that was the only time he took it," said Zaccheo. "If Willie went back and took it again, he'd probably get thirteen hundred."

He had something no high school recruit this side of Le-Bron James had: a Q rating. Williams appeared to be the quintessential 'Cane.

A few days before Miami and Florida State met in the Orange Bowl, Williams boldly announced that the winner would improve its chances greatly of landing him. "I want them to show me something," he said. His declaration opened a few eyes, but that was nothing compared to what would soon follow after he agreed to chronicle his recruiting visits to big-time college football schools for the *Miami Herald.* Williams and his colorful accounts became a full-fledged Internet phenomenon.

Such diaries are often standard fare for most newspapers around the country; full of ho-hum details and aw-shucks observations about how bad the weather was or how cool Coach So-and-so was. But Williams opted to shape his stories in a different tone: Huck Finn meets Jesus Shuttlesworth meets Chris Rock. Williams revealed a world of private jets, surf-'n'-turf dinners, groveling coaches, and personalized pep squad rooting sections. Thanks to the wired Web culture, "the Willie diaries" got posted up on every college team's fan-based bulletin boards and then got e-mailed around more frequently than JPEGs of Janet Jackson's nipple clip. "Fame by forwarding" is how the *New York Times* billed Williams when it did a cover story on him for its Sunday Styles section.

Williams first installment recounted his visit to Florida State, where all of the visiting FSU recruits were taken to dinner at the Silver Slipper, one of Tallahassee's best restaurants. "Dinner was tight," he told the *Herald.* "The lobster tail was, like, $49.99. I couldn't believe something so little could cost so much. The steak didn't even have a price. The menu said something about market value. I was kind of embarrassed so I didn't order a lot. But then I saw what the other guys were ordering, I was like, 'Forget this.' I called the waiter back and told him to bring me four lobster tails, two steaks, and a shrimp scampi. It was good. I took two boxes back with me to the hotel."

The next day Williams got a tour of Doak Campbell Stadium, and when he was ushered into the Seminoles' locker room, he found a jersey with his name on it. "They even had my number, seventeen. I told them, 'Isn't that number retired for [Heisman winner] Charlie Ward?' Coach [Bobby] Bowden was like, 'For you, Willie, we'll bring it back.' "

Williams's next entry, the account of his trip to Auburn, created an even bigger Internet buzz. Williams was appreciative of the Tiger cheerleaders greeting him with chants of "We want you, Willie! We want you!" But he said in the diary that he was put off when several of the school's recruiting hostesses, the "Tigerettes," offered him spinach dip. "You know how it is. Those girls are supposed to be there to cheer you up,"

Williams said. "But I told them, 'I ain't no animal, and I ain't going to eat no plant.' It was disgusting." He also offended the Auburn people by referring to the women on campus as "farmer girls who talked funny."

Installment number three was about his trip to Miami. He was chauffered to campus in Larry Coker's white Cadillac Escalade. "When I saw he was driving the Escalade," Williams told the *Herald,* "I was like, 'Dang, Coach got some taste.'" Williams was given a room at the Mayfair House Hotel in Coconut Grove, called "the Paradise Suite," complete with a Jacuzzi on the balcony.

When the recruits left for a tour of the Orange Bowl, they cruised through traffic lights with a police escort. The UM coaches, having been well versed in Williams's diaries, knew his love of seafood and were ready with shrimp and crab claws. "Coach Coker must be related to Cleo or something," Williams marveled, referring to the television psychic.

His last trip was to the University of Florida. Upon landing, he was greeted by the Gators' coaching staff and whisked away to a dinner party, where Williams scarfed down Swedish meatballs but passed on gator tails. "I ate so many meatballs, the people there started looking like meatballs," Williams said in the diary. "Some guy kept trying to get me to eat these alligator tails, but I wasn't having it. I told him, 'I'm not the Crocodile Hunter.' I don't touch reptiles."

Williams loved the attention. He described it like an addiction. "It's like I'm a fat boy and I love cake," he explained. Williams conceded he loved being fought over by his two main suitors, Miami and Florida State. Heck, how could he not? Here was this kid from a roughneck neighborhood who was so unworldly he thought the Tallahassee Radisson was the Four

Seasons, and now he was being fawned over by coaches and alums everywhere. Could you blame him for developing a warped sense of entitlement or losing some perspective?

The world for a blue-chip recruit, after all, has changed dramatically just in the last five years because of the Internet boom. The Web proved fertile ground for recruitniks; since college coaches aren't permitted to comment publicly on prospects, grass-roots "experts" popped up to fill the void. These men, a collection of former postal workers, housepainters, and community college dropouts, now pontificate online on the exploits of ballyhooed teenagers, scrutinizing and celebrating their every move. The colorful Willie Williams was their moneymaker.

Anytime Williams wanted, he could dial up Warchant.com (FSU's main fan site) or Grassy.com (UM's top fan site) and read hours' worth of Web logs in his honor, many with titles like "Open letter to Willie Williams" or "We need U, Willie!" each reminding Williams of reasons why the young linebacker should choose their school or, in many cases, why he *shouldn't* choose the other—just in case the schools' own coaches didn't already address those things with him.

Both schools had something special to offer Williams. At Miami, the 'Canes were losing five linebackers, so instant playing time (a huge attraction to every recruit) was practically guaranteed. At Florida State, Williams could work in with the 'Noles' great crew of rising star linebackers. Plus, his older sister was an FSU student.

The big announcement that had all of Florida holding its breath was held in the Carol City High library. Walt Frazier, the veteran coach who had developed a slew of NFL players, including former UM star Santana Moss, played emcee.

"This young man's gotten a lot of attention," Frazier said to the crowd of about fifty students, faculty, and media members. "He's enjoyed every moment of it. He probably wants each of us to stand as he walks up [to announce his decision]. And as he makes his decision he wants you to take your hat off and bow. I'd like to bring up the guy that's held everybody in suspense."

As Williams rose from his seat, beaming, his gold teeth shining, he had one family member holding a throwback Jerome Brown Hurricanes number 98 jersey and a UM hat, and another family member holding a throwback Deion Sanders Seminoles number 2 jersey and an FSU hat. He strode to the podium with the family members at his side. "I feel great about today," he said.

Then he shook his head and paused for a few breaths. The audience waited. "I'd like to ask everybody to give me five more minutes just to think about it, if that isn't asking too much," he said as the crowd moaned.

"Coach, can I have five minutes?" Williams sheepishly asked Frazier.

"Why do you always have to be a character?" his mother said to Williams, who whispered to her and his stepfather. The audience was getting restless. The kid loved that he had the crowd hanging on his every word. He chatted with some teammates, then huddled with his family as the TV cameras zoomed in. Finally Williams returned to the podium. "That wasn't quite five minutes; it kind of took a little longer—seven minutes," Williams said. "I talked to some of the players, my family; I already had discussed it with my family. Basically . . ." Williams stammered, then motioned a family member for the Deion jersey.

"Let's see how it looks," Williams said, his voice barely above a whisper. He donned the jersey and pulled the hat on his head. "I feel like I'm a throwback player." Then he yanked off the Seminole shirt and motioned for the 'Canes jersey. His classmates roared. "Jerome Brown would be proud," someone yelled from the back of the room. But then Williams began taking the jersey off. The audience groaned. Williams smiled. "I'm gonna go to UM," Williams said.

With the cameras tracking his every move, Williams plunked down at a table to sign his UM papers. "The reason I made this decision . . . this actually came down to a signing-day decision for me," he said. "I had a lot of pressure on me; it was a big thinking process. Both of them had great academics, a lot of stuff to offer. But this came down to this right here: I feel I can go [to Miami] and be an impact player, wear number seventeen. I don't want to follow in D. J. Williams's footsteps. I want to make my own. I feel like this is my home; I might as well stay here and just represent at UM.

"I can call UM my family—Coach Coker, when I'm there he's going to be like my family. I'm kind of glad it's over, a lot of pressure off me. I feel like I've been through a massage therapy course. I feel relaxed."

Then Williams pulled out his cell phone and dialed up UM linebackers coach Vernon Hargreaves. Williams switched the phone on speaker so the reporters could listen in. "Coach Hargreaves, I'm there, I'm there," Williams said. "I just signed."

Williams then had Hargreaves round up Coker to give him the good news. "Okay, we're on live," Williams told the room.

"Willie Williams?" Coker said when he got on the phone.

"How you doing, Coach?" Williams said.

"You know what, everyone's going crazy down here, man," Coker said, not realizing he was on speakerphone. "I'm doing cartwheels over here. I'm doing great, and let me tell you something: You're going to do great too. You're committed to us; we're committed to you too. Let's do a couple of things—

let's win some championships and let's get your degree. You've got that three-year plan. Let's get it done."

Williams later explained that the three-year plan Coker mentioned was just what everyone thought it was: Williams would play three years at UM and then move on to the NFL.

After the press conference, Williams hopped on another plane to fly to Atlanta to appear on Fox's *Countdown to Signing Day* show that would air later that night at six thirty.

Before he arrived in Atlanta, a bombshell dropped. Word out of Gainesville surfaced that something had happened on Williams's visit to Florida—something that wasn't in the *Herald*'s diaries. Police were investigating three separate sworn complaints against Williams, all stemming from his alleged actions over a five-hour span on January 31, his first night in Gainesville. One of the complaints was sent to the Gainesville state attorney's office Wednesday as a possible felony; the other two were sent as possible misdemeanor batteries, according to police. UF police said they had received a call about Williams discharging three fire extinguishers at about four a.m. Saturday at the UF Hilton, where Williams and other recruits were staying. In addition, Gainesville city police had filed a sworn complaint to the state attorney's office that said Williams was involved in an altercation with another man at the Royal Blue Night Club at two thirty Saturday morning.

Despite Williams's denials, Gainesville police said witnesses at the club claimed they saw Williams punch Akeem Thompson of Gainesville several times in the face "for no apparent reason." Then, according to another incident report by campus police, a female guest at the UF Hilton was hugged by a man she did not know at about eleven p.m. Friday. The report said that when Joanna Braganza of Gainesville realized she didn't know the man, she tried to remove herself from his grasp and he did not let go immediately. That man, she would later claim, was Willie Williams.

The news hit the University of Miami at eleven thirty a.m. on signing day. Doug Walker, Miami PR's contact for football, received a call from a Gainesville TV station looking for a comment. They told Walker a copy of the police report was coming over his fax machine. Walker rounded up UM director of football operations Jeff Merk, who then broke it to Coker. "There was nothing really we could say," said Walker.

Back in Gainesville, Gators athletic director Jeremy Foley tried to distance his school from the incidents, saying this was "not a University of Florida issue. It is a Willie Williams issue." UF coach Ron Zook echoed those sentiments when he was questioned about whether something could have been done to prevent the incidents. Zook's answer? "Yeah, not brought him in."

Could this be? The devilishly charming linebacker who had played the Machiavellian recruiting game for all it was worth had risked crapping out by going all Mike Tyson on his trip to Gainesville? Many in south Florida found it curious that this news was released on signing day. "Do you honestly think any of this would've come out if Willie signed with Florida?" asked Don Chaney, one of Williams's former coaches. Others wondered what Williams's host's role was in all of this, and if, as was rumored, Williams had been drunk, who had gotten him the alcohol? Heck, hadn't the guy the Gators assigned as Williams's host, Channing Crowder, been on probation for misdemeanor battery after kicking someone in the head? Still, the startling allegations about the superstar recruit were followed up by news of Williams's extensive criminal past that was triggered by some routine background checking. His police record showed that Williams had been arrested ten times, mostly on theft-related charges. At seventeen, he was tried as an adult for his most recent burglary arrest, when he pleaded no contest to a charge of stealing stereo equipment valued at $3,800 from Señor Stereo in Pembroke Pines, Florida. (He was caught after making an illegal U-turn at a red light. Police stopped him and discovered the stolen goods in his front seat. Williams admitted to the crime on the spot.)

The kicker? Williams was all set to finish his eighteen-month probationary period just one week after signing day. Williams was now a con man in many people's eyes. He had duped everyone—the recruiters, who supposedly knew every prospect's girlfriend's name and what the kid liked on his pizza; the *Herald*; those doe-eyed recruiting gurus; and the legions of college fans who had been begging him to choose their schools. Everybody thought twice about that nickname of his, Da Predator. Suddenly he was Good Willie Hunting, the brilliant quipster line-backing prodigy who apparently moonlighted on the dark side. UM, just like FSU and Florida and every other school that recruited Willie Williams, ran for cover, claiming they had no clue about his police record. Just as quickly as he became a Web phenomenon, Williams became a pariah.

The UM brass tap-danced around the story, with athletic director Paul Dee issuing statements wrapped in legalese. Miami spokesman Mark Pray claimed athletic department officials were unaware that Williams was on probation, despite routine background checks run on incoming student athletes. "All the reports we got back on him were positive," Pray said. That didn't matter. The feeding frenzy was in full swing. The *Sun-Sentinel* even sent a freelancer to cover a Hurricane basketball game so its Miami beat writer, Omar Kelly, could roam the UM

Convocation Center and try to sneak his way into the private skyboxes where Dee and school president Donna Shalala might be watching, in hopes of ferreting out a comment. With each passing day Miami took a bigger hit public relations–wise. Every time a newscast mentioned Williams's story they invariably paired it with the picture of the U logo. The local papers suggested Miami should shut the door on Williams, regardless of the outcome of the mess up in Gainesville.

Coker's only comment came through a statement: "We will see the attorneys and see all the allegations and take appropriate action. Sure, it concerns us when those things are out there."

The operative words there being *appropriate actions.* Da Predator was facing possible jail time, and UM was facing a dilemma cloaked in its own worst nightmare: Stand by Williams and risk the media flogging that the freshly scrubbed 'Canes were sinking back into the muck, or dump him and look cold, heartless, and hypocritical.

It's six thirty on a damp Tuesday night in December, just about forty-eight hours before Miami faces FSU in the Orange Bowl, and three white men are engaged in a full-fledged bitch session inside the UM sports information office. The men—Mark Pray, Miami's sports information director; Doug Walker; and Josh Maxon, the twenty-four-year-old backup football PR guy—look like they haven't slept in weeks. Normally, the office is empty by now, but all three have lingered to lament their existence. UM football will never live down its colorful and often contemptible past, Walker has come to realize.

"Honestly, what can we do to reach out to people?" Walker asks.

Walker says he's tried to reach out to the media. But for whatever reason, no matter how much spin-doctoring they could try, people, particularly the media, want UM to be villains. "I just don't get it; we haven't had an off-field incident in years, and that's pretty unheard of, and still people think we're the old Miami," Walker said as he shook his head.

UM's grace period from the time people celebrated Butch Davis's cleanup job to the time people started looking at their watches, counting down the moments till the old Miami returned, was indeed short. "The worm turned with that damn Rose Queen," Pray grouses. "That's when the image changed."

The Rose Queen incident happened at a dinner before the 2002 Rose Bowl game between Miami and Nebraska, when Queen Caroline Hsu said that she was rooting for the Cornhuskers because the 'Canes were "rude," after being seated with some UM offensive linemen. The quote was picked up by some papers, but when the Miami PR guys asked several players what it was all about, none of them had a clue. Truth be told, few people in the media had a clue about the Rose Queen "incident."

Perhaps the 'Canes' bad rep still lingers out of ignorance, Walker suggests. Maybe the mostly white, mostly older media has a hard time relating to the mostly black UM team, which seems to have a different look and harder edge than many other teams with similar racial balances. Walker's former employer, Texas Christian, didn't have players who looked and carried themselves like these 'Canes, with their wild dreads and braids and mouths full of gold teeth. Or maybe there's a much simpler reason, Pray says: People just can't get past their hatred of Miami. They hated them twenty years ago, they hated them ten years ago, and they're probably going to hate them twenty years from now.

Walker brings up the case of the media's rejection of Ken Dorsey. The polite, record-setting Miami quarterback was labeled "too boring" by some writers and was practically dismissed as a Heisman Trophy candidate. "It was so wrong how the media treated that kid," Walker said.

"And what's up with ESPN?" he continues. The Miami people say the sports network went out of its way to embarrass the 'Canes in ESPN's College Football Award show in Orlando. "It was like every time they showed a highlight of some guy making a play, it was against us," Walker said. "When they showed [Tennessee punter] Dustin Colquitt, they showed the punt [UM defensive back] Sean Taylor muffed, and I know they had better footage of him kicking longer punts than that."

"I don't know. I just don't get it."

The trouble is, Miami's bad image torments the program like a foul stench coming from its floorboards. Two years before UM had to reconcile how it would handle Willie Williams, it had had to cope with Nate Harris.

A six-foot-one, 215-pound heat-seeking missile, Harris was the top linebacker recruit in Florida in 2001. "The best linebacker I saw that year," said Ohio State linebackers coach Mark Snyder. "Ol' Nate could close on the ball in a heartbeat and would hit anything that moved." He also had a checkered past. When he was fifteen, Harris was arrested and charged with stealing clothes at a mall. He spent six months at Bay Point, an alternative school in north Miami for troubled teens. However, Harris had seemed to have refocused himself and turned his life around. He moved on to Miami's Edison High School and emerged as a punishing tackler and solid student. Just days before signing with UM, Harris pledged to stay out of trouble for the sake of his son, Nathaniel Harris Jr., born just two months earlier. "I've got an even bigger reason to succeed now," Harris said then. "I've got a kid to call my own, and he's depending on me to provide for him. He needs me to be a good father." But just three months before he was scheduled to report to UM, Harris was arrested and charged with armed robbery after he and two other men held up a man at gunpoint who was playing checkers on a street corner in Liberty City. Harris was sentenced to six months in a prison boot camp in Miami, but when he got out, he would have to find a new football team. Coker had announced he had pulled the 'Canes' offer. "It's going to be a while before we can take a kid in that position," a UM assistant said at the time. "We just can't."

In the fallout from Williams's highly publicized case and a scandal at Colorado that first came to light after some CU football recruits were accused of rape in 2001, the NCAA announced it was creating a task force to toughen recruiting rules. College coaches and their athletic directors all across the country also stressed that recruiters needed to dig deeper into a kid's past. But the truth is, most college scouts already chat up every clergyman, school receptionist, and janitor they can find. At UM, former recruiting coordinator Pete Garcia had been doing that for a decade. Much also was made about how doing extensive background checks on a laundry list of recruits might be expensive, but it actually doesn't cost the school a dime to dial up a free state-run Internet database that has profiles of everyone in the Dade County Correctional System almost as detailed as those on the recruiting sites, including those, like Willie Williams, who are on probation. "The thing is, whether we knew the details of his past is irrelevant, man," said one recruiter. "I mean, let's not be hypocrites. We all want Willie because he's a stud linebacker. The big issue is, do you think you can provide him with the type of environment where he can stay out of trouble?

"But now, whoa! It's 'out there' and everyone's running for cover, doing damage control. Puh-leese! We all knew Willie had some shit on his record, man. Hell, just about everybody in the inner city has got a record. Most of them did some stupid shit as a kid. I did. I fucked up too. Those kids [at Florida—Taurean Charles and Channing Crowder] acting as his hosts, they got records too. It's sad but when you're living in the 'hood, in that type of environment, you're gonna mess up. Sometimes they throw you in jail for stuff you didn't even do."

Willie Williams knew the quiet halls of the Bay Point school that Nate Harris had walked quite well. Williams spent time at Bay Point two years after Harris did. Williams was sent there because, in his words, his life was out of control. He said his life took a hard left turn after his father, Willie Williams Sr., a Carol City High assistant football coach with a severe weight problem, died from a heart attack, when little Willie was fourteen. Willie Junior developed a penchant for blowing off classes, running the streets at all hours, and never listening to his mother, Donna Williams. He also had a taste for stealing. That got him a spartan room at Bay Point, which he shared with five other teens.

"Willie was always being silly, always smiling, but after a few months he got serious," said Robert Hipolite, a counselor and assistant football coach at Bay Point. Williams attributed his turnaround to time spent reading the local paper, seeing how his pals were doing on the football field, how they were becoming "big stars." Williams, thinking, "That should be me," vowed to get his act together. He became a model student. He even started reading the dictionary for hours to improve his vocabulary. "When he left here, he'd be using words staff members didn't even know," said Hipolite.

The staff at Bay Point was so impressed by Williams's character that they lobbied the heads of Miami's Monsignor Pace High to admit him. "It is very uncommon for us to take a kid from Bay Point," Joe Zaccheo, the Pace athletic director and football coach, said. "But we got a lot of calls from people at Bay Point saying, 'You need to take a second look at this kid, not athletically, but as a person.'" Williams was accompanied to his interview at Pace by his stepdad and wowed the school's administration. "He just had this great charisma to him," Zaccheo recalled.

Before exiting Bay Point, Williams approached David McGhee, a deeply religious man who served as his counselor at the school. McGhee had spent hours talking to Williams about keeping a positive attitude and maintaining his eye on the future. "Mr. McGhee," Williams said, as his eyes locked on the counselor, "when I get up into the NFL, I'm going to build you a church. Whatever size you want. I'm going to do it for you. Trust me."

"I believed him," said McGhee. "I knew he meant it and I knew he believed that's exactly what would happen."

Two months after Williams enrolled at Pace, he was struck by a drunk driver while he was crossing the street. Williams was hospitalized for a month, undergoing surgery for a broken jaw and other injuries. He ended up missing ninety days of school and wound up failing the year academically. The ordeal, Williams said, made him focus on football and his future even harder. Two years later, as a junior, he led Dade County with an astounding 170 tackles and helped Pace record six shutouts.

Zaccheo called him "another Ray Lewis. This kid can run like no other linebacker I've ever seen. If anyone times Willie in anything over a 4.4 [forty], I'll give them five thousand dollars."

In the classroom, Williams's development might've been even more impressive. He raised his GPA to a 3.3; although, because he'd had to repeat the ninth grade, his chance to get a fifth year of high school eligibility (as a nineteen-year-old) seemed unlikely. His appeal to the Florida High School Athletic Association was denied. However, when he opted to transfer to Carol City High School in the spring, it gave him a second chance to get clearance. Rumors surfaced about whether people at Pace had tried to smear Williams in his appeal by calling him a disruptive influence, a charge Zaccheo denied. In mid-September, the FHSAA, with the aid of a letter from the oral surgeon who had operated on Williams, approved his extra year, making him eligible for the Chiefs—the top-ranked Class 6A team in the state—immediately.

The Chiefs, a long-standing Dade County powerhouse under veteran coach Walt Frazier, looked like a good fit for the ebullient linebacker. Frazier, a onetime National High School Football Coach of the Year, was a no-frills throwback, who always wore his trademark railroad engineer's cap and preached a blue-collar work ethic. The Chiefs wore shirts and ties to school on game day. Trash talk was forbidden; so was profanity. Same for celebration dances. Team weight-lifting sessions, aka Camp Frazier, before school were mandatory, and there was no hip-hop blaring. Players trained in silence, just to the clank of the iron—just like Frazier liked it. "He's pure old-school," Williams said of his new coach.

The kid flourished at Carol City. Frazier was stunned by his new linebacker's football instincts. Rival players said Williams had such a keen understanding of their offenses, he was calling out their plays before they'd snap the ball to run them. In the state title game against Orlando Edgewater, Williams had seventeen tackles, two sacks, and two forced fumbles, and also KO'd the Edgewater QB ten minutes into the game, breaking his arm with a vicious tackle. The Chiefs won 13–0, and Williams was the game's MVP. The dominating performance only added to the growing legend. "Oh, that was just the start of things," Williams matter-of-factly predicted a few days before playing in the U.S. Army High School All-American Game. "We're just getting warmed up."

Williams's next big victory came in the Broward County Courthouse. The only words the loquacious linebacker spoke during his hour-long bond hearing February 13 came in response to the judge's warning that if he violated any of the terms of his release he would be placed into custody again.

"Yes, sir," Williams replied to Judge Michael Kaplan.

The conditions Kaplan decreed: Williams would be under house arrest at his aunt's house; he would be monitored electronically; he would be permitted to attend school but couldn't depart for school until six twenty a.m. (school started an hour later) and must be home by three thirty p.m. (school ended at two thirty p.m.); and he would also have to submit to random drug testing and could not have alcohol or any controlled substances without a prescription.

Williams's attorneys, Paul Lazarus and Bradford Cohen, had successfully lobbied the judge on their client's behalf. Lazarus first spoke about the hundred or so friends and supporters outside the courtroom, telling the judge, "There are in the hallway an untold number of students and members of the football team who would tell you Mr. Williams is respectful of all and does not present as a spoiled star athlete. Judge, none of this is staged," Lazarus continued. "I had to ask people not to come."

Lazarus detailed Williams's academic achievements and then called Williams's "aunt," Adriana Rutledge, to speak on Williams's behalf. Though they are not related by blood, Williams had lived with Rutledge for the previous ten months. "He was friends with my son since he was young," Rutledge said. "He's been a perfect child." Then some of Williams's teachers were asked to speak. Paul Moore, an American Government teacher, said he dreamed of sitting at the inauguration when Williams is elected president.

"He hugs many people at school," Williams's Spanish teacher, Catherine Claiborne, said. "He broke [Moore's] ID [with a bear hug], hugged me so hard he picked me up off a stool."

"It's crazy, man. *Cray-zee*," Luther Campbell said. "It's one big fuckin' conspiracy. It's all fucked-up. This is so fucked-up. Willie ain't no fuckup. People are blowing this whole thing out of proportion like he's some kind of animal. But people don't know this kid. He's a good kid."

Campbell, whose nephew, Mario Alexander, was a friend and teammate of Williams's at Pace, had known the linebacker for years. Some scouts even viewed the rapper as a gatekeeper to Williams. One college linebacker coach sidled up to Campbell at a high school football game. "The dude was like, 'What's going on, Luth-or?' I was like, 'Why the fuck you talking to me?' Then he tells me how he slept on Willie's couch last night, and so I go, 'Well, then I guess I need to give Willie a call.' He was like, 'Nah, why you gonna do that?'"

Campbell scoffed at coaches hiding from Williams's past. He knew all about UM's persecution complex. He said it broke his heart seeing Miami, this new cleaned-up Miami, parade Jay-Z and Puff Daddy on the sidelines, while he was banned for life. Hell, during the 2004 Orange Bowl, religious rocker Scott Stapp, the lead singer for Creed, had a sideline pass. "Miami can't be scared," he said. "They need to stand by this kid, because if they don't, he'll just go to Florida State."

"What a mess," said former UM running back Melvin Bratton. "He was king one day and a piece of crap the next."

Bratton was disgusted by the whole turnaround and subsequent feeding frenzy. He had become like a godfather to Williams. He had met the kid two years earlier through a friend of Williams's probation officer, who thought Bratton would be a good influence. Bratton, a native of the unforgiving streets of nearby Liberty City, seemed an ideal mentor, since his once-promising football career was short-circuited by a horrific knee injury in his final college game. He had forged on to play a few seasons in the NFL and later worked as a scout for the Seattle Seahawks, but he never lost his perspective or forgot his roots. After reading in the newspaper about Nate Harris blowing his scholarship to UM, Bratton tried to help him get a second chance. He had arranged it so Harris had a deal to go to Mississippi State when he got out of boot camp. (That plan eventually fell through when, according to Bratton, the linebacker got in trouble for gambling right before his time was up.) Bratton talked to Williams about maintaining a positive attitude throughout his petition to regain his eligibility and about channeling his intensity on the field. As a nod to his mentor, Williams wore two of the throwback jerseys that Bratton's company produced at his signing day press conference. Right before Williams made his visit to Gainesville, he admitted to Bratton that he didn't want to go. He said he was only going to fulfill his obligation to the *Herald* for their diaries. The *Herald* declined comment.

Bratton, one of the first flashy 'Canes, worried that his old school might bend to the media pressure. "I hope they don't give up on this kid," Bratton said. "Thing is, if he went to Florida State or NC State, it would've been a thing, but not this big a thing. You wouldn't have everybody coming out of the woodwork, saying, 'Look, it's another bad boy; see the old Miami.' But he's not that kid. He's not."

Chaney, the coach back at Bay Point, said that if Miami turned its back on Williams, "It would kill him. It would devastate and destroy him. But if they stand by him, Willie could be an inspiration to millions of kids."

After Williams returned to Carol City and resumed classes, the media frenzy around south Florida went into a holding pattern while the courts determined whether Da Predator would serve jail time. Meanwhile, the scandal at Colorado that saw rape accusations springing up almost on a daily basis took the spotlight away. With each passing week, though, Williams's cause gained more support. Former Miami great Bernie Kosar, the only former player on UM's board of trustees executive committee, came out publicly in favor of the linebacker. "This way gives him a chance at salvation," said Kosar. "The other way puts him out on the streets alone."

Shalala, the UM president, said the school would wait till his legal issues were resolved and then decide. "How it will turn out, I do not know, but we ought to treat this young person fairly," she told the *Sun-Sentinel.* "The true test of the integrity of an institution is not running for cover because someone has an arrest record, but making sure every student is treated fairly, whether or not they play football for us."

Her comments, along with those of some UM coaches, indicated that Williams still had a place waiting for him at Miami. Besides, reasoned Eric Winston, UM's standout offensive tackle, if Miami wasn't going to take Williams, wouldn't the school have cut ties with him initially rather than continue to risk the PR hit?

Perhaps a better question is, Should it even matter now? Had the fortunes of Miami football reached that point? Hadn't the program come far enough that it could insulate such a young man? Or had it, as the cynics chirped, just come full circle?

AFTERWORD

They all gawked. Marvin Lewis, Marty Schotten-
heimer, Joe Gibbs, and a dozen other NFL
head coaches had never seen such a display. Neither had the
350 or so awestruck high school juniors, who, not so coincidentally, also had made a pilgrimage to the University of Miami campus on February 28, 2004. It was Pro Day, the time
when all of UM's NFL prospects would run, catch, lift, and do
virtually anything else to impress the pro scouts.

All over the country dozens of other colleges hold their
own Pro Days for their NFL hopefuls each winter. The size of
the turnout depends on the depth of each college's talent
pool. Getting thirty or forty scouts is considered a good
turnout. In 2003, UM had an unheard-of 115 NFL personnel
types flood the Greentree Practice Fields. (You tend to draw
such a crowd when you're in the midst of a run of an unprecedented thirteen first-round picks over a three-year span.) How-

ever, in 2004, there was a buzz around the NFL that Miami might have a record six first-round draft choices coming out, including three possible top-ten picks. (The record, set in 1968 when Southern California had five first-round picks, was matched two years ago with Bryant McKinnie, Jeremy Shockey, Philip Buchanon, Ed Reed, and Mike Rumph, all of whom just happened to be at UM rooting on their fellow 'Canes.) The number of scouts almost doubled from 2003, as two hundred came to town to check out the show. Houston, Texas, offensive coordinator Chris Palmer said the 'Canes had more first-rounders working out "than we have in Houston right now."

But perhaps of equal significance were the hundreds of baby-faced, droopy-shorts-wearing teens who milled around on the other side of the roped-off workout area who had flocked here for Miami's first-ever "Junior Day." Most colleges stage a Junior Day as sort of a recruiting mixer to give talented prospects who may be on their radar a sneak peak at the school and its facilities and, hopefully, a glimpse at what their program is all about. Combining it with Pro Day, however, was a unique twist. How could a kid not be floored by seeing Marvin Lewis, the NFL's reigning Coach of the Year, paying homage to the U? It also gave those sixteen-year-olds a window to the future to visualize that someday—in the not-too-distant future—that would be them sprinting past those NFL scouts, not Jon Vilma or Kellen Winslow II.

The show drew eighty of the top prospects in the state, including every top recruit in south Florida. There were also blue-chippers who came from as far away as Tennessee and Texas. "I've never seen anything like it," said UM tight ends coach Mario Cristobal, a former all-league lineman for the 'Canes. "It was an absolute mob scene."

Cristobal, a charismatic six-foot-three, 260-pounder with the looks of a supersize *GQ* model, had just returned to Miami after three years helping raise Rutgers to respectability. While working in New Jersey under former UM assistant Greg Schiano, Cristobal had channeled his high-energy style into a recruiting whirlwind that snagged a handful of skilled south Florida kids. At Rutgers, coaches simply have to work that much harder, especially when they're trying to battle for talent in the Sunshine State. That means getting up at four a.m., writing kids more letters, talking to more coaches, and poring over more game film. Cristobal and his colleagues in Jersey landed some prized south Florida kids who wouldn't have known Rutgers from Costco, but they sold and sold and sold some more.

Truth be told, Cristobal had been stunned by UM's drawing power too. When he first returned to Miami, he wrote to the nation's top fourteen tight end prospects, most of whom probably wouldn't even have opened his letters had they come on stationary bearing Rutgers's red-block R. Within one week, he got thirteen responses back telling him they'd love to play for Miami. One came from a kid who had just committed to Michigan. Of course, what hopeful young tight end wouldn't want to play for the school that had just cranked out Bubba Franks, Shockey, and now Winslow?

Cristobal couldn't stop smiling as he watched the recruits standing there with looks of utter shock on their faces. "They're looking in absolute awe at the Kellen Winslows and the Jon Vilmas working out in those tight dry-fit shirts, and their muscles are bulging right through, and we're like, 'Hey, when he came here, he was skinnier than you.'" Some kids' hearts practically stopped when they caught a glimpse of massive Vince Wilfork, UM's 325-pound defensive tackle, who had affixed his game scowl on to prep for his workout. "Heck, they might've scared a couple of those kids away," Cristobal said. Although that's probably a good thing. The 'Canes don't want meek. Each UM assistant who shepherds the group of kids from his recruiting area around the facilities hammers home the same message: If you wanna work your balls off, this is the place for you.

Larry Coker's message to the group is a bit more refined. Coker knows how fickle teenagers can be. He knows that every school will look like a perfect ten with a dazzling smile and luscious full breasts. Hell, if you believe what's been in the news the last few years, some schools might actually provide you with that perfect ten. Over the next year as you sort through your own recruiting process, your feelings are gonna change, Coker tells them, but the facts aren't gonna change.

Coker's point: No one can make a claim that can touch Miami when it comes to the one thing all these kids want most—an NFL career. "You know, I really think we're about to start something like no one's ever seen before," Cristobal said. "I mean, don't get me wrong; what's happened here is already ridiculous, but now it's gonna be taken to a whole new level."

History has a hard time quantifying such levels. It's like comparing the Model-T to a Ferrari. Sure, Notre Dame won four titles in seven seasons in the forties, and Bud Wilkinson's Sooners won forty-seven consecutive games in the fifties, but that was before the NCAA put a limit on scholarships in the early seventies, a rule that prevented the top schools from stockpiling top athletes. Previously, Bear Bryant, Wilkinson, and a select few others would take players just so their opponents couldn't, and this enabled them to have more talent on their bench than most schools could put out on the field.

Also, until 1968, the Associated Press crowned its champion before the bowls, which meant that a school could win a championship and still lose a bowl game. (Five national champions between 1950 and 1964 went on to lose bowl games.) And, all folklore, tradition, and echoes aside, the Fighting Irish, for all their greatness in the forties, never had to play in a bowl when they were selected national champions.

ESPN college football historian Beano Cook calls UM "the greatest dynasty since Caesar." The ironic part of it all is that Cook said if he had been asked twenty-five years ago which program—Rutgers or Miami—would have a better chance at winning a national championship in football, he would've said Rutgers. Perhaps, as Cook said, we need to look farther back for the seeds that helped sprout a Miami. Start with the innovations of air travel and air-conditioning, which sparked Florida's population boom and surely helped change the landscape of college football, considering that places such as Dade County, which had only a handful of high schools in the sixties and seventies, multiplied ten-fold. But the problem is, sheer numbers are only a small ingredient in this mix. Football games are won as much in the heart as they are on the field. When Howard Schnellenberger took over the University of Miami's football program in 1979, it was as though he were inheriting the college-sports equivalent of the Washington Generals—the perennial whipping boys of the Harlem Globetrotters. "Suntan U," as Miami was affectionately known, had long been cannon fodder for traditional powerhouses like

Notre Dame, Penn State, and Alabama. The school's old practice field was part grass, part dirt, and part swamp. Local interest in the team was so nonexistent that the school's radio deal provided Miami with a whopping revenue boost of $50 per week. And somehow, in the midst of all this apathy, a powerhouse rose and changed the way the sport is not only played, but coached too, and in the process "the U" would emerge as a true sports dynasty. Or, as they like to say around south Florida, the 'Canes put the "nasty" in dynasty. That, of course, was born out of staggering success, but out of eye-catching style too. Miami games often take on a pop culture shine. Hip-hop stars, all trying to stay ahead of the curve, flock to the 'Canes. So do heroes from Major League Baseball and the NBA. In 2002, when Jay-Z and his new girlfriend Beyoncé made their first public appearance as a couple, it was on the Miami sideline, when UM faced Florida State.

The Miami Hurricane program is the beast of college football, and it is unlike any other sports powerhouse—a dynasty that's fueled by attitude and aura, not individuals. Even if those individuals who passed through the program were special players, and the coaches have gone on to icon status, it's the *culture* that has allowed the program to dominate college football. The program is the sports world's last true dynasty. The 'Canes have won five national titles in the last two decades— more than Notre Dame, Oklahoma, and Florida State *combined*. They have run off winning streaks of thirty-four games and an NCAA home record of fifty-eight straight games. Since 1984, Miami has also produced forty-two first-round draft picks, including nineteen in the last four years alone. Next best is Florida's twenty-five.

"When you're on the mountaintop, everyone is coming after you," said former NBA great Charles Barkley, who attended a UM bowl practice before the 2003 Fiesta Bowl—as he put it, to get a closer look at greatness. "What they're doing is probably more incredible than what the Bulls did, because [college football] is one and done. They get one loss and they're history. College football is probably the most difficult sport to repeat in. Think about it. In every other sport you can lose some games and still play. These guys for three years have been in a position where they can't lose, and they haven't lost."

Miami went into some much-hyped showdowns against upstart top-ten teams such as LSU, Houston, and Texas, and thrashed them so badly they didn't recover for years. For crying out loud, the Houston Cougars, which in 1991 were the run-and-shoot, run-it-up Cougs and had beaten teams by eighty-four and seventy-three points the previous season, still hadn't recovered more than a decade later from the 40–10 nationally televised prime-time ass-whupping UM laid on them.

Want more proof? Look at Miami's 2002 squad. The team lost three-fourths of its starting secondary in the NFL draft's first round, something that had never happened before in football history, and the *replacements* led the nation in pass defense. The program also lost tight end Jeremy Shockey, one of two NFL rookies (both 'Canes) who were selected to the Pro Bowl, and replaced him with Kellen Winslow II. The son of Hall of Famer Kellen Winslow, "K2" also made all-American in his first season as a starter and is considered to be a better pro prospect than even Shockey or fellow Pro Bowler Bubba Franks of the Packers, who was the tight end who preceded Shockey at Miami. "The school is like no other," said Shockey. "Anybody that comes out of there is going to be ready to play at the next level."

The most remarkable thing about the win streak was that Miami's glorious run was built by five different coaches. These weren't Wooden's Bruins or Red's Celtics or Gretzky's Oilers. This is one program with many voices. It is Jimmy Johnson's team and Micheal Irvin's team and Warren Sapp's team and Vinny Testaverde's team and Ray Lewis's team. "It's the greatest story in the history of college football," said former UM running back Alonzo Highsmith, an NFL scout for the Green Bay Packers. "If Notre Dame or Oklahoma dominated the past twenty years the way Miami has dominated and won all these championships, they'd be building monuments all over campus."